# The Leading Edge of Early Childhood Education

# The Leading Edge of Early Childhood Education

## *Linking Science to Policy for a New Generation*

Nonie K. Lesaux
Stephanie M. Jones
*Editors*

Harvard Education Press
Cambridge, Massachusetts

Library of Congress Control Number 2015954226

Paperback ISBN 978-1-61250-917-4
Library Edition ISBN 978-1-61250-918-1

Published by Harvard Education Press,
an imprint of the Harvard Education Publishing Group

Harvard Education Press
8 Story Street
Cambridge, MA 02138

Cover Design: Ciano Design
Cover Photo: Christopher Futcher/Getty Images

The typefaces used in this book are Adobe Garamond Pro and ITC Legacy Sans.

# CONTENTS

# Introduction

*Nonie K. Lesaux*
*Stephanie M. Jones*

Federal, state, and community agencies across the nation are working on an aspirational and ambitious agenda for the dramatic expansion of children's learning opportunities in the years before kindergarten. This agenda requires that the settings in which our youngest children spend their days offer increasing learning opportunities throughout the day and across the year—a major difference from the existing, decades-old model of childcare. From the dramatic expansion of pre-K in New York City to the Obama administration's Preschool for All initiative to preschool expansion grants nationwide, stakeholders are promoting early learning as a pathway to equalize opportunity for all, particularly at-risk and vulnerable children and families.

This early-learning agenda represents a watershed moment for the field: Americans are focused on expansion at a time when the overall early education and childcare system still needs great improvement, and educational leaders have little knowledge and too few examples in the field of early education to inform a high-quality effort at scale. As developmental psychologists and researchers concerned with promoting young children's healthy development and well-being—professionals who regularly partner with communities and states in the implementation of several of these kinds of initiatives and policies—we are both excited and cautious about today's momentum. To be sure, the central role of early education in a young child's life has never been clearer for the individual and for society. The foundations of lifelong health are established in the earliest years of children's lives. Moreover, young children develop these foundations for learning across the many settings in which they grow and learn, through strong and supportive interactions with caregivers, teachers, and other community members.

But there are very real barriers to going to scale—and addressing these barriers demands a theory of action that is not so much about early learning but about the science of implementation and scaling. In fact, a few key aspects of early education and care must be considered in the design, implementation, and eventual scaling of early learning practices and policies, and these aspects constitute the focus of this book. Recent history shows that even with significant investment of financial and human resources, efforts to promote young children's health and well-being all too often result in small, fleeting impacts. And even with the best of intentions, rapid scaling and expansion can result in unintended, sometimes even harmful, consequences for young children and their families. For today's unprecedented policy initiatives to drive substantially improved learning outcomes, leaders have much to learn and to act upon.

## THE CALL FOR SCIENCE TO DRIVE EARLY EDUCATION POLICY

Today, educational leaders are responding to current policies that call for using research to improve and expand opportunities for children to learn from birth onward. For example, in the fall of 2014, the Harvard Graduate School of Education convened the Leading Edge of Early Childhood Education Initiative, a meeting of nearly three hundred influential leaders, scholars, and practitioners involved in early education around the world, to share their research and perspective on these issues. Focusing on topics such as the constellation of early risk, the promotion of language-rich and cognitively stimulating learning contexts, and the role of technology and media in early childhood, the meeting was convened to make explicit links between science and policy for a new generation of pre-K children. The discussions and synergistic insights gained from all these experts sparked our inspiration for writing this book.

This book brings to the fore the pressing and diverse issues facing the field as educators and leaders meet the challenge of improving the quality of early childhood learning experiences, particularly when there is a call to expand access to those experiences. Many of the contributors to this book attended the Leading Edge of Early Childhood Education Initiative, where we persuaded them to share their expertise in their respective areas. As a group, the book's contributors weave together the most relevant and practical knowledge from the science of early learning and development and share some important lessons from recent implementation efforts.

## THE BOOK'S ORGANIZATION

The chapters in this book cover a range of important issues. They range from systems-level topics, such as strengthening and scaling high-quality early learning practices to more focused, population-level issues, such as high-risk children and families, including children with special needs or negotiating two or more languages. The contributors also examine widely discussed and often-contentious issues salient to today's world—concerns such as effective child assessment and the role of technology in daily learning and teaching.

In chapter 1, Deborah Phillips discusses the particular importance of two fundamental issues confronting the early education community—economic instability and social exclusion—as they are contributing factors to children's experience of *toxic stress* (i.e., strong, frequent, or prolonged activation of the body's stress management system that adversely affects developing brain architecture). Phillips also highlights the promise of early educators as essential actors in implementing effective instruction, protection from stress, and prevention of exclusion. She also calls for adult working conditions that are free from economic and other sources of stress.

Like Phillips, Dana McCoy brings us into the environment of early adversity in chapter 2 but does so more from a neuro-physiological perspective. She summarizes recent research in neuroscience suggesting that executive function and self-regulation play a central role in moderating the impacts of poverty-related stressors and risks on several important aspects of learning, behavior, and health. McCoy also outlines how children's regulatory skills can, and should, be developed within a coherent system of support during the early childhood period, a sensitive period for their development.

In chapter 3, Amy Pace, Kathy Hirsh-Pasek, and Roberta Michnick Golinkoff show that a high-quality language environment is the basis for a high-quality learning environment. They focus on how today's policies ought to focus on the creation of language-rich learning environments. The authors offer six principles of language development derived from the science of learning. These principles can be used to advance high-quality communication in the home, in the classroom, and in the community.

In chapter 4, Gigi Luk and Joanna Christodoulou build on Pace and her colleagues' synthesis, focusing on children from multilingual, low-income households. Examining key findings from research on language and cognitive development among multilingual young children from low-income families, the authors describe the consequences of bilingualism. To take advantage of the benefits of dual-language learning and to offset the disadvantage of low socioeconomic status, the authors discuss and recommend both children's risk assessment that is more culturally sensitive and efforts to build adult capacity.

In chapter 5, Lauren Rubenzahl, Kristelle Lavallee, and Michael Rich describe the role of technology and media in early childhood learning. They argue that to be most effective, media need to be incorporated into the overall curriculum with clear pedagogical intent. Rubenzahl and her colleagues outline fundamental principles and offer practical recommendations for using media effectively in early education settings.

Chapter 6 focuses on the complex issues of early identification and intervention designed to better support children at risk for developmental delays and/or disability. Beth Rous and Rena Hallam map the landscape of assessment types and purposes, taking an approach that recognizes the need for assessment of the individual and the setting. They also present several systems-level issues that prevent educators from effectively gathering and using assessment data to support young children's development and their own classroom practice.

Given the recent press for workforce development and two-generational initiatives, in Chapter 7, Teresa Eckrich Sommer, Terri Sabol, P. Lindsay Chase-Lansdale, and Jeanne Brooks-Gunn extend the conversation to focus more squarely on the adults who support children's healthy development and learning on a daily basis. The authors zero in on two-generation programs designed to improve parents' education and career training and young children's school readiness at the same time with the goal of boosting the life chances of both. They suggest ways to make two-generation programs a reality, including potential funding mechanisms and pilot programming that could help advance the science behind these programs.

In the book's conclusion, we look toward the next steps—the future of the field of early childhood education and these salient issues of expansion and improvement. Specifically, we focus on several key insights and high-impact levers that should be considered when designing and implementing early learning practices and policies, and we raise important questions. In so doing, we draw on the tremendous work represented in this book, the insights and comments of participants at the Leading Edge meeting, and recent advances in the developmental and implementation sciences. Our goal is to contribute to the current dialogue and ongoing policy shifts with science-based, concrete recommendations that are relevant at the level of direct implementation and high-quality practice and to ongoing discussion about the challenges of scaling.

Jacqueline Jones, a visionary and former state and federal policy maker in early education, has contributed an afterword to the book. She remains central to the dialogue, and as president of a national foundation dedicated to supporting optimal development for all young children through high-quality learning opportunities, she exhorts educational leaders to continue this mission and to use this book as a springboard for their work.

## MOVING FORWARD

This book uncovers the important issues that must be addressed if our collective work is to have the very tangible and positive impact we are striving toward. Whether you come to this book as a governmental policy maker, a district superintendent, a head of an early childhood program, a funder or nonprofit leader, a practitioner in a leadership role, or a student in the early childhood field, this book is meant to inform and catalyze your important work. We hope that this resource—which captures an especially important moment in the early education world—can guide your quality improvement efforts, thereby enhancing the lives of the children and families your work serves and supports.

CHAPTER ONE

# Stability, Security, and Social Dynamics in Early Childhood Environments

*Deborah A. Phillips*

The United States has a long history of relying on nonparental early childhood programs to serve a variety of purposes.[1] These purposes range from assimilating immigrant children at the turn of the century to providing care for the children of working mothers on welfare to offering respite care for families at risk of child abuse and neglect.[2] One consistent strand that threads its way through much of this history is the provision of nonparental care to children for the purpose of ensuring their well-being, development, and early learning. This strand has its origins in the day nurseries that ensured the health, hygiene, and safety of young children of impoverished or single mothers, many of them immigrants, at the turn of the last century. During the Great Depression, unemployed teachers were put to work in school-based, educationally oriented childcare programs funded through the Works Progress Administration, and during World War II, the Lanham Act childcare centers provided early education to the young children of women who provided the labor force for the war factories. Head Start has provided early education and family support to young children, initially as part of

**Figure 1.1**
**CHAPTER PREVIEW**
**Challenges to implementing and ultimately expanding quality pre-K education**

1. The design of many policies means that families' access to programs and services often shifts according to their own changing circumstances, such as housing and maternal employment, thus compromising stability and predictability.
2. There are few clear connections and pathways from one setting or sector to another, for example, from preschool to elementary education, or from an early care setting to home visiting services.
3. Early educators' own economic insecurity, combined with unsupportive or unstable working environments, influences their emotional and behavioral self-regulation, undermining their capacities to support these same regulation skills among children in their classrooms.
4. Many early education classrooms are characterized by unhealthy peer dynamics; the most vulnerable children often experience social exclusion, which threatens learning and well-being.

the War on Poverty, for close to fifty years. Early Head Start addresses these same goals for infants and toddlers. State pre-K programs, which provide early care and education as part of a frontal assault on large inequities in school readiness by race, income, and disability status, are the most recent iteration of this child-focused, developmental strand of childcare.

What is new, however, is the exceedingly high expectations of what pre-K and thus pre-K teachers can accomplish for *all* children, not just immigrants, or children whose mothers are temporarily employed during a national emergency, or youngsters growing up in poverty or with a disability. In his 2014 State of the Union address, President Obama pledged to "to help states make high-quality pre-K available to *every* four-year-old." This pledge links early care and education to the long-standing function of public education as an engine of equal opportunity. Favorable cost-benefit ratios associated with high-quality preschool education have extended its potential benefits beyond enrolled children to society at large, lending early care and education a central role in the common good.[3]

In effect, preschool education has now assumed two aspirational and ambitious purposes: as the first step on a trajectory of academic and economic success for all children and as wise economic policy for the nation. At no other time in our nation's history has early care and education been cast so enthusiastically as a potential asset to promote developmental, educational, and national goals.

But despite the promise that pre-K offers, the actual implementation and potential expansion of quality early education faces numerous challenges. We will discuss these challenges individually in this chapter, but figure 1.1 summarizes them broadly.

## THE INTERDISCIPLINARY SCIENCE OF EARLY LEARNING

Science has played an important role in bringing the nation to this watershed moment. The economics of early education, noted above, has coincided with developmental and neuroscience evidence to make a solid, empirical case for the argument that a strong foundation of early skills makes subsequent efforts to promote learning much more efficient in terms of brain development, behavior, and social costs. Both old and new evaluations of pre-K programs have bolstered this evidence with demonstrations that high-quality early education can help build this strong foundation.[4]

The developmental and neuroscience literatures describe the adverse circumstances that derail development and how these circumstances get embedded into the neurobiology of the child to affect expressions of vulnerability and resilience and, in turn, early learning. The evaluation evidence shows the malleability of these impacts, namely, what opportunities exist for redirecting children who have experienced adversity onto more promising pathways toward adulthood. Together, these different types of evidence can tell us if we are trying the right strategies.

Starting with the evaluation evidence, with rare exceptions, the contemporary wave of research on high-quality, at-scale state pre-K programs has documented promising short-term impacts on both academic and social-emotional outcomes.[5] These significant effects extend to children with special needs, dual-language learners, and children at all income levels. New evidence is documenting midterm impacts of several state pre-K programs during the elementary school years, and a longer-term follow-up of a program in Tulsa, Oklahoma, is under way.[6]

An emerging consensus—elaborated on by Amy Pace, Kathy Hirsh-Pasek, and Roberta Golinkoff in chapter 2—has identified some of the essential components of effective pre-K programs, according to existing evidence.[7] One such element is reliance on age-appropriate, evidence-based curricula focused on specific aspects of early learning and development. Coaching and mentoring on the effective use of these curricula and other instructional strategies also appear to be important. The pre-K programs with significant results rely on degreed teachers who have early-childhood certification and are paid on the public school wage scale. Taken together, this emerging evidence on impacts and essential components makes a compelling case for the malleability of early development and the role of high-quality early education in pointing development in promising directions.

Alongside this pre-K research stands developmental and neuroscience evidence that, as described in detail by Dana McCoy in chapter 2, has made tremendous inroads in identifying the neurobiological and epigenetic mechanisms through which psychosocial adversity in the early years of life leaves a lasting signature on development. Four elements of this work are especially important for those interested in early learning. First, from work on adverse childhood experiences, trauma, and stress, the field has drawn important distinctions between positive, tolerable, and toxic stress.[8] Toxic stress—the strong, frequent, or prolonged activation of the body's stress management system—adversely affects developing brain architecture. During the early childhood years, children are especially vulnerable to the effects of toxic stress, given the extent of brain structure and functioning that is under development.

Second, the developing brain is explicitly designed to recruit information from its surrounding environment to shape its developing architecture, neurochemistry, and functioning. For better or worse, the brain is ecumenical. It recruits positive, tolerable, and toxic stress with equal enthusiasm. As a result, all early care and education environments are appropriately viewed as early interventions, even when not explicitly identified as such. The difference is only one of the intentionality and priority that the nation's early childhood policies lend to ensuring that these environments are supportive, stable, stimulating, and protective of early development. This is the case for Head Start and some state pre-K programs and far less the case for other federal and state-funded early care and education programs.

Third, scientists have specified the consequences of chronic and uncontrollable exposure to stress. The immediate impact is a poorly calibrated stress response system that responds at lower thresholds to events that might not be stressful to others and stays activated longer, producing damaging wear and tear on a wide range of neurodevelopmental systems. Such assaults on regulatory, metabolic, and immune systems can have long-term consequences on attentional, emotional, cognitive, and behavioral functioning. Additionally, toxic stress impacts cardiovascular and other chronic disease-related systems, affecting lifelong morbidity and mortality. When children are surrounded by stable, stimulating, and protective relationships, their odds of succumbing to toxic stress are substantially reduced.

Fourth, neurodevelopmental research is revealing the environmental circumstances, beyond the extreme conditions of abuse and neglect, that can produce toxic stress. Children growing up in poverty have been the focus of much of this work. Currently, over one in five American children under the age of six (22.2 percent) live below the poverty line; 45 percent of children meet the criteria for low income (living at or below twice the poverty line).[9] Results from this research are identifying the neurological mechanisms that underlie links between poverty and childhood deficits in language, memory, and regulatory skills. For example, Jamie Hanson and colleagues have examined brain development in healthy children from economically diverse backgrounds (e.g., 4 to 400 percent of the poverty line) from five months to four years of age.[10] Their results revealed significantly slower growth in gray matter volume in the frontal and parietal lobes of the brain for low-income children. These brain regions support information processing, reasoning, planning, attention, memory, and cognitive control capacities. Looking at five- to seventeen-year-olds, Kimberly Noble and colleagues have documented associations between low family income and compromised development of the hippocampus and amygdala.[11] These brain regions are critical to stress management, memory, fear and anxiety responses, and impulse control.

## Implications for Early Education

The scientific evidence on early development is pertinent to concerns about the achievement gap and is thus highly relevant to the equity-related goals of early childhood education. Its implications are especially powerful in light of both the rapid brain development during the early childhood years and the specific behavioral capacities impeded by exposure to adversity. The brain areas and circuits that are hijacked by toxic stress are fundamental to early learning and include the following functions:

- Working memory, which enables children to follow multistep directions and to keep facts in mind while working with them (as in math).
- Control of attention, which affects a child's ability to pay attention and focus, to ignore distractions, and to shift attention as needed when tasks or circumstances change.
- Error processing, which enables a child to notice and correct mistakes while learning and to incorporate feedback.
- Impulse control, which supports a child's resistance to an immediate or a habitual response in favor of a more effective, but less dominant response, such as when children play Red Light, Green Light or Simon Says.
- Emotion regulation, which supports how children manage anger, frustration, social threat, excitement, and other strong feelings.
- Immune and metabolic functioning, which affect how often a child is sick or not feeling well.

With this knowledge base in mind, Jack Shonkoff argues that effective early learning requires "protecting brains, not simply stimulating minds."[12] In other words, in early childhood education, as much attention needs to be paid to the prevention of, and protection from, the consequences of toxic stress as to the provision of enriched learning experiences for every child. Shonkoff's statement directs attention to the broader context within which pre-K operates in the United States and specifically to potential sources of toxic stress among the nation's preschoolers.

## THE BROADER CONTEXT: ECONOMIC INSTABILITY AND SOCIAL EXCLUSION

Today's preschoolers represent a historically diverse generation of children born in the trough of an economic cycle. These current realities confront the early education community with two fundamental issues—economic instability and social exclusion—as they can cause children to experience toxic stress. Economic instability arises from the state of our national economy, with children bearing a disproportionate share of the impacts. The issue of social exclusion becomes increasingly important in view of the growing racial-ethnic diversity of our population, with children at the leading edge of this hugely consequential demographic trend, and because of the growing enrollment of children with special needs in inclusive early care and education settings.

### Economic Instability

We've seen that poverty can compromise young children's neurobiological development. Poverty often brings with it substantial disruption and instability not only in income, but also in children's daily home environments, parents' emotional availability, and the family's network of supports, including their early care and education arrangements.[13] Economic instability is not restricted to families living below the poverty line, but has become a feature of life for families extending into higher income brackets. From 2007 to 2009, at the height of the recession, the number of children under eighteen living with at least one unemployed parent more than doubled, from 3.5 million to 7.3 million.[14] Children under five years are more likely than older children to live in families with unemployed or underemployed parents.[15] Yet, unemployment captures only one aspect of economic insecurity. Recent estimates indicate that over the course of a year, two out of five adults living with children lose one-quarter of their income.[16] The number of homeless children in public schools increased by 41 percent between 2006 and 2008; the number for preschoolers increased by 43 percent.[17] As a result, the developmental implications of economic instability probably affect a broad and growing swath of young children who are receiving early care and education in pre-K programs.

A growing body of research points to the relationship between toxic stress and economic instability, as distinct from more static measures of poverty and socioeconomic status. Gary Evans and colleagues were among the first to document the developmental harm of "chaos," defined in terms of an accumulation of housing problems, family turmoil, exposure to violence, and residential noise and crowding.[18] Most recently, researchers have proposed that poverty exerts its influence on development through a pathway that emphasizes the toxic stress created by instability and chaos.[19] Beyond the impact of poverty alone, composite indices of unpredictability in children's environments prior to school entry have been found to predict risky sexual behavior during adolescence and young adulthood.[20] Other work has found that parental job instability and job loss affect children's educational attainment largely through income instability. Moreover, children's loss of social networks—a loss associated with housing instability—accounts for a significant share of the link between job instability and behavior problems.[21]

### *Implications for early education*

Why is it important for educators to understand the relationship between economic instability, toxic stress, and early development? First, the aforementioned evidence suggests that poverty alone fails to capture the full extent of risk posed to children by their economic circumstances. Consequently, static, income-based eligibility criteria for early childhood programs, including targeted state pre-K programs, may overlook some children who need these programs. If the stresses associated with income fluctuations, especially those that thrust children into and out of poverty, pose challenges to children's capacities to learn, then one-time income cutoffs for pre-K access will fail to capture a notable share of vulnerable children. Second, instability and its associated stresses highlight the importance of promoting families' connections to supportive institutions and people, such as pre-K and pre-K teachers, for families experiencing serious disruption. For example, the McKinney-Vento Homeless Education Assistance Act gives families whose housing has been disrupted the right to keep their child in the school that is connected with the home of origin. Might this strategy be applied to mixed-delivery pre-K systems? Third, instability in young children's lives also creates stressed systems and institutions, including early childhood programs, in the form of extensive mobility among the students and teacher churning.[22] The ripple effects can flow to classrooms as a whole and can affect children whose lives are otherwise quite stable.[23] For all of these reasons, it is important to bolster early childhood programs' capacity to provide stability and security for all children.

*Policy implications*

Evidence of the instability in young children's lives suggests that early childhood policies need to be examined for how well they restore stability and predictability for children and their families. Perhaps we need child security policies just as we have national security policies. Fortunately, stability as a criterion for early childhood policy is beginning to take hold. New regulations proposed by the US Office of Child Care for the Child Care and Development Fund (CCDF) address previously disruptive eligibility rules.[24] For example, once a family's eligibility for CCDF childcare subsidies is determined, the family will retain this eligibility for at least twelve months. This means that even if parents lose their jobs or make a little more money—both circumstances that could change their eligibility—their children can remain in their care arrangement.

Efforts to minimize disruption as young children move from infant-toddler arrangements to preschool early care and education settings and on to kindergarten would also provide much needed continuity to the lives of young children and their families. The new Early Head Start–Child Care Partnerships are a step in the right direction.[25] They support Early Head Start grantees who partner with center-based and family childcare providers who agree to meet Early Head Start Program Performance Standards and to provide comprehensive, full-day, full-year, high-quality services to infants and toddlers from low-income families. Closer links from infant-toddler programs or providers to Head Start and pre-K programs within local jurisdictions are also sorely needed.

Disruption caused by housing loss is partially addressed by the McKinney-Vento Act, noted above, but the act extends only to children in early care and education arrangements administered by state departments of education. A major contribution would be to extend this law to young children across the full range of early care and education settings in this country. The US military offers a model for addressing mobility, given the frequent moves of military families. For example, military children with an individualized education plan (IEP—signaling a child with a disability) are automatically eligible for special education services when they move to a new community and thus a new school, thus avoiding disrupted services while awaiting recertification. The military approach offers a model for all children, whether they have an IEP or are eligible for other federal, but state-run benefits, such as childcare subsidies.

Policies and programs that seek to minimize eligibility cliffs, closely integrate different early childhood programs as children progress from infancy to pre-K and beyond, and minimize the disruption of housing loss and mobility can support the early learning of young children. In sum, we must consider the broader environment of young children's lives, because it both defines a wider role for these programs and affects children's capacity to benefit from high-quality early education programs.

## Social Exclusion

Early care and education settings often provide the stage for children's first encounters with unfamiliar peers and peer groups. As a result, these settings serve as proving grounds for the development of empathy, acceptance, tolerance, and social inclusion. The importance of these developmental tasks is amply illustrated by research on the emergence of social hierarchies in groups of young children and on the peer experiences of children with special needs.

Social hierarchies, in which specific children fall into dominant and subordinate positions within peer groups, have been observed to emerge in the early childhood years.[26] W. Thomas Boyce's evidence suggests that childhood exposures to socioeconomic inequalities establish enduring developmental trajectories, leading to life differences in the rates and severity of medical and mental health conditions and to gaps in educational and occupational achievement. Yet, socioeconomic status alone does not fully explain these differences and gaps. Looking beyond social class, Boyce places his bets on an additional, powerful variable to explain these adverse outcomes: social subordination in early childhood, namely, the experience of being in a subordinate position in early peer hierarchies.

In a study of the emergence and consequences of social hierarchies among kindergarteners, Boyce and colleagues observed that certain children experienced disproportionate teasing; directing; and threatening, physical, and relational aggression—thus, rejection and marginalization.[27] These "subordinate" children were significantly more likely than their peers to exhibit classroom inattention, poor peer relationships, lower academic competence, and higher depressive or internalizing symptoms. The odds of being in a subordinate position were unrelated to socioeconomic status and gender, although associations between subordination and detrimental outcomes were stronger for boys than for girls. Experiences of subordination and exclusion were also associated with dysregulated neurobiological stress response systems.[28] Indeed, subsequent impacts of social stratification on health outcomes have been documented to operate through neurobiological pathways that are activated in response to stress and adversity.

Boyce's work fits into a larger literature documenting the social challenges and threats to which some children—notably those with inhibited and more reactive temperaments—are especially sensitive. More solitary, less socially confident children disproportionately display dysregulated stress response systems, anxious-vigilant behavior, and internalizing symptomatology.[29] In Boyce's work, kindergarten children who experienced the double whammy of being in subordinate positions and being highly reactive to social threat and challenges (a temperamental characteristic) were especially likely to internalize their emotions. Because these children are not disruptive, they can fall between the cracks in early childhood programs. Yet they need as much specialized support as do children with challenging behaviors.

Children with special needs also struggle mightily with peer relationships. Over a decade ago, Mark Wolery and his coworkers estimated that three-quarters of public school pre-K programs included children with disabilities.[30] The proportion is probably higher today. While all children struggle to successfully navigate the social world of early care and education, children with disabilities find this challenge even more difficult.[31] These challenges appear to be especially salient for children with behavior difficulties in addition to developmental disabilities, partly because of their relatively poor self-regulation skills.[32] Michael Guralnick and colleagues' comprehensive review of the literature in 1999 revealed that while inclusive classrooms promote interactions between children with mild special needs and their typically developing peers, these settings do not necessarily enhance sustained social exchanges or friendships.[33] Most children, including those with disabilities, select typically developing children as their preferred playmates and friends.[34]

One of the most profound ways in which early learning settings affect these dynamics is through the practice of suspension and expulsion. Walter Gilliam first called public attention to preschool expulsion.[35] His report found that over 10 percent of preschool teachers in state-funded pre-K programs reported expelling at least one preschooler in the past year: a rate more than three times higher than estimates for teachers of K–12 public school students. In addition to inflicting on a young child the experience of exclusion and accompanying detrimental impacts on development, early experiences of expulsion increase the likelihood of suspension and expulsion in later grades.[36]

A 2014 report from the Office for Civil Rights in the US Department of Education documents the race-, gender- and disability-based disparities in school suspension and expulsions, including during the preschool years.[37] For example, black children represent 18 percent of preschool enrollments, but 48 percent of preschool children receiving more than one out-of-school suspension. Boys represent 54 percent of preschool enrollments, but 79 percent of preschoolers suspended once and 82 percent of those suspended more than once. Children with disabilities are suspended at two times the rate of typically developing children across all grade levels. Children who fall at the intersection of these demographics are especially vulnerable to this form of institutional social exclusion: More than one out of four boys (and one in five girls) of color with disabilities received an out-of-school suspension in the 2011–2012 school year.

### *Implications for early education*

The negative consequences of social exclusion begin in early childhood. These consequences operate through neurobiological pathways that are sensitive to stress and adversity. Early learning environments are the primary setting through which these dynamics first play out for young children. Consequently, the peer dynamics within pre-K settings need to be approached as the crucible that they constitute for young children. Consider the range of developing skills and capacities that are involved:

- How to join a peer group
- How to take turns and sustain a bout of play
- How to identify one's own feelings and those of others (the origin of empathy and tolerance)

- How to deal with others' anger and rejection
- How to express one's own anger, sadness, and anxiety appropriately
- How to help and share
- How to most constructively interpret others' behavior
- When and how to seek support from adults

These capacities pose a special challenge to young children who, for reasons of their temperament or other factors, are especially reactive to social challenges and threats either because they are socially fearful or because they are undercontrolled. Children with special needs are also highly vulnerable to experiences of social threat and exclusion.

Fortunately, there are curricula and strategies that support these capacities, with growing evidence of effectiveness.[38] These approaches include interventions that address the self-regulatory and related social challenges of children with disabilities.[39] Increasingly, such approaches are being integrated with literacy and math instruction, with benefits accruing both to teacher-child and peer relationships and to academic learning. There are also growing efforts—some of which have been evaluated—to tackle explicitly the pressing need to build tolerance among children in the United States.[40] *Sesame Street* is among the television programs that have had a long-standing presence in this area. Taken together, the lessons learned from these efforts indicate that fostering supportive, inclusive peer relationships should be a required element of all early childhood teacher education and professional development.

### *Policy implications*

Beyond classroom-level interventions, explicit attention to and language concerning tolerance and inclusion in state early learning standards could set in motion much greater attention to these issues in teacher training, curricula, and assessments. National leadership from a civil rights perspective is another vitally important arena for attention to issues of social inclusion. Fortunately, the US Departments of Health and

Human Services and Education recently released a joint policy statement on expulsion and suspension practices in early learning settings.[41] The report makes several recommendations, including the development and clear communication of expulsion and suspension policies and the uniform, unbiased implementation of those policies. The policy statement also recommends investing in and continuously improving the skills of the early childhood workforce focusing on children's social-emotional and behavioral health, strengthening partnerships with families, employing strategies to prevent and correct implicit or explicit biases, and conducting universal developmental and behavioral screening and appropriate follow-up. Another recommendation was for educational leaders to set goals and analyze trends in data to assess progress in reducing expulsion and suspensions.

Today, we need to acknowledge the power of peer relationships to either undermine or enhance healthy development in young children, especially in early care and education settings. Casting this domain of the classroom "curriculum" in terms of inclusion, tolerance, and empathy, rather than in terms of behavior management, provides a promising and positive framework for ensuring that today's young children are fully prepared to live full and rewarding lives in our increasingly diverse society.

## RECONSIDERING THE ROLE OF THE EARLY CHILDHOOD EDUCATION TEACHER

There is considerable evidence that early caregiving relationships play an essential role both in the development of the stress response system and in helping to buffer children from the adverse consequences of prolonged, chronic or extreme exposure to stressful events.[42] Responsive, sensitive, and dependable adult-child relationships are developmentally expected and biologically essential; their absence signals a serious threat to a child's well-being, particularly during the earliest years, and activates the body's stress response systems with detrimental, lifelong consequences.[43]

In early childhood classrooms, teachers play an essential role in establishing a safe and supportive emotional climate. In addition to serving as educators, their central job is to establish an environment of relationships that will enable all children to thrive and learn. Teachers are attachment figures, and when they, like parents, provide security to a child, they buffer the child from the toxic impacts of adversity.[44] When teachers do not provide children with responsive, secure relationships, children display rising levels of stress hormones throughout the day in early care and education settings.

In one study, 40 percent of preschoolers in child care displayed afternoon elevations of cortisol—elevations that could be classified as a stress response.[45] Thus, early deprivation that produces stress responses in young children and undermines their healthy development is not restricted to severe cases of physical abuse or highly depriving orphanage care. These responses are seen in the absence of sufficient attention, responsiveness, and protection on the part of a child's caregivers. In particular, intrusive, harsh, and unsupportive teachers can do real damage to young children. These teachers are not attuned to children's needs or bids for attention or help, move children frequently from one activity to another with little regard to the child's engagement in what he or she is doing, and spend long periods in teacher-directed activities that disregard children's interests and needs. And this persistent stress matters: Six months later, rising cortisol levels were associated with higher levels of anxious-vigilant behavior and internalizing symptoms, especially for children who were behaviorally inhibited.[46] Other researchers have reported lower antibody levels and more frequent illness among children who experience elevated afternoon cortisol levels in childcare.[47]

An additional finding from Boyce's work in classrooms characterized by damaging peer hierarchies is of interest. When teachers utilized learner-centered pedagogical practices, the association between being in a subordinate position and higher depressive symptoms was significantly reduced. Learner-centered practices included encouraging students to actively contribute to the learning process, showing respect for and supporting the unique developmental and cultural differences of each student, and explicitly valuing egalitarian interactions among the children.[48]

## Supporting Teachers as a Core Ingredient of Early Care and Education Quality

Links between adversity, stress, and poor emotional-behavioral self-regulation are documented not only for children, but also for teachers, with consequences for their own physical and mental health. These consequences, in turn, affect the teachers' capacity to support the learning and behavioral growth of young children, perhaps especially children who are more difficult to manage or prone to be fearful in groups and who thus most need sensitive and responsive care.[49] Effective early childhood teachers are purposeful, intentional, and reflective in their instructional practices. They deploy proactive management strategies, attend and respond to individual differences among children, offer all children consistent emotional availability, and sustain a positive classroom climate. One might say that early childhood teachers blend the skills of an air traffic controller, a conflict negotiator, a party planner, a detective, and an educator. As is the case with children, the multifaceted social-emotional skills of teachers are precisely the capacities that toxic stress can damage.

Growing recognition of the importance of teachers' own well-being has turned attention to important research questions regarding the adult work environment of early care and education.[50] A new report has documented persistently high teacher turnover in childcare settings, including public-school-sponsored facilities.[51] Between 1990 and 2012, the share of school-based early care and education settings that experienced teacher turnover rose from 23 percent to 51 percent. The actual rate of turnover in these settings that experienced turnover, however, dropped precipitously from 60 percent to 23 percent. Across all types of center-based settings, teacher turnover in centers that experience any turnover is now at 25 percent. It is difficult to offer children a sense of security and dependability when one in four of their teachers leaves the job in a given year.

Reported rates of depression among early education teachers and directors range from 10 percent to 50 percent.[52] A new study of perceived stress among the teachers participating in one state's quality rating and improvement system revealed that over 70 percent worried about being able to pay their monthly bills.[53] Close to half worried about having enough food for their family.

The low wages and high turnover for teachers in the field drive this economic insecurity. US Department of Labor data reveal that the average hourly wage of childcare teachers is now $10.33, and that of preschool teachers $15.11.[54] Even degreed teachers in public pre-K programs earn only 80 percent of the compensation of comparably educated kindergarten teachers. Given what we now know about the toll that toxic stress takes on adult well-being and capacities for responsive interactions with children, this evidence of economic insecurity warrants serious attention by all who are working on expanding high-quality early learning opportunities for children.

### *Implications for early education*

Evidence at the intersection of neurobiology, developmental science, and early education carries vast implications for early childhood teachers. These adults influence children's early development, are responsible for managing many children's first encounters with peers, and provide most children's first experiences with a school-like setting. Because of these critical roles, the teachers' own well-being cannot be ignored. In short, the research evidence ups the ante on what is at stake when children's earliest caregivers and teachers—two-thirds of whom have children of their own—are themselves experiencing economic hardship, low social status, unsupportive and demanding work environments, clinical depression, and other chronic stressors frequently associated with childcare work. It lends new urgency to what Jack Shonkoff and I recommended over a decade ago: "The time is long overdue for society to recognize the significance of out-of-home relationships for young children, to esteem those who care for them when their parents are not available, and to compensate them adequately as a means of supporting stability and quality in those relationships."[55]

### *Policy implications*

While society does now recognize the significance of teacher-child relationships for young children, esteem and compensation for the teachers lag far behind. Furthermore, the portrait of the early care and education workforce painted here will remain largely unchanged until the teachers' status and working conditions are addressed.

One promising first step would be to include these teachers in the two-generation programs that Teresa Sommer and her colleagues discuss in chapter 7. The teachers would be included not just as adults who take care of the children whose parents are the focus of these programs, but as equally economically at-risk adults (and parents) with similar educational and workforce-development needs. Why not build up the capacity of early care and education jobs to provide living wages in the context of these initiatives? A broader agenda, however, needs to be addressed, namely, the need to identify and mobilize a sustainable, dedicated source of public-private funding to upgrade the compensation of those who care for and educate our nation's young children.[56] Additionally, we need rational, equitable, and transparent guidelines that base entry-level wages and salary increases on education, training, experience, and seniority within the early childhood field, as is true of other professions. Finally, we need workplace standards for early childhood teachers—standards that foster, rather than undermine, teachers' capacity to provide children with emotional security, appropriate early learning experiences, and a responsive and caring social-emotional environment. Initial work on these broad goals could begin in the context of state quality rating and improvement systems and in current efforts to revise the Head Start and Early Head Start performance standards.

In sum, economic insecurity, linked to wages, is endemic, especially among teachers who have children of their own. The economic cost of continuing along these lines is considerable for society. As reported by Marcy Whitebook and colleagues, approximately $2.5 billion is spent on public support for which early childhood teachers are eligible—a form of public subsidy for their low wages.[57] The cost to families is felt in skyrocketing payments for early care and education—payments that are going somewhere other than to their children's teachers. And the cost to children of less-than-optimal services is surely profound, but largely uncalculated.

## CONCLUSION

Early education settings, including pre-K programs, have assumed a prominent role in promoting developmental, educational, and national goals linked to equal opportunity and prosperity. Now more than ever, we need to ensure that these settings provide the experiences and supports necessary to meet these goals. Children must be both supported in their early learning and protected from the adverse consequences of toxic stress.

The critical importance of addressing these dual purposes is lent urgency by growing evidence from the developmental and neurobiological sciences. The generation of young children now entering our early childhood programs is growing up in a period of notable economic instability and historical diversity. Their experiences of instability versus security and of acceptance versus social exclusion will have profound effects on their neurological and behavioral development. Because stress can affect brain areas that handle self-regulation and attention skills, the resultant behaviors can greatly influence the child's early learning.

Three implications warrant serious attention: First, early childhood programs need to be viewed as both engines of opportunity and as bases of security for all children. Second, social threat and peer group dynamics pose a major challenge to young children, with some children more vulnerable than others to being undermined by these experiences. Social inclusion is an essential consideration in the environment of ever-growing racial-ethnic and linguistic diversity and the expanding share of children with disabilities in pre-K classrooms. Finally, teachers are the essential actors in implementing effective instruction, protecting children from stress, and preventing exclusion. They require and deserve working conditions that are free from economic and other sources of stress.

CHAPTER TWO

# Early Adversity, Self-Regulation, and Child Development

*Dana Charles McCoy*

The US Census estimates that approximately one in five American children lives below the federal poverty line, with the youngest children facing the highest rates of economic disadvantage.[1] Outside the United States, 89 percent of children—more than 1.9 billion globally—live in developing countries, where economic and health-related adversity is prevalent in everyday life.[2] Over the past several decades, a large body of research has documented the impacts that this exposure to poverty has on children's early health, learning, and behavior.[3] For example, severe and prolonged exposure to socioeconomic adversity in early childhood is associated with higher rates of child mortality, chronic health problems, grade repetition, high school dropout, and emotional and behavioral problems across the life span.[4]

Why is poverty such a salient predictor of negative outcomes over time? Research suggests that children living in poor families and communities are exposed to a number of risk factors that affect their day-to-day life, ranging from instability to violence to malnutrition.[5] Until recently, however, the mechanisms for explaining how these early adverse childhood experiences (or ACEs) get under children's skin were almost entirely unknown. Over the past decade, a technological revolution

**Figure 2.1**
**CHAPTER PREVIEW**
**Challenges to using the existing research on early adversity and child development to shape early childhood education practice and policy**

1. Early adverse childhood experiences have detrimental impacts on brain regions associated with executive functions and self-regulation. High-quality early learning environments can offset, or buffer children against, adversity while simultaneously promoting executive function and self-regulation skills.
2. Many programs focused on bolstering these skills in children in early learning settings are designed without all of the necessary key ingredients for sustained change. For example, many programs focus on discrete classroom strategies without also addressing educators' own experiences of professional stress and adversity.
3. Gains in executive function and self-regulation skills that occur in early education tend to fade or disappear completely when children make the transition into elementary school, largely because of the lack of continuity between these contexts.

in the field of neuroscience has led to vast improvements in the field's collective understanding of the developing brain, biologically sensitive periods, neuroendocrine systems, and genetics. As an increasingly interdisciplinary field, education has reaped immense benefits from this revolution, ranging from enhanced knowledge about the links between the brain and behavior to the identification of targets for classroom-based interventions.

This chapter provides a brief summary of the existing neuroscientific evidence on early adversity and child development and offers suggestions for how this research can be used to shape the future of early childhood education practice and policy. In particular, this chapter will use evidence from the fields of neuroscience, developmental psychology, and education to focus on children's skills in executive function and self-regulation as central links between early adversity and later-life outcomes (figure 2.1). Children's abilities to focus and selectively shift their attention, inhibit their impulsive reactions, remember rules and instructions, plan their behaviors, and control their emotions are critical milestones of the early childhood period.[6] This chapter will summarize research on self-regulation as a mechanism and protective factor in the relationship between ACEs and child learning, health, and behavior. It will also discuss the need for additional research on how regulatory skills can be promoted through integration within and across early learning environments.

## THE NEUROSCIENCE OF EARLY ADVERSITY

### Poverty and Brain Architecture in Early Childhood

During the early childhood period, children's brains grow faster than in any other developmental stage, establishing between seven hundred and a thousand neuronal connections every second.[7] During the first several years following birth, a variety of environmental, biological, and genetic factors interact to support the developing architecture of the brain, strengthening well-used circuits and pruning away unnecessary connections.[8] Although the brain continues to develop and grow well into adulthood, studies have confirmed that early childhood is a principle sensitive period for brain development in regions related to a variety of sensory, language, and cognitive skills.[9] Consequently, positive environmental inputs—including warm, consistent, and responsive caregiving; enriched learning environments; and adequate nutrition—are particularly critical during these foundational years.[10]

Although early childhood is considered a period of great opportunity for brain development, it can also be considered one of vulnerability. Emerging neuroscientific research suggests that exposure to poverty in young children's home and neighborhood environments may have detrimental impacts on children's early brain architecture, particularly for brain regions associated with executive function and self-regulation like the prefrontal cortex, or PFC.[11] In one recent study of more than a thousand children, Kimberly Noble and colleagues used magnetic resonance imaging (MRI) to study the *structure* of children's brains across the socioeconomic spectrum.[12] In particular, the researchers found that increases in family income—particularly at the lower end of the economic distribution—were associated with corresponding increases in the surface area of parts of the PFC. Furthermore, differences in PFC volume were also observed to at least partly explain the relationship between family income and children's skills in inhibitory control and memory, two subcomponents of executive function.

Additional evidence using functional MRI, which examines changes in blood flow in the brain while individuals engage in different tasks, has shown similar poverty-related disparities in the *activation* of different brain regions. One study, for example, showed that when adults who had experienced poverty during their childhood years were asked to downplay negative emotions, the adults showed less activation in their PFC and less suppression of their amygdala—an area of the limbic system associated with strong emotional responses—than did their peers who had not experienced poverty earlier in life.[13] Importantly, the same study revealed that concurrent adult income was *not* associated with neural activation, confirming that early childhood may be a particularly sensitive period for the impacts of economic adversity on neurodevelopment and functionality.

## The Role of Adverse Childhood Experiences, Stress, and Epigenetics

Given that early poverty appears to be deleterious for brain growth and activation, a key question remains: Why? Increasingly, the neuroscientific literature points to ACEs as an important mechanism for explaining the links between poverty and brain development. Children growing up in impoverished environments are far more likely to experience a variety of risk factors in their homes and neighborhoods, including community violence, abuse, neglect, chaos, chronic health problems, and environmental toxins.[14] These ACEs are thought to affect brain development indirectly via several biological mechanisms, which are highlighted below.

The first pathway through which experience is thought to affect children's brain development is biological *stress response systems*. When children experience an environmental stressor, their bodies activate the hypothalamic-pituitary-adrenal (HPA) axis, a neuroendocrinological system designed to help individuals to efficiently cope with threat. Once activated, the HPA axis sends the body a series of neurohormonal stress signals that draw attention to the source of the threat and help the individual to quickly decide how to respond (e.g., through fight or flight). Occasional, mild activation of the HPA axis (e.g., as a result of taking a test or arguing with a friend) is not only considered normative, but actually thought to be positive in that it helps children develop independent coping strategies for dealing with future stressors.

Prolonged activation of the HPA axis, however, is associated with a phenomenon known as *allostatic load*, which is characterized by imbalances in the nervous, neuroendocrine, and immune systems. These imbalances are associated with increased risk for long-term health and behavioral problems.[15] Allostatic load—commonly referred to as *toxic stress* (see chapter 1)—occurs more frequently when children experience severe or chronic ACEs or those that occur in the absence of supportive, buffering relationships with caregivers.[16] Over time, this toxic stress can have direct consequences for children's neurodevelopment. In animal models, prolonged exposure to stress hormones has been shown to have deleterious effects on the structure and connectivity of the brain, particularly in regions associated with emotion, memory, and higher-order cognitive skills.[17] In addition, long-term changes in stress hormones have been associated with diminished activity in areas of the brain associated with reflective self-regulation and increased activity in brain regions responsible for automatic, emotionally driven reactions to stressful situations.[18]

The second pathway through which ACEs may affect brain development involves the substantially younger field of *epigenetics*, which looks at how genes are activated in response to environmental stimuli. A growing literature has found that exposure to ACEs early in life may actually influence how genes responsible for building neural circuits in the brain are expressed. In particular, emerging scientific consensus suggests that adverse environments can produce chemical changes in the body and that these changes control when and for how long genes are "turned on" or "turned off." Although the changes can be temporary, prolonged exposure to environmental stressors is thought to have longer-lasting consequences, not only for micro-level changes to the development of neurons, but also for the larger architecture and long-term plasticity of the brain.[19]

### Variation Based on the Quantity and Quality of Child Experiences

Given this biological evidence, why do some children facing adversity thrive, whereas other children struggle? Several factors determine how ACEs affect children's neurodevelopment. First, the *quantity* of the adverse experiences to which children are exposed varies greatly, even within low-income populations. Whereas some poor children have minimal exposure to major risk factors, others face a host of problems that can accumulate in ways that heighten their risk for negative biological consequences.[20] In addition, research has increasingly highlighted the ways protective factors (e.g., supportive relationships with caregivers and access to community resources that promote learning and health) can either offset the ACEs or protect children from them. To understand this phenomenon, think of children's development as a balancing scale. When children have more ACEs than positive experiences, the scale tends to tip toward negative outcomes. At the same time, even children with more ACEs can enjoy better developmental outcomes as long as they are supported by sufficiently positive home, neighborhood, and school environments. Importantly, this "balancing scale of resilience" also takes into account a child's history, genetics, and temperament in determining his or her individual tipping point. Children with challenging pasts and predispositions tend to need increasing amounts of positive experiences to benefit developmentally over time.[21]

Second, in addition to understanding the quantity of a child's early experiences, we need to consider their *quality*. New theory based on evidence from developmental neurobiology suggests that experiences of threat (e.g., domestic violence, sexual or physical abuse) may have different impacts on children's growth and development than do experiences of deprivation (e.g., institutionalization, neglect).[22] Threatening experiences—or those that are characterized by fear of harm or injury—are thought to have particularly detrimental impacts on brain development in regions associated with emotional processing and regulation. Children with histories of domestic violence and sexual or physical abuse have been shown, for example, to have greater activation in areas of their limbic system when looking at pictures of faces (a sign of potentially heightened levels of emotional reactivity and arousal); these children also show a reduced thickness in parts of their PFC (a marker of potentially reduced capacity for self-regulation).[23]

Experiences of deprivation, on the other hand, are characterized by a lack of cognitive and social inputs that are necessary for healthy growth and development. Children reared in institutional settings, for example, have been shown to have less gray matter in their PFC than do children raised in more traditional family environments that are characterized by higher levels of enrichment and lower levels of stress.[24] Notably, the reductions in gray matter resulting from early institutional deprivation are not merely structural; they have also been shown to relate to reductions in intelligence, executive function, language skills, and academic achievement and to increased symptoms of attention deficit hyperactivity disorder.[25] In addition, the effects of early deprivation may also depend on age and length of institutionalization, with children who were adopted or placed in foster care before the age of two showing greater gains in cognitive functioning than their peers who remained in an orphanage setting until age three.[26]

## THE ROLE OF EXECUTIVE FUNCTION AND SELF-REGULATION AS MEDIATING AND MODERATING PROCESSES

Alongside the rapid expansion of interest in the neurobiology of adversity, the past ten years has seen a notable trend toward exploring and promoting a set of skills called executive function and self-regulation. As is noted above, executive function and self-regulation collectively represent children's abilities to sustain and control their attention, to avoid impulsive actions, to remember and manipulate facts and rules, and to control angry or otherwise emotional responses. Although these skills are often conceptualized as "noncognitive" abilities, evidence from neuroscience has confirmed the roots of executive function and self-regulation are located within areas of the brain like the PFC—areas that are responsible for higher-order cognition, planning, judgment, and concentration. Indeed, neuronal growth in many parts of the PFC occurs most rapidly within the early childhood period, just when children can be observed making their greatest strides in controlling their behavior, attention, and impulses.[27]

At the same time, the PFC is not the only area of the brain linked to children's self-regulatory behaviors. Indeed, self-regulation is often thought to result from a dynamic interplay between lower-order areas of the brain like the limbic system—which are associated with emotional arousal, reactivity to environmental stressors, learning, and memory—

and higher-order brain regions like the PFC and the anterior cingulate cortex (ACC). The relative activation of these different systems within the *corticolimbic circuit* is an important part of self-regulatory processes. For example, executive function is often conceptualized as a "cold" regulatory process completed in the absence of emotional arousal. Emotion regulation and—by some definitions—effortful control, on the other hand, occur within the context of heightened emotional states, requiring the PFC and ACC to work together to either inhibit the emotional response itself or control behavior in the context of emotional arousal.[28]

What role do executive function and self-regulation play in explaining the links between early experiences and later learning, behavior, and health? Research suggests that regulatory processes are important in several ways. First, deficits in children's self-regulation and executive function capacities are considered key mechanisms in explaining the effects of early environmental adversity on later-life academic, social, and health-related outcomes (figure 2.2). As summarized above, much of the neuroscientific evidence on adversity and the developing brain has identified the PFC as a primary target of poverty-related ACEs in the brain. These deficits in PFC growth and activation are thought to make reflective self-regulation substantially more difficult for children, particularly in situations of amplified emotional arousal that frequently co-occur in children experiencing chronic threat and stress

In addition to being linked directly to biological manifestations of adversity, executive function and self-regulation are thought to be core predictors of children's school readiness and later-life success.[29] The ability to pay attention and control impulses is central to classroom learning, getting along with others, and thriving in adulthood. Indeed, although evidence for causality is limited, research has shown that children with better executive function and self-regulation generally perform better on academic assessments, show better behavioral outcomes, have fewer health problems, and exhibit less criminal behavior in adulthood.[30]

**Figure 2.2 Conceptual model of direct relationships between environmental adversity, brain development, and child outcomes**

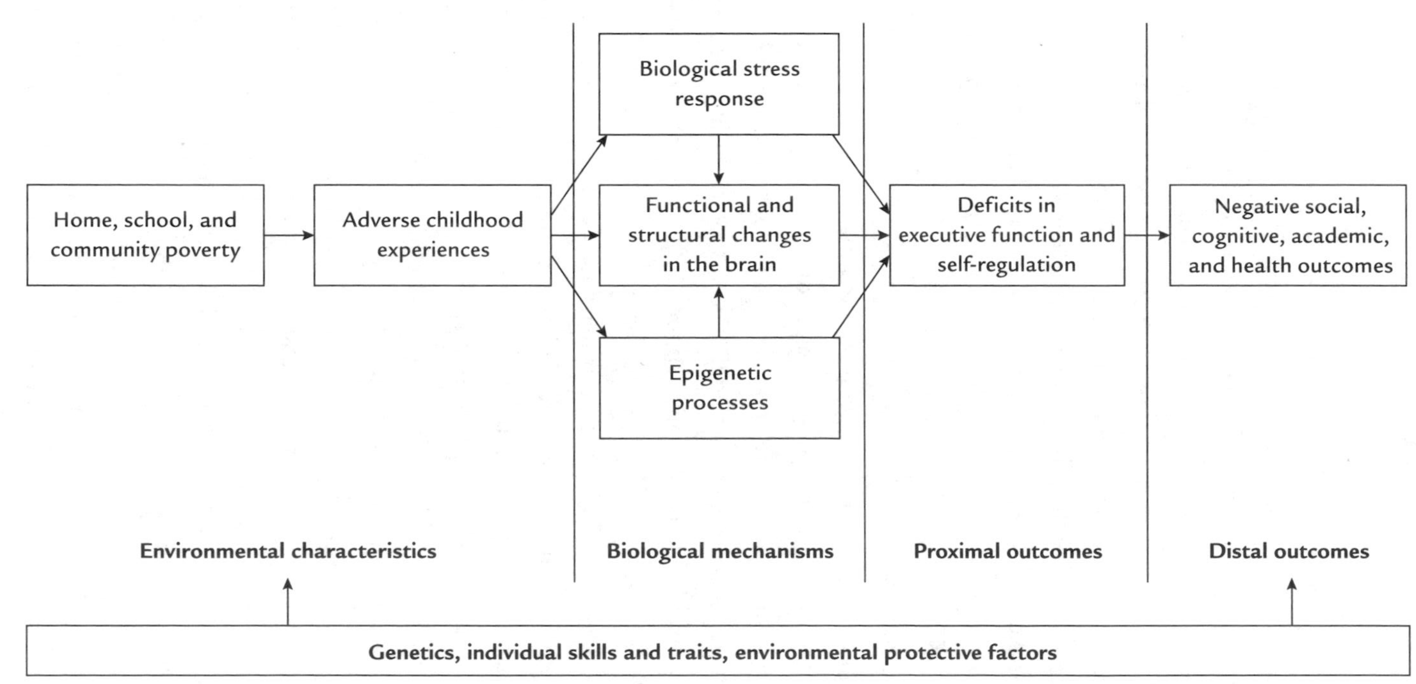

In addition to explaining the impacts of adversity on child outcomes, executive function and self-regulation are increasingly thought to play a role as *buffers* against the negative consequences of subsequent ACEs. The self-regulatory skills that children develop early in life serve as the foundation on which subsequent skills and knowledge can be acquired. When this foundation is strong, individuals facing adversity are better prepared to avoid stressful circumstances, seek out help when faced with challenges, and develop adaptive coping strategies. Indeed, one recent study found that stressful experiences were significantly less likely to lead to aggressive responses in adults with higher levels of executive function than they were in adults with regulatory deficits.[31]

Emerging research suggests that in addition to children's own skills, the regulatory capacities of adult caregivers can play important protective roles by helping children to avoid and cope with adversity.[32] When adults—including parents, teachers, and other caregivers—are well regulated, they are also better equipped to deal with stress, to plan and organize their days, to solve problems, and to control their own anger. These behaviors can help buffer children against ACEs by ensuring the warm, supportive environment that is required for healthy growth and development and serving as a model for children on how to face difficulty.[33]

## RECOMMENDATIONS FOR EDUCATIONAL POLICY AND PRACTICE

The evidence summarized above confirms that self-regulation and executive function play a central role in shaping children's long-term well-being. This research also highlights the potential window of opportunity that is available to the education community in the early childhood period, when children's brains are particularly malleable and amenable to intervention. Finding ways to capitalize on this opportunity and to promote self-regulation and executive function skills during the preschool period is critical not only for improving individual well-being, but also for closing the growing achievement gap.

How can this lofty aim be achieved? Over the past decade, many early intervention programs have explicitly attempted to answer this question. For the most part, these programs have focused on training preschool teachers in two general areas: (1) to consistently manage and respond to the behaviors of children in their classroom (e.g., using behavioral reinforcement strategies such as praise and time out to help children internalize what is appropriate behavior and what is not) and (2) to provide explicit instruction to children regarding social and emotional processes related to self-regulation (e.g., teaching children about what emotions are, what they feel like, and how and when to control them). Although promising, these programs, when implemented broadly, tend to generate only modest improvements in children's executive function, self-regulation, and general socio-emotional competence.[34] How, then, can such efforts be improved? Emerging evidence from developmental neuroscience suggests several ways forward, which are addressed in turn below.

## Reducing Stress and Enhancing Capacities of Teachers

Lessons learned from existing early childhood programs suggest that although many of the components of tried-and-true self-regulatory interventions are useful, they are difficult to integrate into the daily flow of the preschool classroom. Providing basic care and enrichment to large groups of energetic children—particularly when supports are lacking—is in and of itself a difficult task. As Deborah Phillips noted in chapter 1, this challenge is frequently exacerbated by the fact that early childhood educators themselves often experience various risk factors—including financial hardship, depression, and instability—that increase their daily stress levels. Because of these circumstances, these educators often struggle with the same challenges that they are supposed to be addressing in their students: difficulties with organization, planning, stress management, emotion regulation, and the like.

Several complementary approaches can help preschool teachers improve not only their day-to-day practices in the classroom but also their ability to implement self-regulatory interventions for children. These approaches mirror the goals we have for children: both to reduce the number of stressful experiences teachers find themselves in and to improve their ability to tolerate these circumstances when these situations inevitably arise. First, we need policies to *protect teachers from stress and adversity* in their daily lives. Various methods, including increasing teachers' salary to reduce financial strain and lowering the student-teacher ratio in the classroom, can contribute to this goal. From an intervention perspective, growing evidence also suggests that the way curricula and programs are structured makes a huge difference in teachers' ability to implement them with fidelity and success. Programs that provide support with implementation (e.g., through coaching or feedback) or that are designed to be integrated in the daily routine of the classroom (e.g., through evidence-based instructional "kernels") reduce their burden on teachers and are thus more likely to be adopted on a broad scale.[35]

In addition to protecting early educators from undue stress, we need to *support teachers' own capacities* in the areas of self-regulation and executive function. Despite evidence to suggest that the brain is most malleable early in life, the window for growth and development is never fully closed. Recently, several researchers have called for the use of dual-generation programs to simultaneously target the skills of both parents and children.[36] Such programs operate under the premise that parents, as primary caregivers, cannot optimize their children's executive function and self-regulation skills when they, the adults, are dysregulated. As Phillips pointed out and as Teresa Sommer and her colleagues will expand on in chapter 7, similar programs can also be applied for building teachers' capacities in stress management, organization, problem solving, and planning. Enhancing educators' regulatory skills not only improves the flexibility and ease with which they deliver curricular content and intervention programming, but also provides them with additional cognitive and emotional resources for responding to their students in positive ways. This modeling and relationship-building is central to children's ability to develop executive function and self-regulation skills of their own.

## Improving Continuity of Programming Across Context and Time

One of the primary limitations of existing early childhood interventions is that even when they do lead to initial improvements in children's self-regulation and executive function, the effects tend to disappear completely when children move into elementary school.[37] Although several specific theories exist to explain this fade-out, the consensus is that classroom-based interventions may not be powerful enough on their own to permanently alter brain architecture in ways that sustain long-term behavioral improvements.[38]

Two particular approaches warrant consideration for enhancing program sustainability in the future, both of which involve improvements in program continuity. First, a primary critique of early childhood self-regulatory interventions is that they tend to target only the classroom setting. Even children who participate in full-time preschool programs spend a majority of their time *outside* classroom walls, including home, other childcare settings, or other areas of their preschool (e.g., the lunch room, hallway, playground). Within these other situations, children may be exposed to a host of negative experiences—including unresponsive caregivers, bullying from peers, and environmental toxins—that can offset the benefits that they receive in their preschool classrooms and can disrupt the sense of predictability that is fundamental to healthy brain development. To combat this issue, some early education programs—particularly those serving low-income, developmentally delayed, or otherwise at-risk children (e.g., Head Start)—have attempted to integrate home-, school-, and community-based components to complement and enhance the support provided to children within the classroom. For improving self-regulation, the integration of educational programming for parents with training for teachers may be particularly useful by ensuring that children are met with similar expectations for behavior at home and at school.[39] Similarly, within the school, training for administrators, classroom aides, and support staff can help promote continuity, reduce negative experiences outside the classroom, and improve the odds of early identification of children with particular challenges.[40]

Second, to ensure that early gains in self-regulation and executive function are sustained over time, additional efforts are needed to align early childhood environments with elementary school environments. The transition from preschool to elementary school can be stressful for children, as it often requires shifting to an entirely new school building, peer group, and teacher. But for some children—particularly those from low-income communities—moving to elementary school may also be accompanied by abrupt reductions in classroom quality and changes in expectations for how they should behave, interact, and think, often with minimal adult support for navigating this transition. If the benefits of a high-quality preschool environment are to persist for a child, he or she needs additional support during this transition to prevent a "tolerably stressful" event from turning toxic. Although some policies (e.g., open houses, meeting teachers ahead of time) may help prepare children for entry into elementary school, more broad-scale efforts to bring the positive aspects of early childhood education settings to elementary school may offer additional promise. Rather than simply training preschool teachers on how to manage their classrooms, build children's skills, and cope with their own stress, professional opportunities that enhance self-regulation and executive function should be offered universally to teachers across school settings. Again, such integration would improve continuity and lengthen the children's opportunity to build and solidify core skills.

## CONCLUSION

Over the past decade, rapid advancements in neuroscience have opened several doors for understanding and acting to optimize children's early brain development. Exposure to early adversity—including both threat and deprivation—has been consistently linked with changes in children's foundational brain architecture. Such exposure places them at increased risk for immediate difficulty in managing their attention, impulses, and emotions and—over time—more pervasive deficits in academic, social, emotional, economic, and biological functioning. This chapter has highlighted several opportunities to break this negative biological chain of adversity through protecting individuals from environmental stress and stimulating skill development through environmental enrichment. In particular, we need to (1) target children during early childhood, when their brains are growing the fastest and are most malleable, (2) focus additional resources to support teachers and other close caregivers in children's lives, and (3) enhance continuity through integrating core strategies across setting and time. With sufficient attention and care, investments in early brain development, self-regulation, and executive function can create lasting, positive changes in children's lives.

CHAPTER THREE

# High-Quality Language Leads to High-Quality Learning

*Amy Pace*
*Kathy Hirsh-Pasek*
*Roberta Michnick Golinkoff*

Early childhood has finally come of age. Policy makers, educators, and parents appreciate that if we want to ensure strong academic trajectories for all children, these children must be exposed to high-quality learning experiences from birth. In this context, three leading initiatives for early childhood dot the current landscape in the United States. First, programs like Too Small to Fail and Providence Talks, among others, have rallied around the thirty-million-word gap, determined to help parents "Talk, Read, Sing" to narrow the language imbalances between lower-income children and their more affluent peers. In response to the classic study by Betty Hart and Todd Risley, these programs and many others recognize that interactive, meaningful conversations between caregivers and children best prepare them for later entry into formal schooling.[1]

Second, the Campaign for Grade Level Reading, initiated by the Annie E. Casey Foundation, attempts to move the bar by noting that only 20 percent of America's low-income children are reading at the third grade level in third grade. The campaign organizers recognize

**Figure 3.1**
**CHAPTER PREVIEW**
**Challenges to building a strong language base among early learners**

1. Few policies and initiatives aim to increase the quality of children's learning environments by targeting disparities in language-learning opportunities. Early trajectories of language development play a key role in ongoing brain development and learning outcomes—and these trajectories are malleable.
2. Many initiatives and policies focused on stimulating children's language development lack the necessary ingredients for meaningful changes in outcomes. For example, numerous approaches focus expressly on the quantity of language inputs rather than their quality.

that this reading problem begins well before children enter third grade. Thus, they have launched a large campaign that reaches across forty-two states and numerous cities to put measures into place to reverse this trend. Many of these measures include fostering language, because the development of a rich vocabulary and grammatical skills undergird progress in literacy. As David Dickinson, Roberta Golinkoff, and Kathy Hirsh-Pasek argue, "early literacy development is more than code-based instruction. Rather, it is the integral connection of code, content, and language structure."[2]

Finally, high-quality preschool has become a national priority. An article published in the *Atlantic* reported that to date, only nine states have no funding for pre-K programs.[3] As part of the Preschool for All initiative, President Obama has vowed to improve and expand preschool access in ways that will allow all low- and middle-income four- and five-year-olds to attend. Under the new mayor Bill de Blasio, New York City took the unprecedented step of approving preschool education for all four-year-olds. Strong investments in high-quality preschool make both academic and economic sense.[4] As pre-K programs expand across the nation, however, it is imperative to ensure high quality. One mark of high quality is an environment rich in language stimulation.[5] Figure 3.1 summarizes these observations.

These initiatives sit on a common core (pun intended): Strong language development is a hallmark of high-quality learning environments at home and at school. If we want to change developmental trajectories for young children, we must enrich their language environments. In this chapter, we demonstrate the importance of early language for later learning and offer six principles of language development (figure 3.2). These principles, derived from the science of learning, can be used to advance high-quality language interactions in the home, in the classroom, and in the community. Born from nuggets of science offering a distillation of the field, the principles are easy to learn and can be applied widely across cultural contexts.

**Figure 3.2 Six principles of language development**

| **Principle 1** Children learn what they hear most. | **Principle 2** Children learn words for things and events that interest them. | **Principle 3** Language thrives in interactive and responsive, rather than passive, contexts. |
|---|---|---|
| **Principle 4** Children learn words best in meaningful contexts. | **Principle 5** Children need to hear diverse examples of words and language structures. | **Principle 6** Vocabulary and grammatical development are reciprocal processes. |

## FRAMING THE PROBLEM: LANGUAGE AS A KEY INGREDIENT FOR HIGH-QUALITY LEARNING

Language—including both vocabulary and grammar—is the single best predictor of academic success and later literacy.[6] Imagine learning to decode a script into sounds that bear no meaning. Indeed, some children have had this experience after years of going to Hebrew school where words are sounded out but where the children have no idea of the meaning behind those sounds. Oral language ability relates directly to later reading ability and reading comprehension.[7] Longitudinal studies suggest that the language abilities children have at one point in time play a powerful role in shaping their later reading success.[8] For example, fourth grade language skill relates to twelfth grade reading comprehension; first grade vocabulary has been associated with eleventh grade reading outcomes; kindergarten vocabulary has been found to predict reading in fourth and seventh grades.[9]

Oral language skills have also been linked to the development of emotion regulation and to success in mathematics.[10] For example, research suggests that the amount of spatial language that young children hear between fourteen and forty-six months of age predicts their later spatial ability at fifty-four months, and this spatial competency is in turn related to later mathematical ability at age five years.[11] Furthermore, Raquel Klibanoff and colleagues report that the type and amount of math-related teacher talk predicts children's mathematical outcomes.[12] Thus, early language experiences not only are critical for later language and literacy, but also play an important role across the curriculum in STEM (science, technology, engineering, and math) development.

It is well established, however, that by the time children turn three years old, the average oral language skills of children reared in higher versus lower socioeconomic status (SES) homes show robust and well-established differences.[13] A large literature confirms that these SES-related language differences emerge early and tend to remain constant or grow even larger over time.[14] This early disparity is strongly related to intelligence scores and vocabulary size.[15] The language gap also predicts children's processing speed: Young children who receive less language input actually process incoming speech less efficiently, often taking longer to identify the meaning of a word as it flows in the torrents of words that make up sentences and conversations.[16]

Disparities in language stimulation have also been linked to early brain development. SES is an important predictor of neurocognitive performance, particularly in the development of brain areas associated with language and executive function.[17] Gaps in early language experience are particularly profound for children from disadvantaged socioeconomic backgrounds who are also acquiring English as a second language. Though roughly two-thirds of the world's population speaks more than one language and benefits from doing so, bilingual learners in the United States often grow up in poverty and struggle to learn the dominant language. The problem has cascading consequences as these children move into formal schooling.[18]

Fortunately, language trajectories are malleable. Innovative research shows gains in children's language development from early interventions targeting language use at home and increased access to high-quality preschool programs.[19] Preliminary evidence suggests that simply guiding parents to "look at what their child finds interesting and talk about it" can have a profound impact on later language development.[20] Early learning programs hold enormous promise for young children and are particularly promising for the approximately five million US children, ages three to five, from low-income families.[21] The positive results from early learning efforts is not limited to the United States. Across seventy-three low- and middle-income countries, preschool enrollment has been shown to reduce gaps in school readiness.[22]

The accumulating evidence from research being conducted around the world demands that we find ways to increase the quality of language input for all children. This chapter synthesizes that research and presents a set of useful principles that equally apply to young children, whether they are learning one or multiple languages.[23] Through these six language-learning principles, language growth can be advanced in young children, setting trajectories for positive outcomes at school entry and beyond.[24]

## THE SIX PRINCIPLES FOR BUILDING A STRONG FOUNDATION FOR LANGUAGE

### 1. Children Learn What They Hear Most

Frequency matters. Children who receive less language input have slower rates of growth and less developed outcomes across a broad range of measures in oral language than do their peers with more language input. Perhaps more importantly, these differences have an early and cumulative effect. As early as nine months of age, brain development reflects differences in the amount and type of language input infants receive, and many correlational studies have confirmed the strong relationship between the language heard in infancy and later language outcomes and reading levels.[25]

The connection between children's oral language ability and their early language environments has long been observed. Twenty years ago, Hart and Risley documented the thirty-million-word gap in a groundbreaking study that has been subsequently substantiated and extended in research by many others.[26] The Hart and Risley team collected over twelve hundred hours of tapes containing interactions between parents and their children in families that varied by SES. The research revealed that young children from lower-SES homes heard roughly six hundred words per hour as opposed to their more affluent peers, who heard an average of twenty-one hundred words over the same time span. From these data, the researchers estimated that children from higher-SES families heard approximately thirty million more words in the first three years of their lives than did children living in poverty.

This work became an instant classic. Not only has it been replicated with correlational studies, but many studies have also shown long-range consequences for later vocabulary development, grammatical ability, narrative ability, reading levels, and math skills.[27] Perhaps the most striking research came from Anne Fernald and her colleagues, who found that diminished language input at eighteen months of age resulted in slower language-processing speeds or lower language efficiency by two years of age.[28] Slower processing speeds, in turn, are likely to affect children's ability to glean the meaning of unfamiliar words spoken within a linguistic context, setting children up for missed opportunities to learn. Imagine a toddler trying to grasp on to an early word as the sentence continues to speed by.[29]

For children learning English as a second language, research suggests that they lag behind their monolingual peers in English language development. The extent of the difference depends on both their exposure to English and whether that exposure is by a native or a nonnative speaker of the language.[30] Language-minority children with one native English-speaking parent benefit more from English exposure at home than do children with two native Spanish-speaking parents.[31] To compound this issue, 41 percent of children in families below the poverty level in the United States have at least one household member who speaks a language other than English at home, and teachers in early care and education settings in Spanish-speaking communities are frequently nonnative speakers of English.[32]

Living in language-minority communities is likely to affect English language development, and this different pattern of development can exacerbate the effects of poverty for many children. But the principle of language development still applies: Rich and varied language exposure provided by native speakers has a critical impact on learning outcomes. Research with Spanish-speaking bilingual children has shown that first-language skills and growth in Spanish contribute to the development of reading skills in English, and the use of bilingual

**Figure 3.3 Classroom applications of principle 1**

- Enrich everyday activities with language.
- Extend conversations on a single topic, idea, or question.
- Infuse language into daily classroom routines.
- Talk, read, and sing with children every day.

children's first language in instruction leads to higher social, cognitive, and academic achievement levels.[33] Access to high-quality bilingual programming can also assist young bilingual learners in their language and literacy development.[34] Increasing opportunities for children to receive frequent input in *both* languages as early as possible yields better outcomes and may play a role in preventing future language difficulties that bilingual learners frequently encounter.[35] Figure 3.3 lists ways to apply this principle in early learning classrooms.

## 2. Children Learn Words for Things and Events That Interest Them

The learner's interest also plays a critical role in guiding attention, sustaining motivation, and shaping outcomes across learning contexts. The classic work here comes from vocabulary learning in children acquiring their first words. Lois Bloom termed this concept the "principle of relevance" and suggested that "language learning is enhanced when the words a child hears bear upon and are pertinent to the objects of engagement, interest, and feelings."[36] Evidence in support of this principle comes from research showing that young children readily assume that a new word refers to an object they find interesting or perceptually salient rather than to an object they find boring.[37]

How do we begin to foster interest in young children? The key may be building interests together—creating daily routines or interactions that support the mutual development of family, classroom, or community engagement. For children from disparately disadvantaged backgrounds, educators may first need to ensure that children are provided the space and support to develop interests around a concept or an activity. Evidence from the literature on language acquisition suggests that children whose parents talk about the objects and events the children are interested in tend to have larger vocabularies.[38] The research also supports the corollary—children whose parents try to redirect their attention and label objects not of interest tend to have fewer words.[39]

Recent findings suggest that the principle of relevance extends broadly to communicative situations in general. In a study conducted by Katarina Begus and colleagues, sixteen-month-old infants used pointing to solicit information about novel objects. Infants showed superior learning about object function when adults followed the infants' *own* interest to demonstrate the requested toy rather than ignoring the infants' preferences.[40] When adults demonstrated the object that the infant had ignored, the infants failed to learn about the object even though the participants had been equally attentive during the initial introduction of both items.[41]

Together, these findings suggest that if we let them, infants, toddlers, and other children will show or tell us what they are interested in learning about. Applied to high-quality learning environments, this principle suggests that we may boost children's language knowledge by capitalizing on their interests and attention during communicative exchanges (figure 3.4).

**Figure 3.4 Classroom applications of principle 2**

- Observe and listen to determine children's interests.
- Celebrate and support children's unique interests and strengths.
- Provide opportunities for children to discover new interests and to develop deep interests.
- Emphasize child-centered activities, and follow the child's lead.
- Support opportunities for child-to-child conversations and other communication.

### 3. Language Thrives in Interactive and Responsive, Rather than Passive, Contexts

Thus far, we have provided evidence that caregivers' input and the children's interests are important for language and learning. The relationship *between* children and their caregivers—be they parents or teachers—is another essential element of high-quality learning. Passive language exposure is not enough. Instead, teachers and parents must engage with children, offering sensitive and responsive language input that is tailored to the interests and timing of the child's attention.[42] This need for interaction may partly explain why children under the age of three are unlikely to learn language from mere exposure to television or video, even if the media are specifically designed for babies.[43] While there is evidence that children can learn from television from age three and beyond, the interactive qualities of human language offer considerably more varied and adaptive language that builds vocabulary and prepares children for reading.

Catherine Tamis-LeMonda and colleagues noted several qualities central to early interactions, including the timing of the teacher or caregiver response and the adult's ability to respond with actions or language that meaningfully build on the child's contribution to the conversation.[44] Adults who take turns in interactions with young children, share periods of joint focus, are sensitive and responsive to children, and express positive affect provide children with the scaffolding needed to facilitate language and cognitive growth.[45]

Several studies, including the Eunice Kennedy Shriver National Institute of Child Health and Human Development Study of Early Child Care and Youth Development (NICHD SECCYD), demonstrated that caregiver and teacher "sensitivity and responsivity"—a global description of a warm and stimulating engagement—are related to both immediate and long-term language, social, cognitive, and academic outcomes from preschool through the school years.[46] Similarly, Sondra Birch and Gary Ladd found correlations between the quality of teacher-child relationships and academic performance.[47] Other research has shown that the frequency of warmth and sensitivity in teacher-child conversations in preschool classrooms was correlated with the same teachers' tendency to engage in cognitively and linguistically enriching conversations with children.[48] The quality of teacher-child interactions is a key mechanism responsible for learning in the early care and education setting.[49]

Why might responsive interactions be crucial for language growth? Language is learned in a social context.[50] First relationships are essential for helping young children discern adults' intentions, navigate emotional environments, and buffer stress.[51] Indeed, caregiver-child interactions that form the foundation for language occur with children as young as three months.[52] As children and caregivers engage in what Hart and Risley called "the dance" and Hirsh-Pasek and colleagues have termed "conversational duets," a strong foundation for communication is constructed, serving as a platform for ongoing language development.[53] The importance of interaction may explain why children as young as two years successfully learn new vocabulary words over video chat (e.g., Skype) but not over a less interactive television program.[54]

Encouraging conversations—both verbal and nonverbal—between children, caregivers, and teachers who remain attuned to children's attention and interests facilitates language competencies throughout the infant, toddler, and preschool years.[55] Sustained periods of positive interaction build strong relationships, which are known positive predictors of success in school and beyond. A teacher's or caregiver's understanding of children's needs is relevant here. Teachers who are struggling to communicate with children because of large class sizes cannot offer this type of tailored feedback for children who most need it. This challenge to teacher-child interaction is particularly egregious for low-income children and for bilingual learners, who may not be hearing sufficient input in the dominant English language outside of school. When children are a part of the conversation—whether at

**Figure 3.5 Classroom applications of principle 3**

- Learn to recognize and respond to children's verbal and non-verbal bids for communication (a point, a glance, a scowl, or a word).
- Encourage children to take turns during conversations with peers.
- Consider all questions seriously; try posing a question in response to keep the conversation going.
- Stay relevant: Expand and extend children's comments to provide new information and to stretch the conversation.

home, in childcare, or at school—their language learning is more likely to thrive than when they lack opportunities to participate in conversations. To provide these opportunities, educators must consider the individual needs of each student and be sensitive to the wide cultural and linguistic variation encountered in today's diverse classrooms (figure 3.5).

## 4. Children Learn Words Best in Meaningful Contexts

Sparking a child's interest is often a first step in making learning meaningful; it involves encouraging the child to connect new information with a concrete experience or interaction. Catherine Haden and her colleagues have shown that parents support learning when they ask children to recount their experiences to another adult.[56] Indeed, people tend to learn best when information is presented in integrated contexts rather than as a set of isolated facts.[57] Thus, words presented as a grocery list are better remembered than the same list of words presented without context. By the same token, a seemingly random string of letters (e.g., irsfbicianasa) is difficult to recall until chunked into meaningful acronyms (i.e., irs fbi cia nasa).

How does this principle extend to learning environments? Meaningful connections between words develop as children link new vocabulary knowledge with concrete learning experiences. In a preschool classroom, for example, James Christie and Kathleen Roskos found that children who learn related vocabulary for the category of *building* (words like *hammer, tool belts, hard hats*, and *screwdrivers*) better remember these words than children who do not learn in this more integrative way.[58] Amy Booth and Sandra Waxman reported that providing definitions to three-year-olds about what one can do with an object or action promotes better vocabulary learning than does providing static, noncausal definitions.[59] Jennifer M. Zosh, Meredith Brinster, and Justin Halberda found that preschoolers have better memory for new vocabulary words when they learn the meaning through their own inferences than when they are simply told the definition.[60]

Meaning develops not only by connecting words with experiences, but also by hearing words used in sentences with narratives. Play can often provide a rich context for those narratives. *Guided play* involves adults supporting children's active exploration and natural curiosity around a specific learning goal.[61] An abundance of evidence suggests that children who are given the opportunity to use vocabulary in guided play tend to learn it better than those whose only exposure is through direct instruction.[62]

Research from our laboratories shows additional learning benefits from guided play over free play. Parents used spatial language (words describing the spatial features and properties of objects—for example, *big, tall, circle, curvy, edge*) more frequently with their four-year-olds during guided play with blocks than they did in free play with blocks or play with preassembled structures, and children who were engaged in guided play with blocks used significantly more spatial talk than did those engaged in free play.[63]

Enhancing spatial and numerical language through guided play is not just fun and engaging for children—it is also related to later skills in math. One study found, for example, that parents used more spatial language during guided play with puzzles and blocks than at other times and that parents' use of spatial terms was related to children's mathematical skills.[64] Other research found that parents who used more number words when their children were very young—especially when talking about numbers larger than four—had children who did better in number and mathematical tasks, particularly when the children were talking about visible objects.[65] Finally, the amount of teachers' math talk to four-year-olds is related to these children's math skills at the end of the school year.[66] A similar relationship holds between meaningful engagement and preliteracy skills: Doris Bergen and Daria Mauer found that the play of four-year-olds, in the form of making shopping lists and "reading" storybooks to stuffed animals, predicted both language and reading readiness after the children had entered kindergarten.[67]

Meaningful contexts—such as those constructed during guided play—may scaffold learning by heightening engagement and facilitating children's ability to connect new knowledge with concrete experiences. Conversations that take place between adults and children during guided play—conversations that build on children's interests and natural exploration—offer children new lexical concepts that are likely to be retained.[68] Although experimental research comparing vocabulary learning in meaningful versus less meaningful contexts is sparse, correlational studies in language, play, and memory converge to suggest that teaching language in integrated and meaningful situations enriches and deepens children's background experience and thus their mental lexicons.[69] Critically, what is meaningful in one context for an individual child may not resonate as clearly in other circumstances, classrooms, or groups of children. Creating meaningful learning environments will require a richness of representation that carefully considers each child's own interests, knowledge, and experience. Figure 3.6 lists ways to apply this principle in early learning classrooms.

**Figure 3.6 Classroom applications of principle 4**

- Connect the dots; create a web of knowledge.
- Talk with children about what you know.
- Make the link explicit: Highlight connections to enduring themes (e.g., family or recent events).
- Build connections over time by linking routines and activities that span thematic units.
- Extend the classroom beyond its walls to take learning into the world (e.g., walk around the block to find shapes in the neighborhood).

## 5. Children Need to Hear Diverse Examples of Words and Language Structures

Simplifying the language that is used in conversations with young children may actually do them a disservice.[70] On the contrary, introducing diverse and sophisticated vocabulary words—as well as providing these words in complex and varied sentence structures—appears to be beneficial for children's vocabulary growth, grammar development, and communication skills.[71] In fact, linguistic diversity is related to positive language outcomes when measured in terms of rare words and the number of unique (nonredundant) words produced.[72] Diverse input facilitates not only semantic development, but grammatical development as well. In one study, adults' lexical and syntactic diversity, including variety of words, phrases, and clauses, predicted more diverse child speech at forty-six months.[73]

Evidence supporting this principle also comes from interactions between children and teachers in the classroom. Children whose teachers provide more complex and diverse language input make gains above and beyond children whose teachers use language that is less supportive.[74] In a targeted study of language intervention, Janellen Huttenlocher and colleagues asked whether the complexity and diversity of teachers' language (multiclause sentences) with forty-three- to fifty-month-old children was related to language outcomes over the course of the school year.[75] Although teacher language complexity was not related to baseline levels of child language at the start of the year, it was significantly related to children's grammatical levels at the end of the year, even with parental language, child's starting language, and SES controlled. These results suggest that the amount and quality of teachers' language input is directly related to children's language growth.

For children learning more than one language, diversity of input coming from multiple speakers is just as important. One study asked mothers of Spanish-English bilingual twenty-five-month-olds to keep diary entries about their children's dual-language exposure.[76] The number of different speakers from whom the children heard English and the percentage of this input that was provided by native speakers accounted for the variation found in the children's English skills, suggesting that exposure to diverse input from multiple native speakers is important for language learning.

How does diversity support language and learning? Hearing examples of a word presented in diverse contexts helps children develop abstract meanings and make connections beyond the specific instance to build more in-depth knowledge and understanding.[77] If a child hears the word *transportation* when learning about trains, they have a limited connection and may mistakenly restrict their knowledge of the term to train-related travel. If, however, the word *transportation* is introduced as a conceptual theme within a unit that considers travel by boat, bicycle, and airplane, it enriches the child's connection between words and the world. But simply using new words is not enough. Children learn words better when they have the chance to encounter words in context *and* when word meanings are explicitly taught.[78] Though some children benefit from language environments that are designed to ensure adequate quantity and quality of input, many others need more explicit instruction about word meanings and the features of language that are important in formal schooling.[79]

Learning is at its best when children are provided with diverse examples that provide the opportunity to integrate new information. And diverse examples are best presented in meaningful contexts. Dedre Gentner, Florencia Anggoro, and Raquel Klibanoff suggest that comparison, or "structural alignment," is one of the primary mechanisms that allow children to build word knowledge across contexts by pulling out the relevant similarities between diverse examples.[80] These connections are the building blocks for strong language and literacy growth. Susan B. Neuman goes further to suggest that a range of knowledge-building experiences creates "schemas of information networks" that encourage children to question, discover, and evaluate new ideas.[81] Diversity in learning environments requires content- and language-rich instruction to help children continually build on and refine what they already know and can do. Figure 3.7 lists ways to apply this principle in early learning classrooms.

**Figure 3.7 Classroom applications of principle 5**

- Use content-specific vocabulary (e.g., *hypothesis*, *endangered*, or *paleontology*) to build knowledge.
- Define new words during reading and talk.
- Introduce sophisticated language, but ground new words in concrete and tangible learning experiences.
- Use developmentally appropriate clauses and sentence structures that support children's language skills.
- Have one-on-one conversations around content areas that are of interest to the child.
- Use language at the edge of children's current ability, providing language and learning goals that are both challenging and achievable.

## 6. Vocabulary and Grammatical Development Are Reciprocal Processes

Language is more than vocabulary. At the very least, the emphasis should be shifted to include vocabulary *and* grammar. James Dixon and Virginia Marchman argue that words and grammar are "developing in synchrony across the first few years of life."[82] The relation between vocabulary and grammatical development for children's ability to learn more than one language is parallel to that observed in monolingual children. Barbara Conboy and Donna Thal found, for example, that English vocabulary predicted English grammar and that Spanish vocabulary predicted Spanish grammar in bilingual children learning both English and Spanish.[83]

In addition, children learn vocabulary *through* grammar and grammar *through* vocabulary.[84] That is, by noting the linguistic context in which words appear, children gain information about word meanings, and once children have an initial grasp of word meanings, they use this knowledge to construct and comprehend increasingly complex sentences.[85] Critically, learning to use language proficiently requires that children acquire more than object words or nouns; they must also learn verbs, adjectives, and prepositions (such as *on top of* and *between*) to capture the relations that sentences describe. Although verbs and spatial relational terms are more difficult for children to acquire than concrete nouns, they are of utmost importance if children are to comprehend and produce complex language.[86]

A more comprehensive account of oral language must consider children's knowledge of sounds (phonology), meaning (semantics), structure (grammar, including morphology and syntax), and function (pragmatics). Language is multifaceted and iterative. For instance, children often learn the meaning of new vocabulary words by relying on their growing knowledge of language structure. Within the second year of life, for example, children attend to grammatical elements like syntax (i.e., word order), morphological markers (e.g., *-ing*), and sentence structure to help them learn the meaning of a new word.[87] Children learn verbs and spatial terms best when these are presented in sentences and with real-world events that clearly reveal the relationship of "who is doing what to whom."[88]

This principle is key for learning environments because oral language, measured as *both* vocabulary and grammar, is crucial for early literacy and academic achievement.[89] Building vocabulary is not a matter of learning words in isolation, but of hearing words within multiple sentences and in multiple contexts. Complementarily, understanding sentences requires that children comprehend the words that the sentences comprise. Vocabulary is a strong predictor of academic outcomes because word knowledge is critically linked with language comprehension and use. If you take away the language, teaching vocabulary words in isolation is not going to make an impact. Most of us remember learning vocabulary lists for the SAT—few of these words had any sticking power for us after the test was complete. It is time to rethink more effective means of providing children with the tools and strategies for learning new vocabulary words instead of increasing the sheer exposure to sophisticated words with no connection to the rich conceptual meanings that they connote (figure 3.8).

**Figure 3.8 Classroom applications of principle 6**

- Introduce new language structures with familiar topics such as food, family, or toys.
- Pose open-ended questions, provide instructions, and think out loud to promote learning.
- Encourage children to use increasingly complex sentences by modeling them in classroom conversations.
- Encourage the learning of new vocabulary words by presenting them in familiar ways.

## CONCLUSION

Taken together, these six principles of language learning summarize the latest science. They offer what we have called *edible science*—science that is accessible, digestible, and usable. This way of approaching the science-to-practice bridge preserves the integrity of the empirical evidence while distilling themes that might be of use to educators, parents, and policy makers. The principles represent the main findings culled from thousands of published papers, and although much of the research reviewed was conducted with monolinguals, the findings are also relevant to bilingual learners. Several policy implications that emerge from the synthesis of these principles are summarized in figure 3.9.

The principles are also adaptable. For example, some cultures might have more social interaction than others. For this reason, we have presented the requirements for language learning as a set of principles, rather than as more rigid scripts, and thereby allow for diversity in teachers and cultures celebrating individual differences.

We also encourage the use of these principles across many settings where learning occurs—be it cooking, gardening, science, or geography, to name a few. It may be time to expand our model of assessment and outcomes to observe child performance and growth in areas that build on language, literacy, and numeracy—such as art, spatial learning, music, and theater. Language is both the medium of instruction and the mechanism for learning. For this reason, high-quality language experiences can be infused into formal and informal learning situations so that is practiced throughout the day.

Using these principles at home and at school will allow us to change the trajectory of learning for all children in an evidence-based way. And helping children optimize their vocabulary and grammatical learning will prepare them for their journey through school. Involving parents and communities is key. Though academic gains are clearly linked with the time children spend in school, school time represents only a small fraction of a child's experience. Indeed, over 80 percent of a child's

**Figure 3.9 Early language development: policy considerations for teachers, curricula, school organizations, and the wider community**

**Supporting teachers in delivering language-rich instruction**

- Provide opportunities to observe and reliably measure teacher-child interactions through evidence-based assessments.
- Enhance program delivery and child outcomes through coaching, reflection, and professional development so that teachers can see and label effective interactions.

**Starting with a language-rich curriculum**

- Ensure that language is a key part of the curriculum, separate from literacy and other skills or content areas that build on language.
- Adopt evidence-based curricula that connect comprehensive early learning standards to kindergarten standards.

**Promoting classroom characteristics that support language and learning**

- Advocate for higher teacher-to-pupil ratios to enhance the quality and quantity of language-rich interactions.
- Implement early screening, assessment, and progress monitoring to identify target areas for individualized instruction.

**Including families and communities to create language-rich learning environments**

- Create citywide forums—with centralized locations, or *piazzas*—where communities connect and converse with teachers, families, and children.
- Share information about how early language experiences shape children's learning, and mobilize efforts to enhance language environments across families and communities.

waking time, from kindergarten through twelfth grade, is spent *outside* the classroom.[90] Making a difference will require that these principles are applied to informal learning environments as well to promote "lifelong and lifewide learning."[91]

Meeting this challenge will take innovative solutions but does not need to be overly complicated. For example, the Temple Infant and Child Laboratory in collaboration with the Child's Play, Learning, and Development Laboratory at the University of Delaware implemented a subtle and inexpensive language intervention aimed at sparking parent-child interaction in a place families regularly visit: the supermarket.[92] Placing conversation-starter signs at strategic locations within stores serving low-income neighborhoods increased both the amount and the quality of talk between parents and their children. Such simple, cost-effective interventions in everyday environments may be an innovative means of bolstering children's language-rich interactions. It is time to take our knowledge of the science of language learning to meet families where they are: We already have smart classrooms; now we need smart cities and smart communities. We can make large-scale changes with small-scale investments.

In sum, language is a core ingredient in successful academic and social development. We have now amassed enough data in the science of language learning to suggest a set of principles that can be used to help every child reach his or her potential. With the science in hand, we now face the challenge of sharing this knowledge with other educators—including home-based care providers, early educators, pre-K teachers, and all caregivers—to deftly use these principles in ways that augment their daily routines.

For all the policy implications outlined in figure 3.9, the promotion of early learning is key. As we move from discovery to the application of our science, we can begin to narrow the thirty-million-word gap, reach more of the goals of the Grade Level Reading Campaign, and understand the critical role of language as one defining feature of high-quality learning environments from preschool and beyond.

CHAPTER FOUR

# Assessing and Understanding the Needs of Bilingual Learners

*Gigi Luk*
*Joanna A. Christodoulou*

Children from different backgrounds nevertheless consistently embark on language development in similar ways. From birth onward, all children are exposed to oral language and unfurl their natural skills in language learning. While it is important to identify factors that facilitate language development in young children, it is equally important to examine risk factors that hinder it, particularly in bilingual children. Understanding how early life experiences affect language development allows researchers and educators to link these early experiences to subsequent literacy and academic outcomes. Given that language provides building blocks for literacy, cognition, and academic learning, education leaders need to examine the facilitation of, and impediments to, language development in bilingual children to design developmentally and linguistically sensitive educational policy and practices.

In this chapter, we examine language and literacy development for children from linguistically diverse households. We review the risk factors associated with poor language outcomes for all children and how early educational experiences can alleviate these negative consequences. We also look at the cognitive benefits observed in fluent bilingual children

**Figure 4.1**
**CHAPTER PREVIEW**
**Challenges to embracing language diversity and promoting its advantages in early learning**

1. As a primary indicator of bilingual learners' academic achievement, English proficiency may be construed incorrectly as limited learning capacity when children earn low scores on these assessments. In assessments of bilingual learners, home-language proficiency is as informative as English language proficiency.
2. Bilingual learners typically perform better on executive functioning tasks than do their monolingual peers growing up in similar economic circumstances. Yet in most pre-K settings, we do not recognize or capitalize on this important strength.

and the challenges in measuring the childhood language experience. Next, we discuss assessments sensitive to language diversity in young children and how these assessments can be used effectively in school settings. Finally, we argue that language diversity can be harnessed as an asset in US classrooms. Toward this end, we recommend that stakeholders embrace language diversity and advocate for early learning support for children from diverse language backgrounds. Figure 4.1 summarizes the important issues that this chapter considers.

## EARLY LANGUAGE CHALLENGES FOR BILINGUAL CHILDREN IN THE UNITED STATES

Early adversity can put children at risk for delayed learning and development and other difficulties, particularly in the context of education. While bilingualism is not a risk factor for learning and development, it is often associated with social conditions that pose challenges for developing children. For example, at least in the United States, bilingualism is often observed in low-income families. Similarly, poverty itself is not necessarily a risk factor, but limited accessibility to resources due to financial constraints, stress induced by financial crisis, and inadequate parental interactions all act as mechanisms linking poverty to weaker language proficiency. In homes where the spoken language is not the same as the community language, children receive quantitatively less exposure to either single language. The outcome is a persistent achievement gap between monolingual children and bilingual children, two groups that often have disparate socioeconomic backgrounds.[1] Parents and educators need to consider bilingualism in the context of socioeconomic status (SES), rather than consider each independently. Quality language input, regardless of whether it is the child's and parent's native or second language, is important for building a language foundation for subsequent learning.

The American language landscape has undergone tremendous changes, particularly over the last three decades. In an American Community Survey Report, an estimated 60.6 million (approximately 21 percent) of the American population aged five and older reported speaking a non-English language at home in 2011, compared with an estimated 23 million (approximately 11 percent) in 1980. These statistics are probably an underestimate of the bilingual population because the census questions are solely based on home language usage, and therefore children who speak English at home but a different language outside home are not included.[2] Regardless, the dramatic increase in the bilingual population is most apparent in children and adolescents.

Given the increasing population of children from diverse language backgrounds, it is essential to understand language development by isolating the effects of language diversity and risk factors. Furthermore, bilingualism is a life experience that has both linguistic and cognitive consequences. Solely focusing on bilingual children's developing language proficiency—typically English—may not provide a comprehensive picture of their learning potential. In addition to English proficiency, bilingual children's domain-general processing skills, such as executive functions, should be consider in light of their typically weaker language proficiency, because research indicates that their domain-general skills are stronger than those of their monolingual peers. To advance a sensitive and inclusive education agenda, we argue that, according to research on language, literacy, and bilingualism, expansion and improvement in pre-K education could provide more equitable learning foundations for children from diverse language backgrounds.

## LANGUAGE DEVELOPMENT IN EARLY CHILDHOOD

The earliest months of life are already productive language-learning opportunities for children. Language development is so crucial to human development that the earliest experiences set the foundation for later development of language and literacy skills. From birth and onward, children are highly attuned to the specific features of the languages they are exposed to. During the first six postnatal months, children across cultures and locations produce a similar range of sounds as they babble, and by the end of the first year, the range of sounds they produce narrows to those common in their own language environments.[3] Children have a natural ability to become experts in language sounds relevant to their experiences early in their lives, and this tuning becomes the platform for later speech, language, and literacy outcomes.

A significant predictor of these outcomes is socioeconomic status, which is primarily measured through proxies such as parental education and family income. SES indices are understood to represent the range of opportunities available to children and are based on household resources, with greater parental education and income affording greater awareness of, and access to, opportunities. Children from low-income households often attain lower language proficiency and have slower literacy development. More broadly, low SES is associated with negative consequences for academic, neurocognitive, socio-emotional, and physical health domains, particularly during early childhood.[4] Research on risk factors associated with SES has indicated that students from low-SES households are more likely to face multiple risk factors for their development in language and other domains.[5] Low SES, however, is not strictly deterministic, as resilience in these domains has also been evident.[6]

A landmark study by Betty Hart and Todd Risley demonstrated that SES is significantly associated with language exposure at home, with a sharp divide between higher- and lower-SES children increasing over time for vocabulary exposure.[7] The number of words that children heard per hour amounted to about 2,150 for the high-SES group, 1,250 for mid-SES, and 620 for the low-SES group. Children from the high-SES group acquired 60 percent more words than did children from low-SES group. These differences over a sustained period set children up for vastly diverse language characteristics when they enter school, particularly because a child's vocabulary is heavily reliant on his or her language environment. The more words a child is exposed to, the faster the child will build up vocabulary knowledge. A growing body of research bears out the robust relationship between the quantity, and quality, of a child's linguistic input and his or her language and literacy development during school into adulthood.[8]

As Lauren Rubenzahl, Kristelle Lavallee, and Michael Rich discuss in more detail in chapter 5, many families rely on digital technology tools in their daily lives to engage children in entertainment or educational activities, with a disproportionately higher amount of media exposure among young children from low-SES homes.[9] Furthermore, parents or caregivers from lower-SES households overwhelmingly believe that digital resources, in the form of baby DVDs or educational programs on television, can be beneficial.[10] However, early media exposure (at six months or younger) is associated with lower scores on measures of language and cognition.[11] This relation is understood to be driven by a replacement of quality language interactions in the home rather than the content of the media exposure per se. Even background television exposure is associated with decreased quantity and quality of parent-child interactions.[12]

While many digital activities such as watching television offer diverse language experiences, they cannot substitute for, or approximate, the value of learning from another person. Patricia Kuhl and colleagues presented evidence that emphasized the importance of caretakers speaking to children without using digital tools as a substitute.[13] Children were assigned to learn a new language either from an instructor through in-person sessions or by watching videos of the instructor. The group that participated in the human interaction sessions outperformed the other group, lending additional evidence to the critical nature of interpersonal language learning. Furthermore, the study highlights the risk of using screen time at the expense of interpersonal interactions.

## HOW PRE-K EDUCATION CAN ALLEVIATE RISK FACTORS IN LANGUAGE DEVELOPMENT

Before children begin formal schooling, they are students of their home environments, and their caretakers are their primary teachers. Given the clear importance of rich language exposure and experiences early in development, intervention programs have been developed to promote good practice in the home environment and educate caretakers on how to enrich the language environment for their children. Indeed, a focus on early intervention from birth to age five yields the highest returns for individuals and communities, particularly for children in low-SES environments.[14]

The importance of investing in early child development is especially evident among children who have experienced consistent negative outcomes when there is early exposure to stress, poor environments, and limited caretaker involvement and interaction. An important body of research elaborating on this conclusion comes from studies conducted in Romania, where researchers documented the impact of child-rearing inside and outside institutions. The study results show that the earlier a child is removed from an institution and placed in high-quality foster care, the better the outcomes in various areas, including cognitive and language development.[15] Evident from this body of work is the impact of early experiences and the persistently negative influence of significant deprivation.

Access to resources that can support positive child development have been the focus of several intervention programs targeting low-SES households. One example is the Abecedarian Project, which provided early educational intervention to disadvantaged children from birth to age five in a randomized, controlled study with the aim of preventing negative cognitive outcomes. The focus of instruction was predominantly on language but also included socio-emotional and cognitive areas. This longitudinal study recruited children born between 1972 and 1977 and followed them into adulthood (age thirty-five). Results showed that the children who received the intervention had higher scores in cognition, reading, and math and, as adults, went further in higher education and had better health.[16] This work highlights the relevance of early language development and the implications for later academic outcomes, the feasibility of providing high-quality infrastructures for promoting these skills, and the long-term benefit of early intervention at the individual and societal levels.

A major limitation of such longitudinal intervention studies is that on many levels, the children in these studies are very different from today's children. Many scholars who have reviewed the research hesitate to generalize these findings to today's population of students. Unfortunately, this limitation will apply to any long-term study, but it does not eliminate the potential for learning about the growth of core cognitive or language abilities. Despite the limitations of the longitudinal data, the results remain promising and interesting.

## LANGUAGE AND COGNITION IN YOUNG CHILDREN

Cognition, very much like language, also has an early start. During the first few years of life, children's language and cognitive skills change in response to the variability in the environment, such as parents' and other caregivers' language input, parenting style, and level of engagement; the family's socioeconomic status; and the availability of literacy-related materials.[17] One example of children's cognitive development is executive functions, a set of domain-general skills that are critical for efficient and flexible decision making and for goal-directed behavior.

To investigate how language and cognition interact in the context of learning, Christina Weiland, M. Clara Barata, and Hirokazu Yoshikawa reported that executive functions in preschoolers during the beginning of an academic year were predictive of receptive vocabulary at the end of the preschool year.[18] However, there was no equivalent reciprocal predictive power from receptive vocabulary to executive functions in the same sample. These findings suggest that executive functions may serve as a stepping-stone for young children's vocabulary acquisition. To design sensitive and inclusive pedagogy for young bilingual children, educational leaders must understand how children's cognition supports language learning and literacy acquisition.

### Language Development for Bilingual Children

While bilingualism does not entail negative consequences, the need to acquire two languages, sometimes in different situations, may shift the developmental trajectory in language and literacy. Indeed, many researchers have demonstrated that early language development in bilingual children parallels those observed in monolingual children, such as early language perception and discrimination during infancy, efficiency in online language processing, and phonology.[19] The lack of group differences contradicted early research in the 1920s and 1930s suggesting that bilingualism is related to mental confusion.[20] This early research may have set in motion continued misconceptions—ideas still apparent today—about the impact of being a diverse language learner.

Research has shown that bilingual children typically performed better in metalinguistic awareness tasks such as extracting meaning from a context, learning an additional foreign language, and incidental word learning.[21] Children in these studies could be referred to as *bilingual children with two first languages* because they were exposed to two languages early and simultaneously. One pedagogical implication from these results is that young children speaking languages that share the same writing system, such as Spanish-speaking preschoolers learning English, may benefit from Spanish instruction. This is because overall oral language proficiency can be supported through instruction from a language that has similar phonological structures. In other words, instruction or experience in Spanish may support English language development, and vice versa. Given that first-language proficiency, second-language proficiency, and academic outcomes were significantly and positively associated in bilingual children with immigrant backgrounds, young children can benefit from transitional language support that incorporates both their home language and English.[22]

In addition to measuring children's phonological awareness, schools often include word-level assessments, such as receptive and expressive vocabulary. These standardized measures usually adopt nationally representative standardized samples, in which children with diverse language backgrounds are often underrepresented, making interpretation of bilingual children's performance somewhat challenging. On language proficiency assessments using standardized vocabulary measures, children and toddlers from diverse language backgrounds typically have smaller vocabularies in a single language than do their monolingual peers.[23] The bilingual children might have a smaller vocabulary because the testing was conducted in the children's weaker language, to which the children had less exposure. Notably, in terms of conceptual scores, that is, when children are allowed to respond in either language, bilingual children scored as well as their age-matched monolingual peers.[24] These findings support the notion that children from diverse language backgrounds may acquire vocabulary in each of their languages, depending on the quantity and quality of exposure of each language. It is likely that the smaller vocabulary in each language is related to learning and environmental input rather than development and the propensity to acquire language. When evaluating language proficiency in children with diverse language backgrounds, educators need to be mindful of the validity of comparing scores against a standardized sample that is not linguistically diverse.

## Cognitive Effects of Bilingualism

As young children's oral language skills develop, so do their cognitive processes. These processes, or executive functions, include a set of skills critical for efficient and flexible decision making. Typically, researchers compare the performance of monolingual and bilingual children on tasks assessing executive functions such as control of attention, the ability to ignore distracting information, or cognitive flexibility. Compared with children growing up speaking one language, children who are fluent in two or more languages typically performed better on executive function tasks that require little demand in language proficiency, for example, making decisions based on arrows or shapes in different colors.[25] Leah Kapa and John Colombo examined attentional control in English monolinguals, early Spanish-English bilinguals, and late Spanish-English bilinguals.[26] After controlling for age and verbal performance, the researchers found that early Spanish-English bilinguals had significantly faster response time in an attention task. In a bilingual's mind, even when only one language is being used, the other language is never turned off and it interferes with the active language constantly. To successfully manage multiple languages, a bilingual has to suppress the interfering language while focusing on the target language.[27] Because a bilingual child adapts to these increased linguistic demands, he or she has advanced performance on cognitive tasks.

Like language development, the development of executive functions is also vulnerable to risk factors in the environment. While little research has been done on the intersection between bilingualism and SES, the available research demonstrates positive cognitive outcomes, particularly in processing skills that do not rely on content knowledge. Alejandra Calvo and Ellen Bialystok found that SES and bilingualism have dissociable effects on developing cognition.[28] In their study, middle-class children in Canada performed better on language and executive-function tasks than did working-class children.[29] Relative to monolingual children, bilingual children performed better on executive-function tasks but worse on language tasks. The effect size for bilingualism was similar in the two social classes in the study. Furthermore, bilingual children from low-income families in Luxembourg outperformed their monolingual peers in executive-functioning tasks specifically tapping into control of attention.[30] In another study, Greek researchers found no difference in executive functioning between Greek monolingual children and Greek-Albanian bilingual children with matching socio-demographic backgrounds. Nevertheless, there was a positive relationship between efficiency in managing multiple languages and performance in cognition tasks, indicating that the group difference in executive function is not absolute but is influenced by the heterogeneity of the bilingual population.[31]

Overall, research indicated that children growing up with two languages had desirable cognitive consequences but demonstrated limited proficiency in a given single language. Across these studies reporting the seemingly polarized findings on language and cognition, most of the bilingual children spoke a minority language at home while learning a dominant language at school. There is significant heterogeneity in bilingual experiences because bilingualism is not a categorical variable. It is a multidimensional life experience that includes onset age of active bilingualism and functional usage and proficiency in one of the two languages.[32] Lisa Bedore and colleagues showed that parental reports of Spanish-English bilingual children's daily functional usage accounted for more variance in language dominance than did age of first exposure.[33] In our own research involving bilingual Spanish- and English-speaking children attending Head Start programs, we have also identified that home language exposure/usage, but not proficiency in English, is an important quantifiable indicator of preschoolers' executive-function performance.[34] Collectively, these findings suggest that in assessments of bilingual preschoolers, knowledge of their home language exposure/usage is at least as important as is their English language proficiency. In the current education system, however, English proficiency is still the primary indicator for children from diverse linguistic backgrounds.

## Supporting Diverse Language Learners Through Pre-K Education

In light of the globally changing linguistic landscape, education research on children with diverse language backgrounds has increased significantly in the last two decades. Particularly in the United States, this line of research has focused on children who are considered to be English language learners (ELLs). According to the National Center of Education Statistics, approximately 4.7 million children were identified as ELLs in US schools in 2012. Of this population, the majority are born in the United States, attend lower elementary grades in urban schools of large cities, and are concentrated in schools with a high percentage of students eligible for free or reduced-price lunch.[35] ELL children typically speak a home language other than English (most commonly Spanish) and attain lower English proficiency in speaking, listening, reading, and writing. The socio-demographics of the ELL children suggest two major challenges in schools: (1) learning academic content through a developing language and (2) experiencing language delay related to poverty, as described earlier. While there may be a pervasive achievement gap between English-proficient students and ELLs, we argue that providing high-quality pre-K education would enhance the language foundations critical for academic success in young bilingual children from challenging social backgrounds, hence minimizing the achievement gap. Furthermore, with adequate language support in early childhood education, schools could take advantage of language diversity to promote a linguistically inclusive environment.

The transition from home to school is challenging for young children from all social classes and language backgrounds. Children who are developing English proficiency may face a particular challenge when they begin their schooling experience with little understanding of the language medium of instruction. This experience is analogous to what adults with limited foreign language proficiency would face if they were immersed in a foreign language environment. For children from disadvantaged backgrounds, the expansion of affordable, high-quality pre-K education provides them with a stable and predictable learning environment. Indeed, Shannon Wanless and colleagues showed that across the preschool and kindergarten years, the gap in behavioral regulation between low- and high-income English-proficient preschoolers narrowed at the end of kindergarten.[36] However, the ELL children from low-income families did not experience this narrowing of the gap. This finding suggests that ELL children from low-income families are at risk for lower growth in behavioral regulation, possibly because of differences in home and school cultures. In this case, pre-K education exposes children to structured learning before they enter kindergarten. This exposure is especially beneficial to all children from low-income backgrounds, not just those who speak a nondominant language at home.

In a study examining kindergarten retention conducted in Miami, Adam Winsler and colleagues reported that children with ELL status were actually less likely than their English-as-native-language peers to be retained in kindergarten.[37] This finding challenges the view that ELL children were less academically successful because of their language barrier. Indeed, Winsler and colleagues found that, given adequate academic support, ELL children had the potential to succeed academically.[38] Meanwhile, Wanless and colleagues reported that ELL children from low-income families had weaker behavioral regulation across preschool and kindergarten.[39] One implication for such findings is that ELL status does not necessarily lead to compromised academic and linguistic outcomes. When the status is associated with lower behavioral, academic, and literacy outcomes, it is often confounded with SES. However, being an ELL (speaking a minority language) *and* from a low-income family may be a risk factor in the development of behavioral regulation required in the school environment. Therefore, pre-K education offered at an affordable and accessible scale provides similar learning experiences for children who speak a dominant or a minority language, and it could narrow the behavioral differences due to linguistic diversity.

## ASSESSMENTS AVAILABLE FOR DIVERSE LANGUAGE LEARNERS

A challenge in addressing the needs of diverse language learners has been the measurement and identification of these children with the available tools. Table 4.1 offers an overview of assessments to consider for students who are not native English speakers. In the table, we describe the main purpose of each assessment and the considerations for students from diverse language backgrounds. Many assessment tools still lack information both on how to represent students from diverse language backgrounds in standardized samples and how to assess students with limited English proficiency. Clinicians and educators face the significant challenge of limited access to appropriate resources for diverse language learners even before the adults can ascribe any language, literacy, or academic challenges as being due to language proficiency or a language-based learning disability.

**Table 4.1 An overview of prevalent assessments for preschoolers and elementary school students**

| Assessment and year | Constructs measured | Norming sample's demographics and norming age range (year:month to year:month) | Specific considerations for non-native English speakers in examiner's manual |
|---|---|---|---|
| | | *Oral English proficiency* | |
| *Clinical Evaluation of Language Fundamentals, Preschool*, 2nd ed. (CELF-P2, English and Spanish versions); 2004 (English), 2009 (Spanish)* | Receptive language, expressive language, language content, language structure, language memory, core language | Parent education level, age, race/ethnicity, geographic region, sex (3:0 to 6:11) | Bilinguals were included, but all reported English as their dominant language in the norming sample for the English task, while Spanish is the children's dominant language in the norming sample for the Spanish task. |
| *Clinical Evaluation of Language Fundamentals*, 4th ed. (CELF-4); 2003† | Receptive language, expressive language, language content, language structure, language memory, core language | Parent education level, age, race/ethnicity, geographic region, sex (5:0 to 21:11) | "Although the sample included individuals who were bilingual, English was the primary language (used most frequently) of all participants . . . Approximately 15% of the sample lived in homes in which a language other than English was also spoken. Of that group, the following languages were reported: 77% Spanish, 4% Asian languages, and 6.5% other languages . . . About 15% of the examiners reported that the students' language reflected regional and cultural patterns that represent variations from Mainstream American English." (Examiner's Manual, p. 207) |

(*continued*)

**Table 4.1** *continued*

| Assessment and year | Constructs measured | Norming sample's demographics and norming age range (year:month to year:month) | Specific considerations for non-native English speakers in examiner's manual |
|---|---|---|---|
| *Peabody Picture Vocabulary Task*, 4th ed. (PPVT-4); 2007 | Receptive vocabulary | Age, grade, sex, race/ethnicity, socioeconomic status, geographic region, special education status (2:6 to 90+) | No information on language background provided; "English proficient" means "function in an English-speaking environment." |
| *Rapid Automatized Naming/Rapid Alternating Stimulus Tests* (RAN/RAS); 2005 | Rapid automatized naming | Geographic region, gender, race, Hispanic origin, education level, exceptionality status, age (5:0 to 18:0) | Not specified, but "performance on the RAN/RAS tests provide important data on the language skills of many school and clinical populations such as English-language learners (tests can be done in both languages in many instances)." (Examiner's Manual, p. 6) |
| *Comprehensive Test of Phonological Processing*, 2nd ed. (CTOPP-2); 2013 | Phonological processing: phonological awareness, phonological memory, rapid symbolic naming, rapid nonsymbolic naming | Geographic region, gender, ethnicity, Hispanic status, exceptionality status, family income, education level (4:0 to 24:0) | Not specified |

| | | | |
|---|---|---|---|
| | *Measures of reading and writing* | | |
| *Gray Oral Reading Test*, 5th ed. (GORT-5); 2012 | Oral reading abilities: rate, accuracy, fluency (composite of rate and accuracy), comprehension, oral reading index (composite of fluency and comprehension) | Geographic region, gender, race, Hispanic status, education level, household income, exceptionality status<br>(6:0 to 23:11) | None specified |
| *Test of Word Reading Efficiency*, 2nd ed. (TOWRE-2); 2012 | Sight-word identification, phonemic decoding, total word reading efficiency | Geographic region, gender, ethnicity, Hispanic status, education level, family income, exceptionality status<br>(6:0 to 24:0) | None specified |
| *Test of Written Spelling*, 5th ed. (TWS-5); 2013 | Spelling | Age, geographic region, gender, race, Hispanic status, household income, parent education<br>(5:0 to 19:0) | None specified |

(*continued*)

**Table 4.1** *continued*

| Assessment and year | Constructs measured | Norming sample's demographics and norming age range (year:month to year:month) | Specific considerations for non-native English speakers in examiner's manual |
|---|---|---|---|
| *Kaufman Brief Intelligence Test*, 2nd ed. (KBIT-2); 2004 | Verbal intelligence (picture vocabulary, riddles) and nonverbal cognitive skills (matrices) | Education level, race/ethnicity; geographic region (4:0 to 90:0) | Yes; adult norming group restricted to those proficient in English. If English is not the examinee's first language and the examinee is not proficient in English (i.e., cannot carry out normal daily interactions in English), do not test. (Examiner's Manual, p. 43) |
| *Wechsler Intelligence Scale for Children*, 4th ed. (WISC-IV); 2014 | Verbal comprehension, perceptual reasoning, working memory, processing speed, full-scale IQ | Sex, race/ethnicity, parent education level, geographic region (6:0 to 16:00) | Translations or adaptations for multiple languages |
| *Woodcock Reading Mastery Test*, 3rd ed. (WRMT-III); 2011 | Reading readiness (phonological awareness, rapid automatic naming, and letter ID), word-level reading skills (word attack and word ID), reading comprehension | Race/ethnicity, parent education, geographic region, age, grade, educational placement (4:6 to 79:11) | None specified |

* The English and Spanish versions included both monolingual and bilingual preschoolers.
† The norming sample was 15 percent English language learners.

## IMPROVING EARLY LEARNING OPPORTUNITIES

Children from diverse language backgrounds constitute a growing proportion of the school-age population. While initial debates may focus on the best labels to use for these children (e.g., bilingual, second-language learner, language-minority learner), early educational opportunities have the strongest potential to maximize positive long-term academic and socio-emotional outcomes. In pursuing this goal, educators can focus on the connection between language, literacy, and cognition. This foundation can translate to practical outcomes in the areas of assessment, research, training, and instruction.

### Assessment

Early childhood educators work at the front line of a child's academic career. Assessment offers the opportunity to understand how a child's mind works and how various strengths and weaknesses may interact with a child's experiences to date. While not expected to be assessment experts, early educators should be knowledgeable about the team of specialists who can serve as resources in the use of assessments, the interpretation of results, and the results' implications for practice. These professionals primarily include speech-language pathologists, pediatric health-care specialists (e.g., pediatricians), and neuropsychologists and may extend to occupational therapists. Most children will not have had assessments before they start school, but each state is required by federal law to offer services to infants and toddlers, from birth to age three, who qualify on the basis of developmental delays or high risk of delays. Similarly, provisions through the Individual with Disabilities Education Act (IDEA) are available to students aged three to twenty-one.[40]

Over 730,000 children between three and five years old received IDEA-based services in the United States during the 2011–2012 school year.[41] While these data do not clarify the proportion of children in poverty or those who have limited English proficiency, these two factors—poverty and limited English proficiency—can place children at risk for academic difficulties, for different reasons. Although there are federal provisions in place for children with evident or suspected developmental difficulties, many schools offer screening services intended to detect subtle or at-risk factors in the general population. However, there is yet to be a consistent approach to early screening; a quality pre-K program could potentially offer an opportunity for optimizing the potential for screening and early services.

Empowering early educators with knowledge of assessments will position them to (1) understand children who come into their care and who are already identified with a developmental concern and (2) be sensitive to potential warning signs of academic distress or difficulty. These early educational experiences can set the standard for what children expect from their academic lives. Moreover, when pre-K teachers understand why children succeed or struggle, the teachers will avoid common misunderstandings such as assigning labels of lazy, stupid, unmotivated, or inattentive to children who in actuality are struggling to understand or express themselves.

Assessment practices focus on four main purposes: screening, progress monitoring, diagnostic, and outcomes. Screening identifies children in need of extra instructional support and can be given to many individuals at once or administered in a one-to-one setting quickly. Diagnostic measures determine a student's specific instructional needs and are given in a one-to-one setting. Progress monitoring (also referred to as formative assessment or dynamic assessment) ensures that the student is making adequate progress throughout the year. Outcomes measures (also referred to as summative assessment) evaluate overall outcomes. In addition, children in early education have spent the majority of their lives in home environments that influence their current performance or achievement. For this reason, it is also highly relevant to consider using questionnaires about the home environments, including the children's language and academic activities, the language environment, and the amount of time spent on certain activities (digital media exposure, being read to, etc.).

The following recommendations are for early education stakeholders:

- Establish collaborations with assessment experts (speech-language pathologists, neuropsychologists, reading specialists, school psychologists) to identify early screening measures useful for detecting at-risk students.
- Identify at-risk children who can benefit from early intervention or services to counteract the negative impact of early adversity.
- Develop and use assessments that are culturally sensitive and consider the extent of language demands on tasks that are not primary language assessments to allow for improved evaluation of psychoeducational constructs in students.
- Consider the language background of the standardized sample, and document it as reported in standardized assessment manuals.
- Collect data on family background, language skills, and cognitive skills for young children from diverse language backgrounds. School districts often have a home-language survey that assesses young children's language acquisition history. Additional questions about children's home-language exposure using adults' (i.e., caretakers') language usage as proxy would be beneficial.
- Extend and establish partnerships with clinical specialists to encourage recognition and referral of at-risk children.
- Establish a school- or district-based approach to differentiating between English language proficiency and specific learning disabilities in children from diverse language backgrounds.

## Research

To enrich young children's learning experience, all stakeholders of education need to improve and expand pre-K education as a collective initiative. Establishing collaborative research-practice partnerships is key to using scientific findings on bilingualism and child development to design sensitive pedagogy. This is not to imply that one-way information flow should go from either research or practice to the other agent. Education research on the intersection of early life adversity and schooling can inform research in child development and practice in pre-K education.

Much of what we know about child development should be interpreted in context. To advance knowledge in this area, we recommend that researchers study child development in light of the different environments of early childhood learning. Most importantly, we need to understand the interaction between individual child-level differences and school- and classroom-level variability. Furthermore, studies of the long-term impact of pre-K education suggest that this early learning experience provides protection for children who are at risk for academic difficulty. For children from diverse social and linguistic backgrounds, research-practice partnerships need to address a few key questions:

- What are the home-language profiles of the student population? What is the essential information to collect? How can we use this information for improved pedagogy and curriculum design?
- How can we communicate the value of language diversity to families and stakeholders of education?
- What are the best ways to facilitate second-language development (English) via first-language family conversations? How can we improve children's literacy skills through strong oral-language support?

## Training and Instruction

To increase early childhood educators' linguistic and cultural competence, information on linguistic, cognitive, and socio-cultural benefits of second-language learning can be incorporated into early childhood education training. When teachers and administrators have accurate knowledge of diverse language development in children, they can counter the misconceptions that children should be discouraged from learning a new language (or maintaining a native or heritage language). Research on human brain plasticity has demonstrated the brain's potential to learn and adapt. Armed with this research-based information, educators can be sensitive to children and families with diverse language backgrounds. For example, acknowledging the cognitive benefits associated with second-language learning, educators will understand that limited English proficiency is a transition period reflecting young children's process of learning. Teachers and staff in pre-K classrooms can provide high-quality language input for children's developing language, supplementing the child's home-language development and encouraging bilingual development.

An important remaining question about instruction is, Which language should be used in classrooms where English is spoken as a minority language among children and their families? This is not a simple question with one correct answer. Most importantly, recommendations for the language of pedagogy should be considered in context. For example, consider two relatively homogeneous groups of preschoolers in which there are English speakers and speakers of one minority language such as Spanish. In this case, education conducted in English supported by Spanish may benefit both groups of children when they are being exposed to two languages. However, in a relatively heterogeneous group of preschoolers, where English is the dominant community language, but where numerous minority languages are also spoken, the heterogeneity of the sample may complicate the decision of which language or languages should be utilized in the classroom. Increased awareness of the child's home-language environment (information collected in pre-K) and the community's language composition will help educators evaluate and design developmentally sensitive pedagogies for young bilingual learners.

## CONCLUSION

Accessible and affordable pre-K education will benefit children from all language and social backgrounds. Providing common early learning environments for children from diverse social and economic backgrounds may alleviate risk factors for language development associated with poverty and other vulnerabilities in unstable family structure. In addition to having a direct impact on young children, the stable schedule of pre-K programs allowing employment arrangements would also benefit parents. As the first educational experience, pre-K provides predictability in young children's outside-of-home environment, preparing young children for subsequent academic learning. For children with diverse language backgrounds, pre-K is an opportunity for early exposure to English, a second language through which academic learning occurs. Supporting young children's learning one year earlier than formal schooling will facilitate their understanding of the academic language being used in classrooms and will help them establish peer relationships and sustain a positive learning attitude.

All of these benefits cannot be achieved without high-quality teaching staff, an effective classroom environment, family engagement, and developmentally sensitive pedagogy. These determinants of success are adult focused but have a direct impact on young children. Expanding and improving existing pre-K education is one way to harness language diversity in a community as an asset. Such an early learning program supports children with a range of social, linguistic, and cultural background and helps create quality education for all.

CHAPTER FIVE

# Using Technology and Media in Early Childhood Settings

*Lauren Rubenzahl*
*Kristelle Lavallee*
*Michael Rich*

Twenty-first-century society has seen a dramatic change in how we create, integrate, and rely on media technologies for communication, education, and entertainment. We experience these innovations daily; they are so integrally woven into the fabric of our daily experiences that they are barely noticeable. Evolving rapidly from novelty to normality, smartphones, tablets, and other screen media have caused an enormous shift in the experience of childhood. The question for early childhood educators is how these media technologies and young children's engagement with them might be used to serve high-quality pre-K education.

Over the past two decades, children's daily time with screen media has increased exponentially. From 2011 to 2013, children under the age of eight saw a significant jump in their access to mobile media (52–75 percent), while children aged two to four spent on average nearly two hours each day with television, smartphones, tablets, and computers.[1] Any time that children are using media, they are learning from these technologies, whether the exposure is intended to be educational (e.g.,

**Figure 5.1**
**CHAPTER PREVIEW**
**Challenges to using media and other technology effectively with young children, both at home and in pre-K**

1. Technology is becoming widespread in early childhood learning environments and can be deployed to boost learning. Unfortunately, educators lack training in how to use technology effectively, how to assess children's learning with it, and how to apply their own expertise and knowledge when organizing and selecting media and other technology for their own educational practice.
2. In the absence of guidance, parents' beliefs about the role of media in young children's lives are mostly based on personal experience rather than on evidence.
3. There is a substantial disconnect between how children interact with these tools at home and how these same tools are used for learning in early education settings.

a vocabulary-building app), intended to be entertaining (e.g., entertainment TV programs such as *Power Rangers*), or incidental (e.g., a TV playing in the background). In each case, the question is what children are learning and how effectively they're learning it. There's wide variation in how successful media can be at teaching children the lessons that educators would like them to learn, and this variation depends on when, where, how, and which media are used.

The latest technological advancements are often touted as meeting and even exceeding our educational expectations. In the fervor over the new things these innovations can do, media are rarely evaluated or validated, and few experts consider what academic and social experiences the media might displace. Thus, while media can support children's development, they cannot supply everything. Nor can media replace the learning from real-life collaborations between educators and their students or through children's interactions with their peers. The challenge, therefore, is to purposefully consider how to meet children's needs. Rather than automatically assuming that media tools can or cannot support those needs, we have to actively examine which tools are appropriate for which purposes. Figure 5.1 summarizes some of the major challenges we face in using technology as effectively as possible in early education.

## THREE PRINCIPLES FOR USING MEDIA TO SUPPORT PRE-K LEARNING

Three deceptively simple principles can help educators make critical decisions about the effective use of media in pre-K education. First, educators need to choose their learning goals and then determine whether and which media support those goals better than other available pedagogical tools. Second, educators should make sure that the media are specifically designed to work with how young children learn. Finally, educators should use media that motivate interaction of many kinds, whether it is with the medium, with peers, or with adults. This chapter expands on these fundamental recommendations for using media effectively in pre-K classrooms. It explores challenges that arise in accomplishing educational goals and offers recommendations for overcoming those challenges.

### Principle 1: Choose Your Goal, Then Choose Your Medium

Digital media can support many learning goals in the pre-K classroom. Whether you aim to offer access to new information and experiences, provide fodder for classroom discussion, model positive social skills, or facilitate creative expression, a wide variety of media tools can help achieve rich results. Given the burgeoning market of apps and devices, it can be tempting to use any sort of digital media because it is labeled educational (a marketing claim rarely tested by research) or "just for fun," with no clear reason to believe that it will support children's learning.[2] Media gadgets and applications can be powerfully engaging, and children may enjoy them for long periods. Tempting as children's involvement and enjoyment may be, you should not use an electronic device in an educational setting unless there is a clear and compelling reason to use it. Media technologies, like any tool, should serve a purpose. You would not give a child a hammer "just for fun." Rather, you would teach the child how to use it safely to drive and remove a nail, and then give him or her the opportunity to hone and optimize these skills under supervision.

To reap the potential teaching benefits of media use, educators should treat electronic screen technology like other classroom tools: Media devices should be integrated purposefully to achieve explicit, focused learning goals that they are designed to achieve. This holds true both for pre-scripted media content (such as TV programs) and for media tools with which students can create their own content (such as drawing apps). Let's now consider both types of media.

### *Pre-scripted media content*

Many media have predetermined storylines that proceed without regard to the child's input. Such content can be used most effectively with pre-K children when it is based on a pedagogically sound curriculum. Early exposure to such programs—those that are age-appropriate and designed around an educational curriculum—has been associated with cognitive enhancement. In contrast, exposure to pure entertainment (particularly violent content) has been associated with poorer cognitive development and lower academic achievement.[3]

To achieve their intended learning goals, educators must ensure that the content of any media they use aligns with those goals. When it does, such content can be extremely effective in supporting learning. For example, one study found that integrating a brief episode or clip of a children's TV program that models active acceptance of differences can help educators facilitate those types of behaviors and apply them within the classroom setting.[4] Children of this age are both aware of racial differences and open about being friends with children who are different from themselves. Consequently, they can benefit developmentally and socially when teachers use pre-scripted media to reinforce lessons about difference and acceptance.[5]

A well-researched example of such media content is *Sesame Street*, which is both curriculum-based and designed to achieve goals of celebrating diversity and encouraging friendships among children of different races and cultures. The program creates a community of both Muppets and people from various racial and ethnic backgrounds who carefully model cooperation, conflict resolution, and respecting differences. Research bears out the effectiveness of this approach: Watching *Sesame Street* has been associated with positive attitudes toward out-groups.[6] Additionally, viewing prosocial *Sesame Street* content can increase prosocial behavior and decrease antisocial behavior among children during free play after viewing.[7] Other educational TV programs that approach the topic in similar ways have also been shown to positively affect young children's racial attitudes, in addition to broadening their knowledge and increasing their imaginativeness.[8]

Despite the potential benefits of carefully designed and selected pre-scripted media for this developmental stage, such media, well designed or not, are not always the right tools for the job. For example, commercial "skills-and-drills" apps can discourage young children's learning, making the app feel more like a struggle than an enjoyable exploration.[9] For this age group, the learning goals of skills-and-drills apps can be better served by nonmedia tools (e.g., the use of manipulatives and other concrete objects to learn about numbers). An educator must determine whether a media tool is designed simply to grab and maintain a preschooler's attention—a task that can be achieved with no learning goal at all—or to be the most effective possible tool to achieve the educational goals at hand.

### *Open-ended, interactive media*

When used purposefully, open-ended media—those with no predefined outcomes or storyline—can allow children to explore, use their imaginations, and develop problem-solving skills. Such tools can provide a digital environment in which children can draw, write, take photos, shoot videos, and create mash-ups of any combination. Like their analog equivalents, digital tools for creation can encourage imagination, exploration, and self-expression and are thus highly engaging and powerful tools in the classroom.[10] Importantly, they can also motivate creative problem-solving and peer-to-peer collaboration.[11]

Children may demonstrate such creative problem-solving and cooperation through verbal interactions as they use creative apps. For example, they may be more likely to talk with each other while using a drawing app, which does not offer rewards or indicate what success looks like, than while using a puzzle app, which does offer rewards (e.g., "Good job!") and has very particular measures of success (e.g., correctly completing a puzzle). While using the open-ended drawing app, children are more likely to look to each other for feedback and to focus on what they are making rather than on earning rewards from the app.[12]

Open-ended media are most effective when the educator uses them to reach a particular goal that they are ideally situated to achieve. For example, if the goal is for children to reflect on and process what they did during the day, a diary app might help document the day's events with text, photos, and videos that can then be emailed home. However, if the goal is for children to explore color, then concrete materials like finger paints and paper will provide more sensory input and will probably be more effective. Media present unique opportunities, but they are not the only tools that can engage children in creative thinking and self-expression. As with all classroom tools, striving toward clear learning goals will help the educator identify the best tool for the job.

## Principle 2: Choose Media Designed for How Young Children Learn

Every early childhood educator faces the task of choosing the most effective tools for teaching in ways that will foster students' learning and development. When deciding whether and how to integrate media into the classroom, educators should approach the question in the same way that they choose other activities, art supplies, or instructional methods: purposefully, mindfully, and with awareness of their individual students.

The most fundamental consideration for the pre-K educator is what will be most effective for children at this unique stage of development. Whether the choice is finger paints or drawing apps, the tools that educators choose should work *with* how children learn. For example, educational TV can benefit children in formal preschool or day care settings when the programming is, as Daniel Anderson et al. explained, "designed with a research-based understanding of how children use and understand television."[13] Similarly, apps should be based on theories about how software can support student learning.[14] The following approaches tend to work well for pre-K children. Media that use these approaches may be more likely to achieve their—and your—learning goals.

### *Using repetition*

Young children love repeating novel or interesting experiences over and over, both for their enjoyment and to master the experience. Whether they ask for the same book many times in a row or play with a train set for hours, preschoolers learn from repeated experiences. Media that are designed to facilitate such repetitive use can be of particular benefit to preschool children.

Some media capitalize on this developmental preference to help children meet intended learning goals more effectively. The TV program *Blue's Clues* takes advantage of this preference: Each episode airs for five consecutive days, with increasing benefits with each viewing.[15]

Unfortunately, few other TV programs or videos are designed to employ the benefits of repetition in this way. Although DVR and DVDs allow for repeat viewing at the viewer's discretion, TV alone does not facilitate repeated, consecutive viewings. In addition, children cannot typically interact with movies and video in a way that allows them to repeat particularly interesting parts at will.[16]

With the advent of tablets, however, this kind of interaction has become far more accessible to children in pre-K classrooms, even with media content that is not designed with the *Blue's Clues* approach. Because of their portability, intuitive interfaces, and customizability (in this case, one to three children operating a single tablet can each choose what to repeat and how many times), tablets can be useful educational tools for young children. With these devices, children can interact with TV or video content as many times as they would like, for as long as they would like (within parameters the educator sets), and thereby derive more benefit from the content. By attending to young children's developmental preference for repetition—for example, by enabling students to drive their own preferences with tablet technology—educators can help pre-K students get the most out of learning from media.

### *Communicating learning objectives explicitly*

When choosing media with predetermined learning goals and storylines that do not respond to a child's input, an educator should select those that both explicitly define what the educator is trying to teach and present these goals in ways that children understand.[17] *Sesame Street* provides examples of both activities. First, it tells young viewers that today's program is "brought to you by" a letter of the day (with the same letter used across consecutive episodes). The letter is explicitly stated and shown at both the beginning and the end of the program, with the goal of teaching viewers how to identify, sound out, and understand the basic meaning behind both the capital and lowercase symbols.[18] To reinforce the child's understanding of the letter, the program focuses only on one letter per episode, using it across several segments and building narratives around it. The program also includes specific vignettes that portray literacy as helpful, fun, and relevant to the child.[19]

Presenting goals in a way that pre-K children understand—as *Sesame Street* does at the beginning and the end of each segment—is crucial; otherwise, children can easily become distracted by features that are not targeting the objective. In one study, researchers found that even when an app *had* science and literacy learning goals, children did not focus on the science- and literacy-related content when the app didn't direct their attention toward it. Instead, they focused on the game elements, which were engaging but unrelated.[20]

### *Integrating instructions and providing feedback*

Apps should be easy and intuitive for children to use. Specifically, they should include "accessible and understandable instructions and teaching elements" (e.g., the child can replay audio instructions or touch on words or images to hear words spoken) and should incorporate formative, corrective feedback.[21] For example, the Pirate Treasure Hunt app offers corrective feedback through pop-ups and allows users to check their responses before submitting them for a final review. These features make the app particularly effective at helping children formulate and self-correct their answers. The Smart Pants School app takes another approach: It "speaks" instructions to learners, allows users to replay the instructions at will, and offers instructional reminders after an incorrect answer is given.[22] However the assistance is provided, such integrated feedback seems to support learning.

### *Avoiding distracting content*

Many mobile apps and other media technologies enable children to engage in interactive experiences that build toward particular learning goals. However, the seemingly limitless opportunities that media offer can also distract from those goals. When using a medium, children may focus their attention on elements that are unrelated to the goals, thus failing to learn what they're intended to learn.

For instance, enhanced e-books, which augment text with multimedia features, may be less effective than print and basic e-books at achieving content-related goals. The enhanced tools do not demand that the child imagine scenes, sounds, and story elements, and they provide activities that distract from, rather than support, the story and the educational goals.[23] Computerized storybooks can pose a similar challenge: *Arthur's Teacher Trouble* is about a young aardvark who learns how to get along with a demanding teacher. The lesson is that through hard work, he can achieve his goals. Although the narrative and main points are clear throughout the written text, the storybook contains a plethora of incongruent or unrelated clickable content areas. For instance, the child can click on a sink to fill it with water or on a tray of cookies to make them sprout top hats and sing in the style of a barbershop quartet. These attractive but unrelated gimmicks can engage children but can also prevent them from applying the level of cognition necessary to comprehend the narrative and educational themes.[24]

Researchers recommend that educational technologies provide "smooth and distraction-free pathways towards achieving goals" (i.e., no banner ads or pop-ups) to help children focus on the important information in whatever medium they're using.[25] If media contain supplementary materials embedded within a text (such as the clickable content found in the *Arthur* storybook), those materials should *enhance* the narrative or provide different ways of bolstering the child's understanding of the desired learning goals.[26]

### Principle 3: Choose Media That Motivate Interaction

One central feature of quality educational technology arises repeatedly in the research literature: interactivity. But what exactly *is* interactivity? The National Association for the Education of Young Children and the Fred Rogers Center for Early Learning and Children's Media define interactive media as "content designed to facilitate active and creative use by young children and to encourage social engagement with other children and adults."[27] This definition encompasses both interaction with the medium and the human interaction it facilitates.

For young children, interaction with both the environment and other people is essential for development. Preschool children learn about the world by interacting with it and by observing the results of their actions. A unique strength of interactive media, as compared with pre-scripted programs, is that the interactive technology can respond to children's actions. Young children are learning how to work with, play with, and care about others; take turns; share; and compromise. Interactive media can promote these skills in several ways. They provide a safe platform where children can practice reciprocal interactions (such as responding to a character on a video or answering a question in an e-book). The media also deliver a tool that encourages children to ask for help from a peer, caregiver, or teacher. Finally and even more simply, the media are a limited resource that must be shared with classmates.

### *Interactivity by design*

Many kinds of media—even those that may at first seem inherently passive—are designed for interaction with children. For example, TV, still the most-used form of screen media for young children, has long been considered a passive medium, meant for "mindless entertainment." Today, however, children's educational TV is its own industry and includes streaming services, TV stations, and DVDs. Much of this content strives to make the viewing experience interactive, often pausing midstory so that children can answer questions asked in the program; point out certain features; or dance, sing, or move with a beat, song, or character. Despite the fact that the program will be unaffected by how and whether the child responds, such interaction makes a difference in children's learning. Viewer participation increases children's learning—even when the program doesn't truly respond to the child.[28]

One such program is *Sesame Street*, which was specifically designed to encourage viewers to follow along with, think about, and repeat the educational lessons that are presented. Each episode includes educational games formatted to elicit viewer engagement and response. Sometimes, an actor will ask a direct question and then pause while the answer appears on the screen; other times, a character intentionally makes a mistake that young viewers will notice and enjoy correcting.[29]

*Blue's Clues* aimed to elicit active audience participation using similar approaches, with a twist: To encourage mastery of the educational content, producers aired the same *Blue's Clues* episode five times in a week. As previously mentioned, repeat viewing over five consecutive days was found to benefit three- to five-year-olds enrolled in preschool or day care. With each viewing, audience interaction increased, and children could more effectively apply problem-solving strategies modeled in the program when faced with real-life problems.[30]

More overtly interactive media require the child to actually push a button, swipe a finger, or otherwise give direction to the device—which then responds based on the user's action. With the boom of mobile media such as smartphones and tablets, many companies and organizations have been flocking to develop educational apps for children. Such interaction requires the child's engagement if he or she is to play, proceed, or advance.

However, the demand for interaction does not alone make the app effective, as in the case of *Arthur's Teacher Trouble* e-book described earlier. For optimal user engagement and learning, apps should have developmentally appropriate content, provide material that is humorous and fun, offer desirable incentives, and link interactivity to an achievable learning goal. For example, the PBS Kids app Super Why!, a companion to the *Super Why!* TV show, contains four mini-games for children ages three to six. The games are designed to build literacy skills through identifying letters, sounds, and words; spelling and writing words; and completing sentences. The app contains an element of humor (researchers noted that children enjoyed deliberately choosing wrong answers to hear a funny sentence read back to them) and rewards players with virtual stickers, which motivates children to continue playing until their sticker collection is complete.[31]

These apps, however, have their limitations. As children advance in their understanding of literary concepts and increase their vocabularies, apps such as Super Why! become less beneficial, unable to keep up with the children's own intellectual gains as they age. Usability studies note that mobile technologies must pay attention to the physicality of app design, accounting for limited battery life and variations in children's fine motor skills and the dexterity of small fingers when it comes to entering text, swiping, and small screen size. All of these issues can prevent children from achieving the desired learning goals and can vary from medium to medium (e.g., playing a smartphone game on a tablet, or vice versa, presents qualitatively different challenges for children).

*Interactivity with peers*

Another way you can help children achieve desired educational goals when they use media is to choose technologies that encourage peer-to-peer interaction. Child development research has long established the importance of peer play for children ages three to five; they are learning how to share, work with others, empathize, and compromise.[32] Effective learning environments often allow and encourage peer collaboration, enabling children to learn from one another.[33] These experiences can be central to cognitive and social development.[34]

While developmental specialists, researchers, and organizations note that technology should not usurp real-life relationships and social interactions, media can facilitate those connections in ways that promote social development and learning.[35] Many educational technologies are designed to support social development by encouraging children's collaboration with peers.[36] For example, unlike a single-player game, a multiplayer video game (one computer screen with several input devices) can encourage kindergarten children to talk with each other and cooperate on efforts to successfully achieve goals.[37] Social interactions such as those that occur when students work together to solve a game's tasks provide students the opportunity to share ideas and foster understanding, which is a crucial component of educational development.[38]

Media that do not truly respond to children's input can also facilitate peer-to-peer interaction when used with more than one child at a time. Siri Mehus and Reed Stevens observed significant differences between children who watched an interactive TV program (either *Go, Diego, Go!*, *Dora the Explorer*, *Super Why!*, or *The Little Einsteins*) on their own and those who watched with their siblings.[39] When children watch together, they connect with each other in ways that are mediated by the TV program. For example, children coordinate their actions to respond together, elaborate on each other's answers, and engage in conversations spurred by the prompts and responses. Such interaction promotes learning opportunities beyond those inherent to the program. Mehus and Stevens also note that "watching with others not only makes children more likely to engage with a program and benefit from its intended learning opportunities, but also provides a way for children to create their own learning opportunities."[40] Using high-quality media *together* can help children get the most out of them.

### *Interactivity with adults*

Even though media have become increasingly intuitive and children are using them independently ever earlier in their development, the educational benefits of parent and educator mediation—how adults manage children's experiences with media—remain integral to children's overall learning.[41] Young children particularly need such adult mediation because they rapidly acquire many new cognitive skills and need an adult to model and structure the use of those skills.[42] This holds true with technology use as well. When they are involved with children's use of educational media, adults can help improve children's understanding of content, increase language learning, and facilitate engagement in relevant activities.[43]

In the case of educational TV, studies have shown that an engaged caregiver who is present and who comments during the program directs children's attention to important material, strengthens conceptual learning goals, and fosters a deeper understanding of the material presented.[44] For instance, adults can engage children with the educational content presented on *Sesame Street.* They could ask the children questions like "What letter is that?" and wait for a response, following up with feedback that either provides the correct answer or verbally acknowledges the child's correct response. With adult involvement like this, children are better able to identify the letters and numbers shown in the episode than if they view the episode without adult interaction.[45]

Because adults can so dramatically increase children's learning from TV by engaging with children and the program as they watch, it is helpful when the program specifically engages adult attention. As previously discussed, a model of designing such media to encourage adult input and coviewing is *Sesame Street.* Each episode is scripted to contain humor that speaks to both child and adult sensibilities to engage both parties. The program incorporates celebrity guest stars (from comedians like Tina Fey and musicians like Ice Cube to actors like Ian McKellen and political figures like Michelle Obama) that adults recognize and children will enjoy. Segments such as "Upside Downton Abbey" and "RSI: Rhyme Scene Investigation" parody popular adult TV programs while making the narratives entertaining for children and focusing on specific learning goals. When programs engage adults and still provide age-appropriate content for the target child audience, the adults are more likely to watch with the children and help them learn.

In educational or school settings, educator engagement can be similarly effective in optimizing pre-K children's learning with technology. Reed Stevens and William Penuel's term "joint media engagement" describes what happens when individuals learn together with media, whether they do so spontaneously or in a "constructed" experience, such as in a lesson that a teacher designs for students.[46] In one case, preschool educators aiming to teach their students literacy skills implemented a curriculum that included digital videos and online games from *Sesame Street*, *Super Why!*, and *Between the Lions*. The lessons required active mediation by the teachers, asking questions, repeating words, and naming and identifying objects and situations throughout the media experiences. The educators built on the media-based experiences with hands-on activities that explored the principles exhibited in the episodes and accompanying online games. After they completed the curriculum, the students were better able to understand narratives and recognize letters, letter sounds, and words, thus improving their overall literacy skills.[47]

Although adult support and mediation are inarguably beneficial to children's learning, the benefits vary across technological contexts and desired learning outcomes. For this reason, it is essential to select media strategically. When reading stories, for example, adults can choose between print books, e-books, and enhanced e-books (which support highly interactive multimedia experiences). The best choice depends on the learning goals. Basic e-books and print books both encourage actions related to the content of the story, such as labeling, pointing, and discussing—not to mention stimulating imagination, as basic books do not fill in all the blanks. Reading such books with an adult can improve a child's vocabulary, language, and cognitive development. In contrast, enhanced e-books draw out fewer content-related actions and encourage more *non*-content-related actions, such as talking about the device or guiding the child's hands to operate it, which may distract adults and children from the story.[48] Thus, for literacy building, print or basic e-books may be a better choice. However, if the learning goal is to help expand children's experience of the content, the best tool may be an enhanced e-book, which facilitates immediate access to related content on the web, whether the content is videos, images, word definitions, or source material.

## CHALLENGES TO IMPLEMENTING THESE RECOMMENDATIONS

Although some parents, policy makers, and others in the educational community push for integrating screen media tools in the pre-K classroom, there are three significant challenges to be faced. First, children themselves are not media naive; they typically come from households where media use is ubiquitous among parents and older siblings alike. With that previous exposure comes varying degrees of facility and sophistication with media devices, not to mention parental expectations. Second, we face the much-debated idea of the digital divide, an evolving concept that centers on the technological haves and have-nots and what this divide may mean for education. Finally, although education is undergoing a sea change when it comes to technology, educators are not uniformly convinced of its value, and many are less facile with media technology than are the young children they teach. Once convinced that they should bring media into their pre-K classrooms, many educators are overwhelmed by the plethora of products, the rapidity with which they evolve, and the lack of reliable information on the relative values of available devices and content. We explore these three challenges and offer recommendations for addressing them.

### Challenge 1: Out-of-School Media Use and Exposure

Young children live in media-saturated environments and use an increasing amount of media.[49] Media use is a daily part of young children's lives. And despite formal recommendations by the American Academy of Pediatrics and other organizations to discourage screen media use for children under two and to limit older children to 2 hours of quality programming per day, their combined media use at home, at school, and now almost anywhere else often exceeds this amount.[50] On average, children are exposed to 4.1 hours of screen time daily, with 3.6 hours of screen time at home and 0.4 hours while in formal childcare.[51]

Because children are exposed to so much media content in their daily environments, they enter school with various ideas about when and how to use media. Educators should assume that children have at least some experience with media, but they should also know that this experience may not have been provided in an informed way.

Home experiences in particular have a significant influence on what children bring into the pre-K classroom and how educators there can best use these tools. Young children's experiences with media are heavily affected by parents' beliefs about the role of these media in the children's lives, and these beliefs are mostly based on personal experience and anecdotal evidence. In general, parents believe that children need screen media early and often if they are to function in today's world. They tend to see technology as likely to help rather than harm children's development.[52] Still, concerns about potential risks are on the rise, yielding a simultaneous wish to give children access to the newest, most exciting media, while also limiting their exposure to potentially harmful content.

To further complicate matters, parents frequently use screens not for what the technology can teach but rather as a way to occupy or distract children when parents are busy or in public settings. Media time sometimes replaces the time that children could spend interacting with their parents or the environment, developing their imagination, or engaging in open-ended, creative play. Experiences with media as distractions may make it more difficult to support children's development in the classroom through media, as the children may be unaccustomed to using media with a focused purpose.

To support effective in-home media use (which in turn can support effective classroom use, and vice versa), we propose providing parents with more evidence-based and nuanced knowledge about what children need at each developmental stage and how media can serve those purposes. Research does not support the assumption that children need frequent and early exposure to media to succeed. Indeed, the technology with which they will be working as adults will be dramatically different from what we use today. It is more important that their media use be purposeful and directed than that it be frequent. The exposure children have, both in the home and in the classroom, will influence their assumptions about the use of media in the context of education.

*Recommendations*

1. Educators should recognize that children bring prior media experience to school with them. They can help children access that expertise in the classroom by asking them about media and, when appropriate, having them demonstrate what they know. Educators can create clear classroom rules and expectations that delineate the differences between classroom and home uses of media. Because students will probably bring prior experience of technology with them, their understanding of technology and its uses may need to be examined and relearned so that they can use these tools more purposefully.
2. Educators should provide students with the skills necessary for using media mindfully, in developmentally optimal ways for learning.
3. Educators should provide parents with clear, concrete resources, guidance, and support for using media at home with the same goals and in the same ways that students use the technology in the classroom.

## Challenge 2: The New Digital Divide

The digital divide, the concept that some children have greater access to computer technology than others do and are thus at an educational advantage, has been a focus of discussion among educators. Originally seen as an issue of haves and have-nots, a disparity of hardware access based on the economic status of families, neighborhoods, and schools, the phenomenon of the digital divide has changed with the rapid evolution of technology and resulting economy of scale.[53]

As personal computers became ubiquitous, the digital divide evolved into a differential in facility with the technology. Those who had a computer at home had more time with the technology and, using it not only for educational exercises but also for entertainment and communication, became more adept with technology than those who waited in line to do their homework on a school or library computer. The evolution of the computer into toy and telecommunication as well as tool fueled the subsequent iteration of the digital divide—between those who had broadband connectivity and those who did not. The bandwidth disparity has subsequently been blunted (though not eliminated) by the next evolution of technology: mobile devices, which make connectivity accessible even to those of limited economic means.

The development of mobile media has also made technology accessible to very young children. Not only are the devices physically manageable, but the touch-screen interface is far more transparent and intuitive than a keyboard and a mouse. Parents proudly show off their infants' facility with tablets and mobile devices—a practice that has seemingly become *de rigueur* when toddlers join their parents for a dinner out. Because of this early and near-constant exposure, young children's comfort level and facility with technology is developed early and quickly, frequently outstripping that of their parents and educators. As a result, the digital divide we currently face is between preschoolers (and their accompanying confidence with technology) and those who oversee their formal education.

### *Recommendations*

Just as educators must abandon the preconception that integrating computer technology is always a benefit, our use of technology in educating preschool children must accept and embrace the children's abilities and natural adeptness, engaging them as teachers as well as learners. Even very young "digital natives" learn the grammar of communicating with these devices much more quickly and intuitively than do adult "digital immigrants," who must first "unlearn" established patterns of thinking and ways of operating technology. While educators "must become strong advocates for embedding meaningful, developmentally, and culturally appropriate uses of technology into our teacher preservice and in-service training," we can also learn from our students by having the humility to observe and learn from how they interact with technology and even to ask them what they are doing and how they are doing it.[54]

## Challenge 3: Lack of Educator Training

As mentioned, educators are not always confident in their ability to use technology effectively and may lack the training to assess children's learning with technology.[55] Teacher education can contribute significantly to effective use of educational technology in the pre-K classroom.

### *Difficulty in using media*

Whether and how educators use media in the classroom depends in part on how they conceptualize media in children's learning. Like parents, many educators believe that media technology is beneficial for children, particularly when it supports cognitive development.[56] In fact, many educators are asking not *whether* but *how* to use media technology in the early childhood classroom.[57] However, educators' acceptance of technology doesn't necessarily mean that they have the training to use it. Additionally, many educators are unconvinced or have mixed feelings about technology use in the classroom. For example, some teachers believe that media can interfere with the teacher-student relationship.[58] Without the proper training, such barriers are more difficult to overcome.

### Recommendations

To help support educators in their endeavors to optimally integrate media and other technology in their classrooms, change must occur at the policy level as well as the individual school and classroom level:

1. Policy makers should recognize the importance of educator training in this field and provide opportunities for professional meetings. One possibility is to dedicate a certain number of the required continuing education hours to training in this area.
2. Administrators should recognize the need for faculty training in educational technology and provide ample opportunities for teachers to obtain the necessary knowledge, both before implementation and in an ongoing way thereafter, so that teachers stay up-to-date not only within but also beyond the classroom.
3. Teachers should recognize the need for training to close the digital divide between themselves and their students and should seek out ways to expand their competence and confidence with educational technology. They should try not to implement any technology unfamiliar to them until they understand how it will meet their learning goals, how children will use it, and how it will affect students.

Following the steps outlined above can help ensure that educators feel equipped, empowered, and supported when they are faced with implementing new technologies in their classrooms.

### *Difficulty in identifying high-quality content*

Complicating the issue of high-quality content is the lack of clear distinction between entertainment and educational media—the two are not mutually exclusive. TV programs such as PBS's *Word World* may be entertaining for kids *and* be built around an educational philosophy that aims to teach preschoolers basic literacy skills and increase their social awareness.[59] Still, not all content that claims to be educational is the best choice for students. As an unintended consequence of the Children's Television Act of 1990, which mandated that all broadcasters provide at least three hours of educational or informational content each week, some media producers and broadcasters are declaring some questionable programming to be educational or informational.[60]

Such blending of education and entertainment (referred to as *edutainment*) in media technologies designed for children is a practice riddled with controversy, especially when these technologies are formally implemented in preschool and pre-K classrooms. For example, the *Muzzy* series could be one teacher's "mindless cartoon" and another's way to introduce a foreign language.

Part of the challenge is that though media may label themselves as educational, such labels are unregulated and rarely substantiated by evidence. With apps, for example, it can be difficult to evaluate education value because so many apps carry the "educational" label with no evidence to back it up.[61] This lack of oversight can challenge teachers who are trying to decide which media are curriculum-based or designed with particular learning goals in mind.

## Recommendations

When considering integrating any new media or technology into the classroom or curriculum, educators must remember that they are the ones who are equipped with the background knowledge and skills needed to determine what is best for their students. Just as educators apply their expertise and knowledge of education, child development, and their individual students' interests and aptitudes when deciding which physical materials, like paints, construction supplies, print books, and games, will be utilized in their classrooms, so too must they rely on this same knowledge when curating media and other technology for their students.

Consequently, educators must conduct the due diligence necessary to familiarize themselves with and learn about the technologies they use. After ensuring that the content is developmentally appropriate for their students, educators should then make sure that the educational claims of a specific tech tool align with the curriculum goals of the class. For example, an educator looking to teach the students coding skills may allow children to free-play with a tablet app such as ScratchJr, which contains explicit learning goals of teaching children how to code and supporting materials and tools for teachers, should they wish to apply them in their classrooms.[62]

Once a technology tool is selected, educators should use, watch, read, or otherwise interact with the new medium themselves to make sure that it will integrate well within their lesson goals and classroom environment. For example, a teacher wanting to implement ScratchJr in the classroom should first engage with it himself or herself to determine whether it can help students achieve the desired learning goals in developmentally optimal ways that also complement the children's learning styles.[63]

Finally, as with all classroom tools, an educator should monitor, interact with, and assist students when they are using new media technology and should continuously assess how the students engage with and learn from media. During this assessment period, an educator should note what works well and what needs to be improved. For example, a teacher may observe that, while students learn the desired coding skills with ScratchJr on their own individual tablets, students who use the app in groups of two or three on one tablet are more social and better able to learn how to cooperate and solve problems collaboratively. By applying their own expertise and experience, early childhood educators can identify high-quality media and other technologies that align well with their students' developmental stage and that are best suited for the children's needs and educational goals.

## CONCLUSION

In this chapter, we have outlined best practices for educators to consider when developing curricula that include media and other technologies. These best practices include taking into account the child's developmental stage, understanding and accounting for the digital divide, and choosing media that are grounded in curriculum, that actively engage students, and that require a level of interaction between themselves, the technology, their peers, and their teachers.

To use these tools effectively, we must move past preconceived notions about media and how they may help or hinder children's learning. Rather than being dogmatic or reactive, we must look to the research evidence (incomplete as it may be), implement these powerful tools in mindful and focused ways, and observe children and their progress. When we incorporate media content and exercises into the curriculum, we should do so only with clear pedagogical intent. They must be aligned with nonmedia materials and activities to meet explicit learning goals. Simply because a product labels itself as educational does not mean that it is useful to the serious twenty-first-century educator. Educators must determine for themselves exactly which products and exercises advance their overall educational objectives. Additionally, open-ended apps not explicitly designated as teaching tools can be implemented in creative and imaginative ways. We must be prepared to observe and learn from children as they use these media, collecting empirical findings in our classrooms and using findings from prior research. We must also allow ourselves to be surprised, as much by the bold new discoveries that the children will make as by disproving the preconceptions we hold.

We must recognize media as the tools that they are: far-reaching information-aggregators and flexible instruments of creative expression, but not always the best tool for every learning task. For example, a print book remains better than an enhanced e-book for encouraging flights of imagination and child-adult interactions. To integrate media effectively in the preschool classroom, interactivity between the child and the technology, his or her peers, and the teacher are key goals. Media tools in preschool education should always be implemented with an eye toward increasing the flow of ideas and activities between the virtual and the real world; ideas first discovered online can then be explored in the classroom or on the playground. Shared use of media between children or between a child and an educator achieves both didactic and social-emotional objectives and provides a powerful bridge from the virtual to the real, from what is learned to what is lived.

As we examine technology in light of early childhood education, we must clearly distinguish media tools that nurture developing minds from those that are attractive because they are new rather than because they are useful. We must be cautious not to subject this new generation to a vast uncontrolled experiment, saturating early education with the latest media technologies simply because we can, but rather to instruct children, using technologies that have been thoughtfully selected, assessed, and proven to benefit young children's learning and development.

CHAPTER SIX

# Screening and Supporting Children at Risk for Developmental Delay or Disability

*Beth Rous*
*Rena Hallam*

The expansion of high-quality pre-K programs brings the promise of improved educational services to preschool children and their families. Such growth in these services creates the opportunity for the early identification of children at risk for developmental delays, the provision of needed intervention and services to children and their families, and increased inclusive placement options. As defined by the Division for Early Childhood (DEC) and National Associate for the Education of Young Children, there are three key features of successful inclusion for young children with disabilities: (1) *access* to the physical and instructional environments, (2) *participation access*, meaning the children's participation in those environments, and (3) *system and organizational support*.[1] Central to these key features is accurate and appropriate early childhood assessment. We need to gather information about young children's learning and development to understand an individual child's

**Figure 6.1**
**CHAPTER PREVIEW**
**Challenges to screening and assessing young children's development**

1. Screening is misunderstood as an assessment rather than a starting point of a universal identification strategy. Without effective screening, many children miss intervention opportunities during critical periods of their development.
2. Current policies depend most often on early educators for developmental screening, referrals for diagnostic assessment and services, and monitoring children's progress. Unfortunately, many early educators are inadequately prepared to carry out these functions.
3. Children from culturally and linguistically diverse backgrounds are at risk for either being incorrectly identified or being overlooked for developmental delay or early learning issues. The frequent result is inadequate or inappropriate services, or no services at all, for children who need them.

developmental status. We also need this information to design effective instruction, adapt interventions and learning opportunities, and track children's overall development and learning through their participation in pre-K programs.[2]

Key problems and issues related to appropriate developmental screening and child assessment are at the center of pre-K expansion. Figure 6.1 outlines the three greatest issues that often prevent children from obtaining the services they need. In this chapter, we examine these difficulties and make recommendations to overcome them.

## PURPOSE AND TYPE OF ASSESSMENTS

Appropriate and adequate assessment is central to the successful identification of young children with, or at risk for, developmental delays.

In this chapter, we focus on child-level assessment, as opposed to environmental or program-level assessments, like those often used in quality rating and improvement systems (QRIS; e.g., environmental rating scales). At the child level, various types of assessment are used for different purposes. Regardless of the type, assessment of young children is complex. Assessments are often misused, or the results are often misrepresented, or both.

Good assessment requires a nuanced understanding of typical and atypical child development as well as the fundamentals of appropriate and rigorous assessment practice. While assessments are typically organized by developmental or content domain, teachers must recognize that the domains are interrelated, and growth in one area often affects growth in another (e.g., a child's ability to complete a puzzle requires skills in three areas: fine motor, self-regulatory, and cognitive). Across the continuum of assessment practices to support early identification, the type of assessment varies according to its purpose. Assessments play three critical roles in the early identification of, and intervention for, young children with developmental delays or disabilities: (1) developmental screening, (2) diagnosis and eligibility determination, and (3) instructional assessments for planning and ongoing monitoring (figure 6.2).

## Developmental Screening

Developmental screening is designed to identify children who may have developmental delays or concerns.[3] The brief screening includes a few assessment items that can provide general information about a child's developmental status. Screening tools can be designed to cover one or more developmental domains. Most of these tools are easily administered by early childhood professionals after training. In pre-K settings, all children should be screened to determine those who might need further assessment and support.

While many programs and teachers may screen children, children for whom areas of developmental concerns are identified must be

**Figure 6.2 The early screening, assessment, and progress monitoring process**

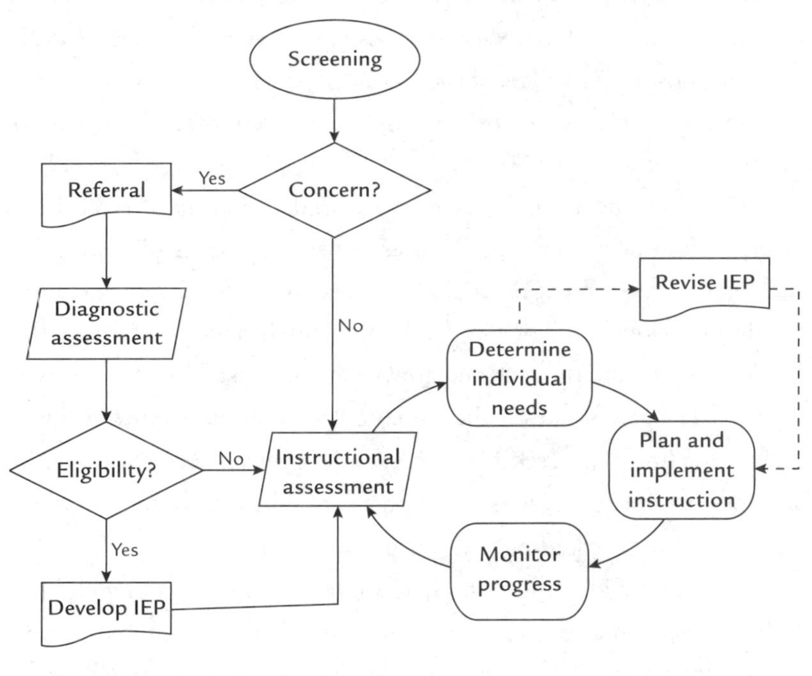


*Note:* IEP, individualized educational program.

subsequently referred for further assessment. Note that developmental screening is considered part of the pre-referral process for children who may be eligible for special education services under the Individuals with Disabilities Education Act (IDEA). Samuel Meisels and Sally Atkins-Burnett recommend three actions, depending on screening results: Children who demonstrate no developmental concerns generally require no modifications to instruction or the curriculum. Children who have inconsistent results, depending on the setting, the domain, or who is contributing information to the screening may require rescreening. Between screenings, these children may need more-individualized instruction or modifications to instruction or the curriculum. Children for whom screening results are concerning should be immediately referred for further diagnostic assessments, so that eligibility for special education services can be determined.[4]

## Diagnostic Assessments and Eligibility Determination

For children whose screening identified concerns, diagnostic assessments provide specific information about a child's health or developmental status as a basis for identifying the type of specialized services needed. This diagnostic step, often referred to as a child evaluation, includes the specific procedures used to determine both a child's initial eligibility for special services under the IDEA and his or her and continued eligibility for these services.[5] Because diagnostic assessments provide this information and indicate where a child falls within developmental norms, they are often referred to as standardized assessments.

There are five areas in which a child may be eligible for specialized services under IDEA: cognitive, communication, physical/motor, social/emotional, and adaptive/self-help. Stephen Bagnato, John Neisworth, and Kristie Pretti-Frontczak recommend that diagnostic assessments incorporate multiple measures, settings, and informants.[6] Typically, a team of professionals (e.g., special educators, occupational therapists, physical therapists, speech or language therapists) who have received specialized training conduct the assessments. While diagnostic assessments help determine a child's eligibility for services, the information from these assessments is not useful in determining specific instructional support children may need. Therefore, additional instructional assessment is needed.

## The Use of Assessment for Instructional Planning

Instructional assessments can be based on a fixed standard of performance (criterion-referenced) or on a normed sample of children (norm-referenced).[7] However they are conducted, the assessments are designed to record children's skill development several times during a period (e.g., one year). Rather than direct testing, assessment data are gathered primarily through observations, work samples, and interviews. These types of assessments are often linked to a specific curriculum. All children in pre-K programs should be assessed daily in their routine activities, and the findings should directly influence the curriculum and instructional approaches to support the children's growth and development.

When used appropriately, instructional assessments provide information about the individual needs of children and can thus be used to inform individualized education plans (IEPs) for children who have special needs. These assessments also ensure "that children are making progress."[8]

## LINKING SCREENING, ASSESSMENT, AND PROGRESS MONITORING

Regardless of the assessment used, it must include the multiple stakeholders supporting the child (professionals and families). The assessment must also be individualized to meet the child's specific needs and be integrated into instruction. For children who qualify for special education services under IDEA, documentation of the referral, eligibility, and IEPs should also be integrated into the process.

To address early identification and assessment practices within an expanding pre-K environment, we apply an ecological lens. We start with the fundamentals of classroom practice and then expand to examine how administrative and systems issues affect teachers' ability to effectively gather and use multiple types of child data.

## CLASSROOM-LEVEL POLICIES AND PRACTICES

In 2014, DEC released an updated version of recommended practices in early education for children with disabilities.[9] These recommendations are designed to link research to practice as a way to better support practitioners and families in facilitating the optimal growth and development of young children with disabilities. The DEC identified several specific practices to that help children with disabilities have full access to, and participate in, services and other support in natural environments and inclusive settings (figure 6.3). These practices cover a range of assessment options for young children as defined previously: screening, eligibility determination, instructional and individual planning, and progress monitoring.

## Linking Curriculum and Assessment

At the heart of early identification is the link between instructional assessment and curriculum. This relationship is especially critical for young children with or at risk for developmental disabilities. Both the National Association for the Education of Young Children (NAEYC) and DEC offer specific recommendations related to these connections.[10]

Teachers play a large role in developmental screening. Depending on the screening tool selected by the program, they are trained to administer screens in collaboration with the family. For example, the Ages and Stages Questionnaire (ASQ-3), a commonly used developmental screen, does not require technical training and includes a parent-completed tool.[11] Most screens include manuals for those who are administering the tool, information on how to share results with families, and guidance on when results indicate a need for further diagnostic assessments.

Should diagnostic assessments be warranted, teachers may not conduct the actual evaluation of the child. They can, however, play a key role in determining the child's eligibility for services because they have unique information about the child. Among other things, they could provide input on support and instructional approaches needed to achieve the goals and outcomes on the child's IEP. Unfortunately, although teachers are considered members of the IEP team, they are seldom given enough free time to participate in IEP meetings where these decisions are made. Thus teachers often have limited input into

**Figure 6.3 Recommended practices in assessment**

1. Work with the family to identify family preferences for assessment processes.
2. Use assessment materials and strategies that are appropriate for the child's age and level of development and that accommodate the child's sensory, physical, communication, cultural, linguistic, social, and emotional characteristics.
3. Conduct assessments that include all areas of development and behavior to learn about the child's strengths, needs, preferences, and interests.
4. Conduct assessments in the child's dominant language and in additional languages if the child is learning more than one language.
5. Use a variety of methods, including observation and interviews, to gather assessment information from multiple sources, including the child's family and other significant individuals in the child's life.
6. Obtain information about the child's skills in daily activities, routine, and environments such as home, center, and community.
7. Use clinical reasoning in addition to assessment results to identify the child's current levels of functioning and to determine the child's eligibility and plan for instruction.
8. Implement systematic ongoing assessment to identify learning targets, plan activities, and monitor the child's progress to revise instruction as needed.
9. Use assessment tools with sufficient sensitivity to detect child progress, especially for the child with significant support needs.
10. Report assessment results so that they are understandable and useful to families.

*Source:* Adapted from Division for Early Childhood, "DEC Recommended Practices in Early Intervention/Early Childhood Special Education," Division for Early Childhood of the Council for Exceptional Children, April 14, 2014, www.dec-sped.org/recommendedpractices.

the child's IEP or the instructional approaches that would best help the child meet these goals and outcomes.

A primary role of teachers is in instructional and individual planning and the monitoring of children's progress. To accomplish this, teachers must regularly assess students and use the results to plan and implement the curriculum through their own intentional instruction. Teachers should choose culturally relevant assessment tools that are both appropriate for the children being assessed and implemented in ways and settings that are as close to the child's everyday activities as possible. Through ongoing assessment, teachers can adjust their approach, either in teaching practices or in curriculum planning. For example, depending on the scope and sequence of the selected curriculum framework, teachers can use assessment data to determine if children need additional opportunities to practice specific skills to support mastery.

## Applying Principles of Universal Design

For children with developmental concerns or disabilities, teachers can ensure enable full participation in the curriculum through the use of accommodations or modifications to the environment, materials, or instructional approach. After these changes have been employed, assessment can document how successful they were. Because of the important link between assessments and curriculum, assessments of children with, or at risk for, developmental disabilities or delays should address two key concerns.[12] First, it must be sensitive enough to differentiate small, incremental rates of growth and development of young children, especially children with more significant delays. Second, it must produce sufficient information to identify socially valid goals and outcomes, such as the ability of children with delays to function in the normal activities within the classroom.

Embedding principals of universal design at the classroom level can help ensure greater learning opportunities for all children.[13] These principals include multiple means of representation, engagement, and expression. To apply universal design, teachers use assessment results to understand children's particular strengths and areas of need. From there, they can augment the curriculum to support children's full participation.

For multiple means of representation, a variety of formats are used to allow children with different learning styles and developmental levels to access and participate in classroom activities. For example, a teacher may use verbal cues, a printed schedule, and pictures to help children navigate the daily schedule. In this case, teachers of children with developmental delays can use cue cards or pictures to better navigate the class schedule, rather than relying solely on verbal cues (e.g., "time for circle").

For multiple means of expression (e.g., text, speech, print, music), children demonstrate their knowledge and learning in a variety of ways. Consequently, a teacher could allow children to choose from a variety of options for active participation in an activity. For example, a child identified as having a language impairment may point or use a communication device to answer questions posed during circle time by the teacher, while another child may role-play or act out a response.

For multiple means of engagement, the curriculum uses choice and autonomy to respond to children's different needs and approaches in the activities and routines of the classroom. This approach can include simple measures, for example, providing a variety of materials and activities (e.g., manipulatives, computer games, board games) to help children learning basic mathematics. In this way, a child identified as having a sensory impairment may prefer to interact with a computer rather than participate in a board game or practice math using manipulatives with their peers, or the child may want to participate in an art activity using a paint brush instead of finger paints.

### Additional Considerations for Culturally and Linguistically Diverse Children

The US population is becoming increasingly diverse. Most recent national estimates indicate a 15 percent increase in the proportion of children of Hispanic ethnicity, and the number of children learning English as a second language in the public schools has increased dramatically—an estimated 44 percent since 1990.[14] However, the majority of preservice teachers are not representative of the child population.[15] The expansion of pre-K programs must strive to meet the needs of the increasingly diverse population through a variety of means.

The complexity of early childhood screening and assessment is amplified for children and families from culturally and linguistically diverse backgrounds. In the preschool classroom, a teacher may struggle to accurately assess children as they navigate differences in language and cultural practices. To effectively gather and use assessment data, pre-K teachers must be familiar with the unique issues of second-language learning, have access to appropriate assessment tools that meet the needs of a diverse preschool population, and be culturally responsive to children and their families.

Children from culturally and linguistically diverse backgrounds are, paradoxically, both sometimes incorrectly identified for developmental delay and sometimes overlooked in this regard. For language development specifically, young children learning a second language are often inadequately identified because of the difficulty in "distinguishing between language differences and language disorders."[16] Children learning a second language are commonly overidentified when educators misinterpret dual-language use as a language delay. Conversely, the identification of language delays in a home language can be particularly difficult for teachers and related service personnel who are not proficient in the home language. These issues create particular challenges for appropriately identifying language and literacy delays and can clearly have an impact on other areas of learning and development. Although such difficulties could lead to either over- or underrepresentation in early childhood special education, a recent analysis of the nationally representative birth cohort of the Early Childhood Longitudinal Study (US Department of Education) sample suggests that by forty-eight months, young children from culturally diverse backgrounds are underrepresented in intervention services.[17]

The National Research Council cites a lack of adequate assessment measures to assess dual-language learners across all assessment types, including development screening and curriculum-based and norm-referenced assessments as well as a shortage of qualified teachers and practitioners prepared to assess this population as key issues to improve service delivery in preschool programs.[18] As the diversity of the preschool population continues to increase, we need to make sure that screening and assessment policies and practices are responsive to the needs of the children and families served in pre-K programs and that teachers and related service personnel are adequately prepared to engage in effective and culturally responsive assessment practices.[19]

### The Role of Families in Early Identification

Families play a critical role in the early identification, assessment, and intervention processes. A child- and family-centered approach is key to ensuring that the child's strengths and needs are appropriately identified and addressed.[20] Family members can provide information about the child's functioning across settings and should be seen as equal, contributing partners.[21] Teachers in pre-K programs can keep family members engaged in the process through regular communication and updates on the child's growth and development in the classroom, while continuing to gather information from families on the child's status in other settings.

## PROGRAM- AND SYSTEM-LEVEL POLICIES AND PRACTICES

Effective early identification and intervention practices in the classroom require three kinds of support at both the program and the system level. First, high-quality assessment relies on prepared teachers who have access to appropriate child assessment tools and strategies—and who receive ongoing support in their implementation. Second, teachers need technically sound early childhood assessment tools to gather instructionally meaningful data. And finally, interagency and interdisciplinary collaboration helps promote the effective planning and tracking of child progress within and across settings. Figure 6.4 summarizes all our recommendations for program- and system-level improvements in early identification and assessment of at-risk children. We will now examine each of these requirements.

## Preparation, Support, and Increasing the Numbers of Pre-K Teachers

As documented in this chapter, the collection and use of assessment data in pre-K programs ensures high-quality instructional practice for

**Figure 6.4 Program- and system-level recommendations for identifying and assessing young children in pre-K classrooms**

1. Recruit and retain pre-K teachers who have formal training in both early childhood education and early childhood special education.
2. Select child assessment tools using the best available evidence for linkage with curriculum or intervention and for technical adequacy.
3. Prepare and support pre-K teachers and related service personnel to appropriately use selected child assessment tools.
4. Provide time for collaboration among teachers, related service personnel, and families to discuss and use assessment data to inform instruction.
5. Invest in additional research to address the lack of technically sound child assessment tools for the diverse preschool population served in pre-K programs.
6. Increase the number of early childhood teacher candidates prepared to implement inclusive practices and to be culturally and linguistically responsive.

young children. As pre-K programs expand and diversify, teachers need adequate preparation and support to implement developmentally appropriate assessment practices. Both the NAEYC and the DEC/Council for Exception Children outline specific teacher competencies regarding child assessment.[22] These competencies articulated for teacher preparation programs provide the foundation for teacher knowledge and practice in early childhood assessment. Unfortunately, current estimates suggest that only 57 percent of states currently require that pre-K teachers have a bachelor's degree.[23] This finding illuminates two critical components of pre-K expansion—adequate professional preparation of pre-K teachers and an increase in the number of qualified early childhood teachers practicing in pre-K classrooms.

Even with professional guidelines, current early childhood professionals in the field have called for additional assistance in the area of appropriate child assessment. In a national study of early childhood practitioners serving young children with or at risk for disabilities, the top five training needs in early childhood assessment included appropriate assessment tools; appropriate assessment for culturally and linguistically diverse populations; developmentally appropriate assessments; appropriate modifying assessment for special populations, such as children with disabilities and culturally and linguistically diverse populations; and the use of child assessment data to plan instruction.[24] Further, 27 percent of the respondents indicated they did not feel knowledgeable about child assessment processes.

Daily classroom practice in high-quality pre-K classrooms integrate a range of assessment strategies. Although specific child assessments may be required or mandated by different groups such as public schools, Head Start, or childcare rating systems, these data can only benefit children if the information is used to improve instructional practice and become part of a cycle of data-informed instruction. As part of this cycle of gathering and using child information, pre-K teachers must gather informal assessment information to gauge children's progress across developmental and learning domains. These informal approaches, such as observation and analysis of children's work samples, allow the teacher to modify lessons, the classroom environment, and other instructional aspects to better meet the needs of individual children. These ongoing assessment approaches require an in-depth understanding of the constructs being assessed as well as an unbiased lens on child performance. Prior research suggests that teacher subjectivity can influence ratings of child performance in social-emotional and math competence.[25] However, emerging research suggests that the reliability of teacher ratings can be enhanced with intensive professional development and support.[26] Consequently, professional attention and support are another essential systemic component of pre-K expansion.

## Need for Technically Sound Assessment Tools

In addition to the preparation of teachers to adequately use child assessment data in pre-K programs, the field of early care and education suffers from a paucity of technically sound assessment tools appropriate for young children.[27] The National Research Council and others have called for more attention to the scientific basis for early childhood assessment tools, because their use or misuse has significant implication for children, their families, and the programs that serve them.[28] As state policy makers and administrators design and enhance pre-K initiatives, they need to consider the selection of high-quality assessment instruments. To date, several products have been developed to aggregate reliability and validity data for early childhood assessment tools.[29] Further, research in this area has grown, with new findings providing additional guidance.[30] As pre-K programs expand across the country, it is critical that investment is made in the study of existing measures and the development of new measures for assessing the development and learning of young children.

## Interagency and Interdisciplinary Collaboration, Transition, and Continuity

Pre-K programs can be expanded and enhanced through collaboration among professionals, families, and agencies. Collaboration at the classroom level creates a team-based approach to instructional planning for young children with disabilities and their families. Program- and system-level interagency collaboration, which allows information to be shared across settings, is particularly useful for young children with disabilities who may be moving from another setting or who receive services in multiple settings.[31]

Once a child has been identified as eligible for special education services, an IEP is developed outlining the child's goals, outcomes, and services. The child may then begin receiving services from a number of professionals (e.g., a special education teacher) and related services personnel (e.g., occupational, physical, and speech and language therapists). This team of professionals determines where the child's specialized services will be provided. Services can be provided within the pre-K setting or in another setting such as at home, in childcare, or in a Head Start program.

Effective communication and collaboration between these professionals, the pre-K teacher, and the family is critical to the child's ability to make progress on individualized goals, thus improving overall child outcomes.[32] Team members should collaborate and share information related to assessment, specific intervention strategies, modifications to the curriculum, and children's progress. To support this collaboration, programs should provide joint planning time to allow staff to meet to discuss specific children. As mentioned earlier, arrangements must be in place so that pre-K staff can participate in a child's IEP meeting.[33]

State pre-K programs vary in terms of their operating schedules, from part-day (43 percent) to full-day (20 percent), with an additional 33 percent of states allowing schedules to be determined at the local level.[34] This means young children must sometimes navigate multiple programs and service systems across a day or a school year.[35] Children with disabilities often navigate more-frequent and more-complicated transitions than do children without disabilities.[36] For example, once children are identified as having a disability, they often receive specialized services from multiple professionals as described above.

Program-level practices that provide continuity between services have been linked to better academic outcomes for young children. Consequently, educators need to address the continuity and alignment of the service delivery system (e.g., programs, curricula, and expectations) of pre-K programs, especially related to supporting children's adjustment into the preschool program and specialized services and has been linked to more successful transitions.[37] In doing so, pre-K professionals can work with community partners to develop transition policies and procedures for children moving into and out of pre-K classrooms to ensure continuity between programs.[38] Pre-K programs can be situated within the larger framework of other early childhood services (e.g., early intervention services, childcare, and home visits) and thus strengthen an integrated early care and education system that serves all young children and their families.

## CONCLUSION

To meet the needs of all young children, including those with, or at risk for, developmental delays or disabilities, early identification and assessment should be considered a vital part of pre-K expansion efforts. A holistic design and implementation of child assessment practices connects the realities of classroom practice with the administrative and systems-level support needed to sustain high-quality child assessment. No longer can early screening be viewed in isolation; it must be viewed instead as a starting point for understanding the developmental needs of a young child so that he or she can realize the long-term benefit of education. As the very foundation of a child's education, the appropriate use of screening and assessment tools helps ensure that all children, particularly those with disabilities or at risk for developmental delays, are diagnosed accurately to support their individual educational needs. No longer can we afford to miss this opportunity by having inadequately prepared, and inadequate numbers of, early childhood teachers. The recommendations we have presented throughout this chapter suggest classroom-, program-, and system-level ways to implement these early identification practices.

CHAPTER SEVEN

# Two-Generation Education Programs for Parents and Their Young Children

*Teresa Eckrich Sommer*
*Terri J. Sabol*
*P. Lindsay Chase-Lansdale*
*Jeanne Brooks-Gunn*

The United States has a long history of developing and expanding early childhood education as a key policy for improving education and economic outcomes for children. Indeed, the focus of this entire volume is to draw on this extensive knowledge to examine and document what is needed to bring high-quality early childhood education to scale in the twenty-first century. Deborah Phillips (chapter 1) and Amy Pace, Kathy Hirsh-Pasek, and Roberta Michnick Golinkoff (chapter 3) synthesize over forty years of evidence regarding the benefits of high-quality early education, especially model programs from the 1960s and 1970s, on outcomes later in life.

The observation that high-quality early childhood education programs can make lasting change for young children is encouraging.[1] However, as model programs have been scaled up, the strength of impacts has varied by program type, implementation, and quality.[2] Some

**Figure 7.1**
**CHAPTER PREVIEW**
**Challenges to two-generation education efforts for young children and families**

1. Despite parents' critical roles in young children's lives, early childhood education initiatives rarely include program elements that foster parents' own education and degree advancement, a key to supporting child well-being.
2. Parents with limited education are less likely to provide stimulating learning environments at home than are parents with higher levels of education.
3. Parents with low levels of education often experience daily adverse experiences (e.g., financial stress, housing instability, nonstandard work hours) that undermine their capacities to support their children's learning and growth and that diminish the effects of early childhood education on their children's development.
4. Low-quality or limited childcare options are cited as a primary barrier to full participation in traditional postsecondary education and training programs, significantly limiting the programs' success in helping parents advance their own education.
5. Early childhood education programs are staffed by experts in child development. Two-generation education programs require additional staff who are specialists in adult education and workforce training.

recent state pre-K programs demonstrate impressive effects on children's academic outcomes in the short term.[3] Yet, evaluations of other programs, including Head Start, suggest more modest short-term impacts on child development.[4] In addition, numerous recent evaluations have found that the positive effects of Head Start diminish over time and, for some evaluations, disappear.[5]

In the face of this evidence, we propose an alternative possibility to maintain the benefits of early childhood education by targeting parents' and children's education together through two-generation programs. The idea is to use early childhood education as a platform to support parents' own educational advancement, specifically linking children's programs with postsecondary education and workforce training for parents. Parents facing economic hardship tend to have low levels of education, with 50 percent having no more than a high school degree.[6] Children whose parents have low educational levels and the often-corresponding low income are less likely to be prepared for elementary school, to graduate from high school, or to complete postsecondary education.[7] This educational disadvantage sets both parents and children up for increased disadvantage and limited life opportunities over time.

In this chapter, we address two-generation education programs that are designed to promote educational advances for parents and their young children. Some researchers posit that two-generation education programs will be more beneficial for children than early childhood education programs alone.[8] For example, increased education might help parents raise their income, invest in their children's learning, reduce their own stress, or become better role models. Because few researchers have yet examined these ideas, there remains a tantalizing question: Does improving parents' education and career skills provide a significant additional benefit to children's early education?

Early education for four-year-old children (and perhaps for three-year-olds as well)—whether through pre-K, Head Start, or community-based programs—is likely to become universal in the twenty-first century. For this reason, educational leaders and policymakers need to examine the feasibility of integrating education and career training for parents within the early childhood landscape. The recent innovations in adult workforce training and education make this an opportune time to consider two-generation programming.[9] Figure 7.1 summarizes the major challenges confronting the implementation of two-generation programming.

In this chapter, we explore the possibilities of using two-generation programs to promote deeper and longer-lasting benefits of early child education. We examine the frameworks and empirical evidence underlying education programs for both children and parents. We review the advantages and disadvantages of adding programs for parents to different types of early childhood education settings, including state-funded pre-K programs, Head Start, and community-based programs. We also examine the literature on education and workforce development for parents and other adults and highlight key innovative elements that could be integrated into two-generation programming. We draw lessons from the ongoing evaluation of one of the most advanced two-generation programs, CareerAdvance. Finally, we offer suggestions on how to make two-generation programs a reality, including cross-agency partnerships, potential funding mechanisms, and pilot programming that could help advance the science behind two-generation education programs.

## FRAMEWORKS AND EVIDENCE UNDERLYING TWO-GENERATION EDUCATION PROGRAMS

Historically, several early childhood education programs, particularly those funded through Head Start, have provided direct services for parents. Most often, these programs focus on improving parenting skills and knowledge (e.g., classes on home literacy or positive discipline practices) as a way to foster children's development. While promoting effective parenting practices is critically important, our emphasis is on programming that directly targets parents' education and subsequent employment and income, also known as human capital. These two-generation programs are distinct in that they strengthen parents' human capital as a way to influence parenting and child outcomes over time.

Parents' education is consistently related to children's development.[10] Even a one-year increase in a low-income mother's education is related to better academic achievement among children.[11] We hypothesize that improving parents' education may be particularly beneficial for children who are already experiencing the positive effects of early childhood education, although this premise warrants more study than it has yet received.

Increased education helps parents secure more-stable jobs and reduce nonstandard work hours, which would give them a better work-family balance and more time to spend with their children. These benefits could in turn reduce unpredictability or instability in the home. The increased family income often resulting from additional education could decrease stress as well and promote well-being for both parents and children. Parents with higher levels of education are also likely to provide home environments that are more cognitively stimulating, and they are able to tailor their interactions to better suit the developmental needs of their children than parents with lower levels of education.[12]

Although parents' education plays a key role in fostering social and cognitive development among young children, past education interventions for parents have had limited success.[13] In the 1980s and 1990s, several programs were created in response to concerns that too many teenagers were becoming parents without completing high school (e.g., the New Chance Demonstration, the Learning Earning and Parenting Program, and Teenage Parent Demonstration). These programs, designed to help parents complete their General Educational Development (GED) test, provided a range of services, including basic academic skills instruction and occupational skills training. Experimental studies, however, suggest that these programs had limited success in helping parents advance their education or employment.[14] Importantly, many mothers in these interventions and in more recent studies of programs that provided scholarships to young low-income parents in community colleges cited childcare as a barrier to education activities.[15]

Early childhood education addresses the biggest impediment to career advancement for parents—the safe and trusted care of their children—and thus is a key lever to promote parents' educational success. Yet, these learning environments for children are much more than childcare. Early childhood education programs foster trusted, connected communities for parents as allies in the shared goal of enriching children's development and fostering future school success.[16] On the day-to-day level, as parents watch their young children thrive and learn in early education programs, they may be more motivated to improve their own education and career opportunities, especially because two-generation programs help them see the vital connection between their own educational attainment and their children's learning.[17] The two-generation approach capitalizes on early childhood education to attract parents into education and training and has the untapped potential to promote parents' educational success.

While early childhood education may be an effective platform for offering training and education for parents, few such models exist. Whether two-generation programs are warranted within the current early childhood education landscape is currently being debated. On one hand, early childhood education should focus on improving classroom and teacher quality, not advancing the education and skills of parents. This position is aligned with the primary aim of early childhood education programs, which is to offer effective educational services to promote children's readiness for school. On the other hand, because parents play a critical role in the lives of their young children, any program element that fosters parent outcomes could be considered an essential way to support child well-being.

To examine this debate in detail, we reflect on four central questions. First, what types of early childhood education programs are well positioned to support parent-centered education and career training programs? Second, which features of parent-centered services would best suit the needs of parents, especially low-income parents? Third, what would a combination of early childhood education with training and education for parents look like? (We answer this question with a case study of an innovative two-generation model being conducted in Tulsa, Oklahoma.) Finally, what are the key implementation issues that early childhood education providers should consider when adding parent-centered programming?

## EARLY CHILDHOOD EDUCATION PROGRAMS WITH POTENTIAL AS A TWO-GENERATION PLATFORM

Early childhood education and care comprise a diverse range of program types, arrangements, providers, and funders. For children with low socioeconomic status, the three main types of early childhood education programs are pre-K, Head Start, and community-based organizations, and each varies in its scope, mission, and capacity to support two-generation programming.

### Pre-K

Pre-K programs provide early childhood education to three- and four-year-olds for no charge to families and are controlled and funded by local and states monies. Because of their design, these programs may not be the most feasible environment from which to launch a two-generation intervention. The mission of pre-K programs is to prepare children for entrance into elementary education. To date, parents have not been central to the aims of pre-K. In fact, the National Institute for Early Education Research definition of pre-K programs includes state-funded early childhood education programs that offer parenting classes, but excludes programs that mainly address parent education or work status or that tie child eligibility to either. Education and training for parents would be a large departure from the traditional focus of pre-K.

Although some pre-K programs are located with Head Start or placed in community-based or faith-based organizations, the majority are embedded in the K–12 system, which may provide various barriers for two-generation programing. Typical K–12 barriers include reduced flexibility in staffing roles and limited funds to support parent outcomes. Yet co-location with elementary education may benefit two-generation programs by providing continuous services from pre-K through elementary school and engaging parents and children across the elementary school years. Many other types of early education programs serve children for only one or two years, potentially limiting the amount of time to help parents make educational gains.

Pre-K programs can also serve a wide range of children. Programs targeted for low-income and at-risk children would be an effective platform for two-generation services. On the other hand, universal programs, which serve children across a range of income levels, may not be as appropriate for two-generation education programming, particularly if parents already have higher levels of education than parents in targeted pre-K.

## Head Start

Head Start, the nation's largest federally funded preschool program, may be more amenable to two-generation education programming than pre-K because, from its inception in the 1960s through former President Lyndon B. Johnson's War on Poverty, it has had a whole-family, antipoverty approach. Indeed, many advocates and leaders consider Head Start the original two-generation program. In particular, every family in Head Start is assigned a family support advocate to provide case management and emergency services support. In addition, Head Start already provides various parent-oriented services, such as parenting classes, mental health support, financial coaching, and GED services.[18]

New findings from the Head Start Impact Study reveal that parents whose children were randomly assigned to Head Start were more likely to increase their *own* educational attainment over time than were parents of control group children, particularly among those who had some college experience at baseline.[19] Formalizing a more explicit education program for parents could add to this promising base.[20]

Indeed, on-the-ground momentum is growing within Head Start to provide more intensive two-generation education programing. In 2011, the federal Office of Head Start established the National Center on Parent, Family, and Community Engagement, which provides technical assistance to Head Start centers throughout the country to support parents. More recently, the National Head Start Association and Ascend at the Aspen Institute held a conference in February 2015 to discuss two-generation innovation in Head Start and to highlight models with promise.[21] The Office of Planning, Research and Evaluation in the Administration for Children and Families is currently supporting Head Start University Partnership Grants for dual-generation programs.

### Community-Based Centers

Community-based organizations or private centers that serve children whose tuition is subsidized through state-administered federal monies from the Child Care and Development Block Grant have mixed potential for offering two-generation education services. One of the most important design elements of these subsidies is parental choice. Parents may select any legally operating childcare provider that meets state health and safety requirements; offerings include center-based care, licensed family childcare homes, and more informal settings (although for purposes of two-generation programs, we focus on center-based programs only). Community-based centers could provide the opportunity to integrate parent education and career-related training by providing a safe and trusting environment that parents selected themselves, assuming the program's mission is sufficiently parent-oriented. These providers may also be especially supportive of working parents as subsidies require labor market participation, and higher income eligibility thresholds permit parents to earn higher wages than parents with children enrolled in Head Start, in which income requirements are stricter.

One challenge of working with community-based programs is that the quality varies widely across center-based programs that serve children who receive subsidies, with recent evidence suggesting that these children may often attend low-quality care that is associated with poorer outcomes at kindergarten entry.[22] Although the quality of pre-K and Head Start programs varies as well, community-based programs often do not have to adhere to the same quality benchmarks (depending on their funding source) as do pre-K and Head Start. Thus, there is a greater concern that community-based programs may not meet minimum levels of quality. To ensure positive benefits for both parents and children, two-generation programs seek providers that use high-quality early childhood education programs as a platform.

## PARENT-CENTERED SERVICES BEST SUITED TO TWO-GENERATION PROGRAMS

One compelling reason for the idea of two-generation education programming in the twenty-first century is the progress made in the 2000s in identifying better strategies for implementing adult-oriented education and training. Past attempts to improve the education and employment of low-income adults have had modest impacts, and interventions and research on these programs for low-income parents specifically (with the exception of teenage parents) have been limited.[23]

Community colleges—the most common point of postsecondary entry for low-income students—typically provide a wide range of disparate and sometimes confusing educational and training options. Adults receive limited guidance on how to select and complete required coursework, and they get an incomplete picture of how their coursework relates to future education and employment. (As community college expert Davis Jenkins points out, however, there are notable exceptions to this unfocused approach at community colleges.[24]) These issues are especially concerning for low-income students who typically have inadequate knowledge and skills to navigate the system and are less likely to take advantage of scarce career services.[25]

Lessons from behavioral and cognitive science suggest the need for a different approach. Students are most likely to succeed when their choices are carefully delineated and divided into manageable sequential steps; when feedback and support are offered regularly; and when the pathways to completion are well defined and monitored.[26] New developments in adult workforce training and education align with these principles and include these six approaches, which we describe in the following sections: sector-based training, stackable career credentials, contextualized curricula, connections to employment, coaching and peer support, and compensation for performance and other financial support.

## Sector-Based Training

Sector-based training programs improve a prospective worker's chances for securing stable employment and higher wages by identifying and targeting growth areas of the local economy.[27] For example, market analyses of Tulsa, Oklahoma, revealed that jobs were expanding in the health-care sector so the two-generation program focused on health-care careers.[28] This strategy may be especially beneficial to low-income students who are likely to have inaccurate and incomplete information about career training options and the consequences for employment and earnings, and who may need guidance in narrowing their career choices.[29]

## Stackable Credentials

Students earn stackable credentials through step-by-step career training that leads to increasing levels of employment and commensurate wages.[30] For example, students in a nursing pathway can progressively receive certification as a nursing assistant (e.g., $9 to $12 per hour), licensed nurse practitioner (e.g., $16 to $20 per hour), and registered nurse (e.g., $20 to $30 per hour), entering and leaving employment and school as needed to achieve certification, to practice skills, or to improve income.[31] Stackable credentials offer parents of young children a well-defined path and the flexibility that is likely to improve work, family, and school balance, especially given the shifting developmental and care needs of young children. A parent might decide to pursue short-term certification when a child is in early childhood education, minimizing the time demands on the family when a child is very young, and then progress to more challenging and time-intensive college-level career training when a child enters elementary school.

### Contextualized Curricula

Adult students are more likely to be engaged in learning and motivated to persist educationally when their coursework is connected to their career goals.[32] Two-generation programs have a distinct advantage in that they can design coursework relevant to both the parent's career and experiences of parenting. New two-generation models are exploring ways to align curricula of parents and children. For example, English language learner classes for parents of young children can be based on developmental objectives used by teachers in their children's classrooms (e.g., math, "My daughter can name shapes," or socio-emotional learning, "My son can make friends") while also advancing English language skills.[33]

### Employment Support

Workforce intermediaries serve as matchmakers between the broader needs of the local labor market and the skills of the workforce.[34] Examples include workforce development organizations and community college bridge programs that bring together employers and workers, private and public funding streams, and students and educational institutions. Early childhood education centers have been underutilized in this role to date but can help identify skilled and educated workers for existing workforce intermediaries. And in so doing, early learning organizations would be helping parents find employment that offers security, family-friendly hours and conditions, and family-supporting wages.[35]

### Coaching and Peer Support

Peer support, mentors, coaches, and counselors have been shown to be effective for low-income students in general, although there have been fewer studies of these services for low-income parents specifically.[36] Career coaches with specialized knowledge of the local training and education market may be especially effective in helping student parents prepare for and succeed in an education system that typically offers limited academic support. The coaches can work with small groups of parents and offer regular opportunities to reflect and assess progress.[37] Low-income parents facing educational barriers may be more likely to overcome them when working in tandem with other parents who share similar life experiences and career goals. For example, parents could share childcare, transportation, problem-solving approaches, and encouragement.[38]

### Incentives and Other Financial Support

Incentives can promote persistence in college; likewise, extra support (e.g., before and after childcare) can help parents balance the competing demands on their resources.[39] Incentives may include cash payments for regular monthly class attendance or for the completion of educational milestones such as career certification or degree completion. Past studies suggest that even modest financial support to low-income parents and their families can promote child well-being. Parents returning to school may also require additional care for their children beyond pre-K or other early learning programs. Two-generation programs may choose to cover the cost of wraparound childcare while parents attend classes or participate in on-the-job training.

In sum, programs that incorporate these innovative parent-centered elements in an early learning platform may be more effective for low-income parents of young children than programs lacking them, although experimental studies are needed. The advantages for parents (and, by extension, their children) could be substantial, given a postsecondary education system that is poorly designed to meet parents' particular strengths and challenges. While the number of parents pursuing college has grown over the past several decades, rising from 20 to 27 percent among students who are enrolled in undergraduate institutions, most parents cannot attain an advanced certificate or degree through traditional two- or four-year institutions.[40] Within six years of starting, only 33 percent of parents who enroll in higher education institutions attain a credential or degree, compared with 53 percent of nonparent students.[41]

## PULLING IT ALL TOGETHER: A CASE STUDY OF A TWO-GENERATION PROGRAM

An Oklahoma antipoverty organization called the Community Action Project of Tulsa County (CAP Tulsa) is testing the feasibility of adding these six innovations (sector-based training, stackable career credentials, contextualized curricula, connections to employment, coaching and peer support, and financial support) through its CareerAdvance program. The program is showing initial signs of promise.[42] We, the authors of this chapter, are leading three ongoing federal evaluations of the CareerAdvance program, examining how a blended pre-K and Head Start early childhood education program can serve as an effective platform for advancing the future education and employment opportunities of parents and children alike. CAP Tulsa's model is an example of original simultaneous programming for parents and children that is possible within an early childhood education context. Although experimental results are not yet available, research on program implementation, including focus groups with parents and staff, highlights the experiences and perspectives of providers and participants in the program. On the following pages, we present some of these findings.

### Key Elements of CareerAdvance

The CareerAdvance program prepares parents of children enrolled in CAP Tulsa's Early Head Start and Head Start programs (which also receive pre-K funding) for careers in the health-care field (e.g., nursing, health information technologies, medical and dental assisting), a growing sector of the local economy. Through cross-agency partnerships with Tulsa Community College and Tulsa Technology Center, CAP Tulsa purchases entry-level classes and pays tuition for college-level career training for parents accepted into the CareerAdvance program. The agency also offers GED and college preparatory classes geared to the health-care field for parents not yet ready for college. To support employment, CAP Tulsa connects students at each level of certification with local health-care providers in search of job candidates with similar skills and training.

CareerAdvance participants engage in group (weekly) and individual (monthly) meetings with career coaches. The groups consist of fifteen parents, all of whom have at least one child (six months to five years) enrolled in CAP Tulsa's early childhood education programs. Topics at peer partner meetings range from soft skills (e.g., time management and job interview skills) to course selection and employment opportunities.

The CareerAdvance program covers student tuition and all school-related expenses. Program participants are eligible to receive up to $3,000 annually in cash transfers for attendance or performance-based incentives for achieving certification and employment. Parents also receive tutoring assistance and additional childcare coverage as needed to fulfill educational requirements.

### Early Childhood Education as a Platform

CAP Tulsa's CareerAdvance program serves as a model two-generation program and uses pioneering service strategies to connect parent and child programming. First, the program has expanded the Head Start's family support team to include career coaches with expertise in education and careers. Second, it delivers parent education and training programs while children attend school. Last, it intentionally and intensively promotes the skills of parents and children at the same time, which may lead to synergies in learning across generations.

CareerAdvance coaches serve as an extension of the Head Start family support team. Each family advocate is assigned to work with a career coach and a small group of parents enrolled in a career training track. Family support staff members help parents cope with the day-to-day challenges of raising children with limited resources, and career coaches build on this foundation to promote economic self-sufficiency over the longer term. The perspective of one parent exemplifies the experience of many:

> My favorite part is so much support we're getting. We can pretty much call her [the coach] anytime . . . We constantly have the support not only from our classmates but also from our teachers and our coach . . . And when I was in college before, it was just me against the world, basically . . . So if I dropped out, nobody cared . . . I was only just disappointing myself. Now if anybody is missing too much class, we'd call them and are, like, you know, "Where are you at? Come to class."

CareerAdvance coaches provide information, support, guidance, and direct accountability to parents according to principles of effective practice for adult students.[43] Working with parents in small groups to foster peer relationships, the career coaches also often succeed in creating community, as suggested by this parent participant: "I know if I tried to leave this program, I would have some people on my phone. And that's the good thing about us being . . . a small group of people. If one of us tried to leave it, oh, we gonna be on that phone quick: 'Wait a minute what are you doing?'" Parents, coaches, and family advocates expand the trust that has been built from a foundation of early childhood education.

The CareerAdvance program offers training and education services for parents during early childhood education center hours of operation, a critical support to parents that allows them to take advantage of other key features of the program. The synchronization of schedules helps parents in that they have time available while their children are safe and in care to pursue their own goals: "I like how they've made the program fit around the youngest child's schedule," said one parent. "How they've tailored it to fit around those hours, which really would tailor around all school-age children's hours. So only during clinical times do you have to really worry about before- and after-care. But for the most part, all of us can still take the kids, kiss them good-bye, do our thing, and then be there to pick them up." Parents may be more motivated to engage in education and career training knowing that their children are learning and thriving in early education, although this idea has not been tested empirically.[44]

CAP Tulsa has invested heavily both in children's development and in parents' education and skill building. Program participants are beginning to identify connections between the two, especially for their older children, who benefit immediately from parents' improved skills to support their school work:

> I have found, on a positive note, what school has done in our house. Like, my nine-year-old has always struggled in math. And I have always struggled in math. It's never been a strong suit. I've always told her that, you know, "Sorry, I can't really help you." And she's relied on that. "Well, mommy can't help me. She doesn't get numbers." Well, when I got put in this math tutoring class, I felt like I could then relate to her more, and I felt like it was empowering me because it was giving me those skills that I left behind somewhere in high school and junior high. And so when I would get home, for the first couple of weeks, I'd be like, "I can help you." She's like, "No you can't, you don't know how to do this." And I was like, "No, really, I know how to do it now." So I feel like I wasn't getting so upset with her, because now I know the material and understand it and I'm getting it. So it's helping her

> to feel better about herself, and I feel better about myself because for all those years, it was embarrassing to tell your nine-year-old, "Sorry, I can't help you with this because I don't know it myself." So I feel like that's been a positive—is that I can guide them better. Now that I have the information, I can help them better.

This parent links her new skills with improved family life, including her increased confidence, reduced stress at home, and a healthier relationship with her older daughter, which in turn benefits her preschool-aged daughter. We are testing these associations by studying the CareerAdvance program's effectiveness and whether the program promotes children's well-being above and beyond what early childhood education provides on its own. We have also found that CAP Tulsa's early childhood education teachers and staff support parents' education and training advancement. They engage with the objectives of CareerAdvance (e.g., through in-service training sessions), and they play an important role in celebrating and supporting parents' day-to-day school success.

### Preliminary Evaluation Results

As of this writing, the main evaluation of CareerAdvance is still ongoing, but preliminary results are promising, as parents in the program have attained relatively high levels of education. After sixteen months in the program, 76 percent of parents achieved at least one workforce-applicable certificate.[45] This progress is remarkable, considering the rates of average community college degree completion across the country. Only 27 percent of full-time students and 15 percent of part-time students complete a degree after six years in community college.[46] These findings suggest that—in addition to preparing children for school—early childhood education programs could provide parents the tools for increasing their education and eventually reducing economic hardship over time. A CareerAdvance participant explains this viewpoint: "This program has changed my life; it's changed my future, my family's future definitely. I mean, this has opened up so many opportunities for me and my family."

## KEY IMPLEMENTATION ISSUES

As previously discussed, early childhood education programs vary in their scope, mission, and capacity to support two-generation programming. Those that embrace an antipoverty mission (e.g., Head Start) may be especially well suited for adding parent-centered education services. Other important considerations for two-generation programs from an early learning platform include the types of parents to serve, the kinds of cross-agency partnerships needed to support them, potential funding opportunities for these efforts, and pilot programs to help gather evidence on the effectiveness of two-generation programs.

### Types of Parents to Serve

The education, skill level, and career goals of parents as well as the financial circumstances and characteristics of the household (e.g., single parenthood) may vary widely among parent populations served by various types of early childhood programs.[47] Two-generation education programs may choose to target specific parent subpopulations and should tailor their services accordingly. Programs interested in serving fathers, for example, may develop career training services in more traditionally male career fields (e.g., manufacturing or transportation logistics).[48]

### Cross-Agency Partnerships

Most early childhood education programs do not have the organizational capacity and expertise to deliver parent-centered education services themselves; typically, cross-agency partnerships with local educational providers (e.g., community college and technical schools) and employers are needed. These partnerships are most successful when they are mutually beneficial to both organizations.[49] For example, when employment opportunities that suit the needs and interests of parents of young children (e.g., career field, wages, hours, benefits) match the job openings of local employers, the likely result is sustainable partnerships between early childhood education centers and businesses in the same community.[50] When partnering with adult education providers, early childhood education centers may choose to purchase separate classes for parents. In doing so, the centers increase the opportunities for tailored instruction and social networking among parents while also securing a funding source for the educational service provider.

## Funding Strategies

Inventive funding strategies for two-generation programs hold promise for advancing the field. These strategies include blending child funding streams, combining adult and child funding sources, reallocating public dollars within a single funding stream, and testing low-cost two-generation pilots.

### *Child-centered funding sources*

Candidate programs that receive federal and state funding sources for children include pre-K, Head Start, and home visiting, all programs with a solid evidence base (although the strength of the impact varies) and relatively broad political support.[51] Other federal sources for children include the Child Care and Development Fund, Race to the Top Early Learning Challenge grants, and Preschool Development Grants.[52]

### *Adult-centered funding sources*

Federal funding source options within the adult sphere include the Workforce Innovations Opportunity Act (WIOA), which took effect July 1, 2014; Temporary Assistance to Needy Families (TANF), the federal welfare program passed in 1998 to replace Aid to Families with Dependent Children; and Pell Grants and the Federal Supplemental Educational Opportunity Grant (FSEOG) program.[53] WIOA, the first reauthorization of the federal workforce training system since 2000, seeks to support job seekers through education, training, and employment. The legislation fits well with the purposes of two-generation strategies and, as a new mandate, may be more likely to support innovation. TANF, part of President Clinton's Personal Responsibility and Work Opportunity Act, emphasized work over education and training. This act may be reauthorized and may offer new opportunities to expand allowable educational activities. And because FSEOG focuses on students with the highest level of financial need, these grants could be especially beneficial to early childhood education programs serving the most vulnerable families with young children.

### *Braided funding*

The strategy of combining funding may have a particular advantage over single funding sources for two-generation education programs. For example, braided Head Start and pre-K models build from the strengths and opportunities provided by both services. Improved labor market outcomes such as family-supporting wages may take many years and thus require a longer-term investment than an investment for pre-K programs alone, which typically fund children for a single year. Braiding funding sources also can help overcome the tendency to serve parents and children in separate programmatic silos despite the deep connection between the well-being of parents and that of the children in the same family.[54]

### *Funding reallocation*

Within a single funding source like Head Start, existing dollars may be reallocated to support two-generation programming while not detracting from child services. For example, Head Start centers could apply for waivers to expand or reallocate family support services dollars, of which $1 billion are spent each year, such that the centers offer tiers of services for different subgroups. One type of family support staff could focus on existing family support functions such as emergency assistance, crisis counseling, and case management services for families experiencing high levels of emotional and financial distress. Another type of staff, with a different set of skills and content expertise, could serve as career coaches for parents who have educational and career goals and who are ready to enter programs in developmental education, career certification, or degree attainment. Staff at the Administration of Children and Families within the US Department of Health and Human Services have shown some interest in such staffing diversification models in Head Start.[55]

## Pilot Programming

Another way to gather research on the effectiveness of two-generation programs is to test low-cost models that do not require the braiding or reallocation of federal funding but use existing public dollars, which may be augmented by private and other community resources. One such model offers classes in career exploration and soft-skill development to parents within a network of local employers and community providers with expertise in serving parents, children, or both. Ascend at the Aspen Institute has funded such a pilot program in Evanston, Illinois—the Evanston Two-Generation Initiative—through a partnership with the Evanston Community Foundation and Northwestern University.[56]

At this juncture, we know little empirically about the impact of adult training and career services offered from a base of early learning on child, parent, and family well-being. Yet pilot models in early childhood education centers are currently under way.[57] Several inexpensive and low-intensity two-generation approaches are available to help parents and children. For example, services for first-generation immigrants include the translation of postsecondary transcripts to assess the value of educational credits attained outside the United States.[58] Other programs provide short-term transportation to parents' places of employment while helping parents build savings to purchase a car of their own (e.g., Friends of Children of Mississippi's TANF to Work and Ownership Project).[59] Family members can take technical training and community college classes at an early childhood education center or elementary school (e.g., the College Access and Success Program of Educational Alliance).[60] Finally, there is a wide range of financial support offerings to encourage economic self-sufficiency and asset building. Efforts include helping families with credit repair, budgeting, completing the Free Application for Federal Student Aid (e.g., Evanston Two-Generation Initiative), and the establishment of individual and child savings accounts, especially for college (e.g., Corporation for Enterprise Development, or CFED).[61] While these approaches do not have an evidence base yet, they hold promise for improving the labor market success of low-income parents and their children.

## CONCLUSION

Empirical evidence shows strong associations between parents' education and income, on the one hand, and children's development and academic success, on the other. In this chapter, we have considered the value of adding education, workforce training, and career services for parents to early learning settings, and whether this is achievable. Two-generation programs may be a viable and reasonable approach to protect and sustain investments in early learning by advancing the education and labor market outcomes of low-income parents, thus improving the likelihood of school success for their children. We hypothesize that supporting the education of parents and children together may strengthen the benefits of early childhood education programs to children over time. This chapter does not prescribe a definitive direction for pre-K or other types of early learning programs as to whether they should add a focus on parents' human capital. We do, however, suggest approaches worthy of additional consideration. Combined pre-K and Head Start programs and agencies willing to extend beyond a business-as-usual approach to add education, employment, and career services for parents are especially well suited to model ways to support parents and children together so that families might escape poverty when their children are still young.

# Conclusion

*Nonie K. Lesaux*
*Stephanie M. Jones*
*Julie Russ Harris*

This book highlights the array of diverse and pressing issues facing us at this pivotal moment in the early education sector—a moment that demands that we engage in the hard work of substantial quality improvement within the system with an eye toward scaling. Building on the rich and exciting work featured in the previous chapters, we now present some implications for the system and key recommendations for advancement and improvement. The following sections are organized around five high-impact leverage points to consider in the design, implementation, and eventual scaling of the next generation of early learning practices and policies. In each section, we summarize the central scientific insights that inform these leverage points; some common pitfalls that impede advancement in these areas; and actionable suggestions for bringing relevant strategies to bear on today's settings that serve and support young children and their families.

## FIVE HIGH-IMPACT RECOMMENDATIONS

### Identify and support children facing adverse life circumstances and experiences that impede learning.

Decades of research have illuminated the impact of adverse childhood experiences on development and learning. Experiences of adversity "get under children's skin," having long-lasting effects on children's early brain architecture, particularly for brain regions associated with executive function and self-regulation. But we also know that risk is not deterministic. Early learning practices and policies, when focused and targeted, can buffer the impacts of adverse experiences on children's development by providing protective and enhancing effects.

The first step to securing children's access to protective and enhancing experiences is identifying the children who face adverse experiences known to affect their health, well-being, and learning. When it comes to identifying vulnerable children and families and channeling resources to buffer the impacts of risk, what's becoming increasingly clear is that we cannot rely exclusively on socio-demographic indicators, especially in today's socio-political and economic environment. In fact, data suggest that adverse experiences hurt development, regardless of socio-demographic context (although the magnitude of effect is greater for some groups than it is for others). For example, while growing up in poverty is a key socio-demographic factor linked to adverse life experiences, in today's economic environment, economic *instability*, or turbulence, cuts across income brackets. Economic instability affects children who might not necessarily be identified as experiencing risk according to screening practices based solely on static measures of poverty and socio-economic status. Moreover, adverse life experiences tend to co-occur, meaning, for example, that children exposed to economic instability may also live in poor housing conditions where they are exposed to environmental toxins or community violence. Children exposed to poverty tend to suffer more frequent and more intense health problems, including ear infections and asthma. In addition, adverse life experiences cascade, creating other challenges that influence children's everyday lives. For example, economic instability is likely to disrupt children's daily home environments, parents' emotional availability, and the family's network of support, including early care and education.

Yet simply identifying and understanding the effects of the risks or challenges that children experience in their daily lives is not enough. Connecting children and families to targeted and meaningful support is essential. For such support to make a genuine difference for children, it must (1) focus on the mechanisms that buffer risk and promote a development-enhancing environment and (2) include specific strategies that are implemented in a manner consistent with their design.

Why focus on buffering mechanisms for impact and implementation strategies? While many early learning policies and initiatives do indeed promote environments that buffer the impact of adversity on children's learning, they often target areas that do not necessarily correspond with practices that the science of early learning suggests would have the highest impact. Described in more detail in the sections that follow, early care and education policies and initiatives must prioritize stable, nurturing relationships and inclusive environments, through support and interventions that target children, the adults who care for them, and the variety of settings in which they learn and play.

There are existing policies designed to mitigate the impact of risk on development and to promote protective factors that also offset risk. For example, caps on classroom size and adult-child ratios are in place for health and safety reasons, but also because they can lay a foundation for adults and children to form and maintain high-quality, connected, and nurturing relationships. The challenge is that the *implementation* of the policy (i.e., small classroom size) can undermine the second goal (high-quality adult-child relationships) and cause unintended negative consequences for children. Imagine the situation in which complex and sometimes unpredictable teacher schedules (e.g., absences, early morning, late afternoon coverage) prevail. Children arrive at school unsure of which classroom to go to or which teacher they will be with or are moved around from room to room to maintain ratios. Both cases interrupt relationship quality, stability, and predictability—all central mechanisms for buffering risk. Such scenarios serve as useful reminders that mandates must be accompanied by training, support, and oversight that place greater value on the multiple intentions behind the policy or practice.

### Implement universal screening systems to identify children at risk for developmental delay and to drive comprehensive prevention efforts.

Early childhood practices have not been data-driven historically. Yet good practice—whether educational or clinical—starts with universal assessment. There are legitimate reasons why assessing young children has been unpopular; when assessment systems result in high-stress experiences for children or add unnecessary burden to already taxed teachers or administrators, we should all be concerned. However, neglecting universal screening systems not only results in missed opportunities to help children when the timing may be optimal (i.e., before an early indicator becomes an actual delay) but can also result in costly and time-intensive (and often unsuccessful) efforts to remediate more entrenched problems later. Remember that in early childhood, remediation and enrichment have a similar look and feel to the young child. This is not the case for the eight- or nine-year-old who has experienced sustained difficulties.

Though many disciplines (e.g., developmental psychology, public health, economics) agree on the benefits of early identification and few would suggest that children at risk for developmental delay should be denied access to intervention or development-enhancing learning experiences, standard universal assessment practices (or the lack thereof) prevent such timely identification. Given the extensive evidence base, why is this still the case? As Rous and Hallam highlight in chapter 6, we often confuse screening with assessment. Rather than using screening as the starting point and following it with more comprehensive assessment and links to services as indicated, screeners are often deployed as a substitute for the whole process. By design, screening tools should identify the need for further assessment, flagging anyone who may be at risk according to either an early, subtle indicator or a more obvious one. But as commonly used, screening has become misconstrued as a tool to find services only for children already demonstrating overt difficulties. Consequently, we are systematically missing children whose developmental concerns are not necessarily clear—children who are showing early signs of difficulty and for whom additional, targeted assessment is warranted.

Implementing universal screening for prevention efforts requires both practical and conceptual shifts. Not only must we use developmental screeners as they were intended, but we must also identify common touch points where all children have access to screening. We then need to provide training and support to professionals working in these common settings so that they can administer screening tools, provide follow-up guidance, and make connections to the variety of settings in which children spend their days. As Rous and Hallam point out in chapter 6, screening efforts need to encompass multiple agencies and settings that cut across sectors and developmental stages. Typical settings include the following:

- Public education facilities providing pre-K education
- Early learning and childcare settings, including home and family childcare
- Pediatric offices

Importantly, because these settings are already laden with responsibilities, we must be cautious about loading them with additional obligations. But by design, the screening process is brief; it includes a limited number of items that can provide general information about a child's developmental status. What's more, most screening tools are easily administered by early childhood professionals after training.

As indicated, universal screening via any of these touch points is only a first step. It must be followed by intensive and targeted preparation and support for the adults who conduct screenings. This preparation includes

(1) training in screening administration and (2) training in follow-up practices that connect potentially at-risk children to diagnostic assessment or targeted support services, or both.

This two-part focus is critical. Not only is the collection of screening data important, but how professionals use it is equally important. We must do better at sharing across agencies, settings, and networks. Those charged with caring for young children, and especially those implementing screenings, must be armed with knowledge of the available options for diagnostic assessment, support programs and services, so they can connect children and their families to appropriate services.

### Provide consistent high-quality early learning experiences over time.

As noted in the introduction, this book was spurred in part by today's ambitious agenda for dramatic expansion of pre-K. This momentum gives rise to both excitement and concern. Throughout this book, we clearly see that child development exists along a continuum. It does not comprise disconnected stages (e.g., infancy, toddlerhood, preschool), but instead represents the ongoing accumulation of experiences that build from one period to the next. Although this is not a new concept, it is nevertheless an accurate view.

When we become overly invested in certain periods (or outcomes), we risk losing sight of this continuum. For example, recent history shows us that, all too often, early education initiatives have suffered from an overly narrow focus:

- They focus on the expansion of one aspect of the early learning system without attending to how this expansion affects other parts of the system.
- They invest in a particular period through multiple (and even redundant) avenues while allowing for gaps in support so that results diminish over time (e.g., focusing on early intervention and universal kindergarten without addressing the years in between).

We cannot, at scale, invest in one developmental moment to the exclusion of others, under the false notion that this investment alone will mitigate the effects of past and present adversity and will inoculate against future difficulties. Instead, if we truly believe that child development is the result of ongoing experiences starting at birth (or even before), then early education leaders planning early learning practices and policies should create a blueprint of the early learning options and providers in their region and analyze this blueprint with an eye toward several issues:

- *Gaps in services:* These gaps may be due to cutoffs in eligibility, housing loss or a mobile family life, or aging restrictions.
- *Programmatic redundancies:* These ineffective measures cause confusion among stakeholders.
- *Avenues for alignment:* Effective interventions connect early childhood programs within communities, from infancy to pre-K and beyond.

### Address both severe and subtle instances of systematic exclusion from and within settings by attending to their root causes.

Children can only learn when they feel a sense of security and emotional safety. This is because children's adverse experiences, which challenge their sense of security and emotional safety, hijack the very skills and competencies they need to take advantage of the learning opportunities offered.

Most of us have heard of horrifying stories of severe child abuse that damaged children's health, ability to learn, and sense of well-being. However, as Deborah Phillips reminds us in chapter 1, early deprivation that undermines healthy development is not restricted to severe cases of physical abuse or to the sometimes extreme social deprivation characteristic of orphanage care. On the contrary, even relatively "subtle" instances of neglect, instability, and exclusion can produce stress responses that inhibit children's learning and development. For example, in early learning settings, children's sense of emotional security and safety can be compromised, and their stress responses triggered, by experiences of intrusive, harsh, or unsupportive interactions with caregivers; rejection or marginalization from peers; and unpredictable, chaotic environments (e.g., churning of students and teachers between classrooms). For this reason, we must now not only attend to severe instances of abuse and neglect, but also put into place policies and practices that address the more subtle, chronic, and common versions of these adverse experiences that similarly (though there is a difference in magnitude) compromise development and learning.

While the field has attempted to address less severe, but just as damaging adverse experiences, many of these efforts have ignored the root causes of the issues at play. In these cases, we have often unintentionally created situations in which new problems, with similar root causes, arise. For example, we have mandated inclusive practices without providing educators with the requisite training and support to cultivate nurturing and stimulating inclusive communities. In such cases, more subtle versions of exclusion, such as peer rejection and marginalization, can unfold, and children's learning and development continue to be compromised. Addressing both severe and subtle adverse experiences means mandating practices *and* providing the support necessary to mitigate root causes and promote the intended practices. Where should these efforts be focused? We suggest zeroing in on two places:

- *Stability:* instituting policies and practices that ensure consistency and predictability within learning environments. A focus on stability means turning around common practices such as continuous changes in staffing patterns, within and across years; frequent shifts in classroom groups because of individual behaviors, maintenance of adult-child ratios, and eligibility cutoffs (e.g., those based on family income, housing, and employment).

- *Relationships (adult-child and peer-to-peer):* instituting policies and practices that build and enhance children's experiences of acceptance and inclusion. A focus on relationships means adopting and supporting the use of curricula, and accompanying support, that use and build on peer groups as a platform for the development of social skills, especially those associated with empathy, tolerance, and emotional expression. It means being more intentional and intensive in educator training focused on preventing and correcting implicit or explicit biases as well as training focused on supporting children who are most vulnerable to social threat and exclusion (i.e., children with special needs; children with challenging behaviors; and children who are more solitary, less socially confident, and more sensitive).

A focal point for ensuring that children are cared for in environments that truly guard against severe and subtle neglect, exclusion, and instability is the focus of our next strategy: supporting early educators themselves, many of whom experience several risk factors in their own lives and all of whom are engaging daily in a physically, emotionally, and cognitively demanding profession.

## Support the adults caring for and educating young children through continuous and meaningful learning opportunities.

Children's healthy development is promoted through positive and supportive interactions with caregivers, teachers, and other community members, making adults fundamental to children's positive development. In this sense, adults' development and well-being is inextricably linked to children's development and well-being. In chapter 7, Sommer, Sabol, Chase-Lansdale, and Brooks-Gunn present an innovative avenue for improving adult well-being and focus on professional education: the integration of education and career training for parents within the early childhood landscape. This two-generation approach to supporting children shows great promise, but we need not stop there. We also learned from Phillips (chapter 1) and McCoy (chapter 2) that our idea of two-generation approaches should not be constrained to the two generations in households. Educators should consider how to focus on both "generations" in classroom and childcare settings. Indeed, the success of today's early education initiatives rests on their quality, and quality itself rests on the early educators and caregivers on the ground. To date, many reform efforts have failed to effect lasting changes in the early learning environment because they are not genuinely two-generational. The failed efforts paid insufficient attention to the adults' skills and knowledge necessary for high-quality implementation.

To improve children's outcomes in all early learning settings, we can no longer stop at the instructional tools and support that target children's needs; we must be just as intentional and intensive in supporting the educators who serve the children. Consider that to cultivate a high-quality learning environment, the educator must encourage children's social-emotional learning, build their content knowledge and language, and manage the challenging behaviors that inevitably arise during the day. In these learning environments, there is an emphasis on relationship building and there is a sense of emotional calm, all the while children's skills, knowledge, and competencies are building over time. For such a learning environment to become commonplace, we must provide educators with professional learning opportunities and support that recognize and are responsive to their own needs. As a consequence, interactions between adults in the system are enhanced, and supportive professional networks are enhanced and deepened. In turn, across the setting, there is increased cohesion of practices to promote children's behavioral and academic development.

How can today's early education stakeholders accomplish this two-generational approach? As McCoy reminds us, we need to protect educators from stress and other adversity in their own daily lives. Education stakeholders can accomplish this by taking these steps:

- Providing educators with livable, equitable, and transparent entry-level wages and salary increases, like those enjoyed in other professions. As Phillips notes, this means identifying and mobilizing a sustainable, dedicated source of public-private funding to upgrade the compensation of those who care for and educate young children.
- Enhancing educators' own self-regulatory and executive functioning strategies for the classroom or childcare setting. Most existing initiatives focus on improving educators' technical skills or supplying children with tools to regulate their own behaviors. Clearly, our initiatives to build workforce capacity must emphasize early childhood educators' continued development and deployment of self-regulation necessary for managing the high energy and time demands inherent in early childhood education.
- Providing educators with both the tools (e.g., curricula) and support (e.g., coaching) necessary for improved learning and teaching. Concrete tools and process-based support must work in tandem if either form of assistance is to be optimally effective. Such tools and support improve both the learning settings to which children are exposed and the educators' working conditions and satisfaction, thereby also enhancing their own well-being.

## LOOKING AHEAD

The strategies and recommendations delineated here represent the wealth of knowledge of the many contributors to this book. These recommendations were truly co-created; they arose from collaboration that produced insights beyond what any one of us could have achieved on his or her own. For this, we are deeply indebted to the contributors to this volume, to discussions with attendees at the Leading Edge meeting, and correspondence with others in the field. But the work does not stop here. We encourage our readers to respond to today's challenge of both improving and expanding children's opportunities to learn from birth onward by engaging with us in this burgeoning community of action—one focused on designing, implementing, and scaling the next generation of early education. The recommendations offered here in the conclusion, combined with the deep and practical insights embedded in each chapter, are for us educators to design and implement together. It is our hope that, collectively, we will accelerate transformative action within today's early learning community, cultivating strong and supportive early learning environments for all children.

# AFTERWORD

In 2015, there is much to celebrate in the world of early care and education. A growing body of science around child development has made great strides by providing new insights into the importance of the interactions between the biology of development and the environmental influences young children experience. We understand, more than ever before, that healthy learning and development is as reliant on the efforts to buffer young children against the damaging effects of chronic stress and adversity as it is on providing supportive and nurturing relationships and high-quality educational experiences. Local, state, and federal funding is supporting increased numbers of early childhood programs and systems-building efforts. In addition, the growing public awareness of the importance of healthy and nurturing experiences in the early years of life is making early childhood education one of the more bipartisan issues in an often politically fractured environment.

In general, the impetus for early care and education programs springs from the desire to counter the harmful effects of poverty on young children's learning and development and to close the achievement gap between black and white children and between the economically disadvantaged and their better-resourced peers. The children and families most in need of these services often have multiple risk factors and vulnerabilities that must be recognized and understood in the program design. Policy makers and the early childhood administrators and teachers who are charged with implementing these programs have a huge task. Children grow, develop, and learn within their families and communities, and early learning interventions must address young children's developing needs; respect families, communities, and cultures; and buffer children from the harmful consequences of poverty, inequality, and discrimination.

We can now observe the trajectory of mature state-funded programs such as those in Georgia and Oklahoma and in a select group of low-resourced school districts in New Jersey. At the local levels, we see emerging efforts to provide high-quality early learning and development experiences in cities such as San Antonio and New York City. Although the now decades-old Perry Preschool and Abecedarian Project have been held as models of successful early care and education programs, there are promising results from more current efforts such as the preschool program run by the Boston public schools.

Yet, for the programs being brought to scale and for those that are long-standing, there is reason to step back and reflect on this moment. The urge to scale up quickly to high quality and demonstrate strong child outcomes is compelling. However, this impulse must be tempered, because these are complex systems that take time to develop and implement if young children are to enjoy any strong and lasting benefit.

Continued funding and public support will rely on confidence in the ongoing effectiveness of early education. Yet, these programs do not spring to life and function effectively simply through the provision of a space and staff. Successful efforts that result in strong outcomes for young children need to be based on the careful development and tenacious nurturing of a system that provides high-quality experiences to young children, their families, and the early care and education professional who are charged with program implementation.

During the first term of the Obama administration, senior staff in the Departments of Education and Health and Human Services created the framework depicted in figure A.1 to conceptualize the complexities of early learning and development systems. High-quality programs consist of early learning standards, comprehensive assessment systems,

**Figure A.1 The multifaceted nature of high-quality early learning and development systems**

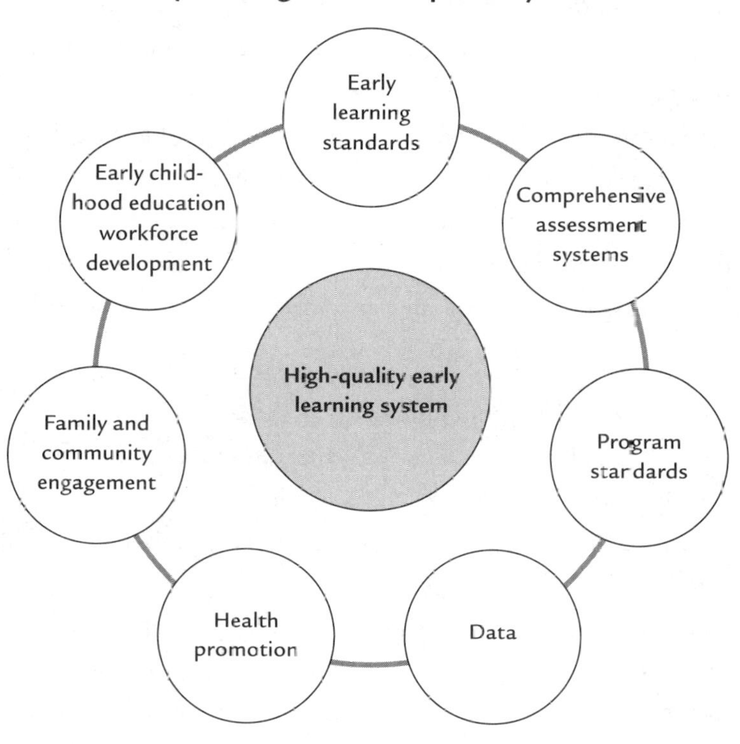


*Source:* Department of Education; Department of Health and Human Services.

program standards, data systems, health promotion strategies, family and community engagement efforts, and workforce development.

Policy makers and program administrators cannot expect any individual program component to bring about lasting change. Rather, these components are interrelated, and implementation requires a competent workforce of early care and education teachers and administrators who understand the contributions of each of these components and the importance of their interactions with each other.

*The Leading Edge of Early Childhood Education* is designed to outline our most current knowledge about the science of early learning and development so that today's early-learning agenda is more likely to succeed. Responsible use of public and private funds requires that we take a very careful look at what happens between the allocation of funds and the evaluation of a program. Early care and education interventions need to be delivered as intended, under the most beneficial conditions to the target populations. With an eye toward continuous improvement at all stages of implementation, policy makers and programs administrators should pose questions such as these:

- Which characteristics of the implementation best explain the impacts on children and families?
- Under what circumstances is implementation most effective?
- Are curricula being delivered with fidelity?
- What teacher and administrator characteristics are associated with high quality and positive outcomes?
- Does the quality of implementation vary by geography? Does it vary with the characteristics of the target populations, such as socioeconomic status, race or ethnicity, or linguistic background, immigration status, and so forth?

Supporting children, families, and early childhood educators is not an easy task. While the work of maintaining existing programs and scaling of new ones is valuable and can be life changing, we should not view it as one-dimensional. Rather, we must understand the most current research and the key elements that can have an impact on specific populations.

This book takes on the challenge of presenting the complexities of bringing programs to scale and supporting existing programs by providing a solid research base from a broad range of domains and offering examples from program implementation. The contributors to *The*

*Leading Edge of Early Childhood Education* have created an important resource. Their work provides a solid foundation for understanding the basic components of early learning and development programs that can support early childhood educators as they strive to make lasting improvements in the lives of young children and their families.

*Jacqueline Jones*
*President and CEO*
*Foundation for Child Development*

# NOTES

### *Chapter 1*

1. Joan Lombardi, *Time to Care: Redesigning Child Care to Promote Education, Support Families, and Build Communities* (Philadelphia: Temple University Press, 2003); Deborah A. Phillips, "Day Care: Promoting Collaboration Between Research and Policymaking," *Journal of Applied Developmental Psychology* 5, no. 2 (April 1984): 91–113.

2. Barbara Beatty, *Preschool Education in America: The Culture of Young Children from the Colonial Era to the Present* (New Haven, CT: Yale University Press, 1995); Sally S. Cohen, *Championing Child Care* (New York: Columbia University Press, 2001); Sonya Michel, *Children's Interests/Mothers' Rights: The Shaping of America's Child Care Policy* (New Haven, CT: Yale University Press, 1999).

3. W. S. Barnett and Leonard N. Masse, "Comparative Benefit–Cost Analysis of the Abecedarian Program and Its Policy Implications," *Economics of Education Review, The Economics of Early Childhood Education*, 26, no. 1 (February 2007): 113–125; Timothy J. Bartik, William T. Gormley, and Shirley Adelstein, "Earnings Benefits of Tulsa's Pre-K Program for Different Income Groups," *Economics of Education Review* 31, no. 6 (December 2012): 1143–1161; James J. Heckman et al., "The Rate of Return to the HighScope Perry Preschool Program," *Journal of Public Economics* 94, no. 1–2 (February 2010): 114–128; Arthur J. Reynolds et al., "Age 21 Cost-Benefit Analysis of the Title I Chicago Child-Parent Centers," *Educational Evaluation and Policy Analysis* 24, no. 4 (December 21, 2002): 267–303; Arthur J. Reynolds et al., "Age 26 Cost-Benefit Analysis of the Child-Parent Center Early Education Program," *Child Development* 82, no. 1 (January 1, 2011): 379–404.

4. M. E. Carolan, K. C. Brown, and W. S. Barnett, "Publicly-Supported Early Care and Education Programs," in *Handbook of Early Childhood Programs, Practices, and Policies*, ed. E. Dearing and E. Votruba-Drzal (New York: Blackwell, in press).

5. M. W. Lipsey et al., "Evaluation of the Tennessee Voluntary Prekindergarten Program: End of Pre-K Results from the Randomized Control Design" (Nashville, TN: Vanderbilt University, Peabody Research Institute, 2013); M. W. Lipsey et al., "Evaluation of the Tennessee Voluntary Prekindergarten Program: Kindergarten and First Grade Follow-Up Results from the Randomized Control Design" (Nashville, TN: Vanderbilt University, Peabody Research Institute, 2013); William T. Gormley et al., "Social-Emotional Effects of Early Childhood Education Programs in Tulsa,"

*Child Development* 82, no. 6 (2011): 2095–2109; William T. Gormley et al., "The Effects of Universal Pre-K on Cognitive Development," *Developmental Psychology* 41, no. 6 (2005): 872–884; J. T. Hustedt et al., "The New Mexico PreK Evaluation: Results from the Initial Four Years of a New State Preschool Initiative—Final Report" (National Institute for Early Education Research, 2009), http://nieer.org/pdf/new-mexico-initial-4-years.pdf; Christina Weiland et al., "Associations Between Classroom Quality and Children's Vocabulary and Executive Function Skills in an Urban Public Prekindergarten Program," *Early Childhood Research Quarterly* 28, no. 2 (2013): 199–209; Vivian C. Wong et al., "An Effectiveness-Based Evaluation of Five State Pre-Kindergarten Programs," *Journal of Policy Analysis and Management* 27, no. 1 (December 1, 2008): 122–154.

6. D. Bassok and L. C. Miller, "Do Children Benefit from Widely-Available Public Preschool? Evidence from Florida's Voluntary Prekindergarten Program" (paper presented at Annual Meeting of the Association for Public Policy Analysis and Management, Albuquerque, NM, 2014); K. A. Dodge et al., "Impact of Statewide Early Childhood Programs and Policies on Educational Outcomes Through the End of Elementary School" (paper presented at Annual Meeting of the Association for Public Policy Analysis and Management, Albuquerque, NM, 2014); Heather D. Hill et al., "The Consequences of Income Instability for Children's Well-Being," *Child Development Perspectives* 7, no. 2 (June 1, 2013): 85–90; E. S. Peisner-Feinberg and J. M. Schaaf, "Summary of Key Findings: Long-Term Effects of the North Carolina More at Four Pre-Kindergarten Program" (Chapel Hill: University of North Carolina Frank Porter Graham Child Development Institute, 2010), http://fpg.unc.edu/node/2059; Deborah A. Phillips, William T. Gormley, and Sara Anderson, "The Long-Term Effects of the Tulsa Pre-K Program on Academic Outcomes," Annual Meeting of the Society for Research on Educational Effectiveness, Washington, DC, 2015.

7. Hirokazu Yoshikawa et al., *Investing in Our Future: The Evidence Base on Preschool Education* (Society for Research in Child Development and Foundation for Child Development, 2013), http://home.uchicago.edu/~ludwigj/papers/Investing%20in%20Our%20Future%20Preschool%20Education%202013.pdf.

8. National Scientific Council on the Developing Child, "Excessive Stress Disrupts the Architecture of the Developing Brain," working paper 3 (Cambridge, MA: Harvard University, 2005, updated 2014), http://developingchild.harvard.edu/resources/wp3/.

9. C. DeNavas-Walt and B. D. Proctor, "Income and Poverty in the United States: 2013," Current Population Reports (Washington, DC: US Government printing Office, 2013); S. Addy, W. Engelhardt, and C. Skinner, "Basic Facts About Low-Income Children: Children Under 18 Years of Age" (New York: National Center for Children in Poverty, 2013).

10. Jamie L. Hanson et al., "Family Poverty Affects the Rate of Human Infant Brain Growth," *PLoS ONE* 8, no. 12 (December 11, 2013): e80954, doi:10.1371/journal.pone.0080954.

11. Kimberly G. Noble et al., "Neural Correlates of Socioeconomic Status in the Developing Human Brain," *Developmental Science* 15, no. 4 (July 1, 2012): 516–527, doi:10.1111/j.1467-7687.2012.01147.x.

12. Jack P. Shonkoff, "Protecting Brains, Not Simply Stimulating Minds," *Science* 333, no. 6045 (August 19, 2011): 982–983, doi:10.1126/science.1206014.

13. Heather Sandstrom and Sandra Huerta, "The Negative Effects of Instability on Child Development: A Research Synthesis," Low-Income Working Families Discussion Paper 3, (Washington, DC: Urban Institute, 2013).

14. J. B. Isaacs, "Unemployment from a Child's Perspective" (Washington, DC: First Focus and the Urban Institute, 2013); N. Mossaad, M. Mather, and W. O'Hare, "Children with Unemployed Parents: Trends During the U.S. Recession" (paper presented at Population Association of America Annual Meeting, Washington, DC, 2011).

15. Marybeth J. Mattingly and Kristin E. Smith, "Changes in Wives' Employment When Husbands Stop Working: A Recession-Prosperity Comparison," *Family Relations* 59, no. 4 (October 1, 2010): 343–357, doi:10.1111/j.1741-3729.2010.00607.x.

16. Gregory Acs, Pamela Loprest, and Austin Nichols, "Risk and Recovery: Documenting the Changing Risks to Family Incomes" (Washington, DC: Urban Institute, 2009).

17. Children's Defense Fund, "The State of America's Children, 2011" (Washington, DC: Children's Defense Fund, 2011).

18. Gary W. Evans and Kimberly English, "The Environment of Poverty: Multiple Stressor Exposure, Psychophysiological Stress, and Socioemotional Adjustment," *Child Development* 73, no. 4 (2002): 1238–1248; Gary W. Evans and Theodore D. Wachs, *Chaos and Its Influence on Children's Development: An Ecological Perspective*, 1st ed., Decade of Behavior (Washington, DC: American Psychological Association, 2010).

19. Clancy Blair, "Stress and the Development of Self-Regulation in Context," *Child Development Perspectives* 4, no. 3 (December 1, 2010): 181–188, doi:10.1111/j.1750-8606.2010.00145.x; Clancy Blair and C. Cybele Raver, "Child Development in the Context of Adversity: Experiential Canalization of Brain and Behavior," *American Psychologist* 67, no. 4 (June 2012): 309–318, doi:10.1037/a0027493; Gary W. Evans and Pilyoung Kim, "Childhood Poverty and Health: Cumulative Risk Exposure and Stress Dysregulation," *Psychological Science* 18, no. 11 (November 2007): 953–957, doi:10.1111/j.1467-9280.2007.02008.x; Hill et al., "Consequences of Income Instability for Children's Well-Being" (working paper, *Early Childhood Research Quarterly*).

20. Jay Belsky, Gabriel L. Schlomer, and Bruce J. Ellis, "Beyond Cumulative Risk: Distinguishing Harshness and Unpredictability as Determinants of Parenting and Early Life History Strategy," *Developmental Psychology* 48, no. 3 (2012): 662–673, doi:10.1037/a0024454; Jeffry A. Simpson et al., "Evolution, Stress, and Sensitive Periods: The Influence of Unpredictability in Early Versus Late Childhood on Sex and Risky Behavior," *Developmental Psychology* 48, no. 3 (2012): 674–686, doi:10.1037/a0027293.

21. Ariel Kalil and P. Wightman, "Parental Job Loss and Children's Educational Attainment in Black and White Middle Class Families," National Poverty Center Working Paper Series (Ann Arbor: National Poverty Center, University of Michigan, 2009); Ariel Kalil and Kathleen M. Ziol-Guest, "Parental Job Loss and Children's Academic Progress in Two-Parent Families," *Social Science Research* 37 (2008): 500–515; Rucker C. Johnson, Ariel Kalil, and Rachel E. Dunifon, *Mothers' Work and Children's Lives: Low-Income Families After Welfare Reform* (Kalamazoo, MI: W.E. Upjohn Institute for Employment Research, 2010); Kathleen M. Ziol-Guest and Ariel Kalil, "Long-Run Impact of Childhood Housing Instability on Adult Achievement," working paper (Chicago: Harris School of Public Policy Studies, University of Chicago, 2013), http://fcd-us.org/sites/default/files/APPAM%20Kalil%20Ziol-Guest%20housing%20FINAL.pdf.

22. Sandstrom and Huerta, "Negative Effects of Instability."

23. E. O. Ananat et al., "Children Left Behind: The Effects of Statewide Job Loss on Student Achievement," working paper 17104 (Cambridge, MA: National Bureau of Economic Research, 2011).

24. For details, see US Department of Health and Human Services, Office of Child Care, "HHS Announces Actions to Improve Safety and Quality of Child Care," accessed October 22, 2015, www.acf.hhs.gov/programs/occ/child-care-rule.

25. For details, see US Department of Health and Human Services, Early Childhood Development Office, "Early Head Start–Child Care Partnerships," accessed October 22, 2015, www.acf.hhs.gov/programs/ecd/early-learning/ehs-cc-partnerships.

26. W. Thomas Boyce, "A Biology of Misfortune," *Focus* 29, no. 1 (2012): 1–6; W. Thomas Boyce, Marla B. Sokolowski, and Gene E. Robinson, "Toward a New Biology of Social Adversity," *Proceedings of the National Academy of Sciences of the United States of America* 109, no. suppl. 2 (October 16, 2012): 17143–17148, doi:10.1073/pnas.1121264109.

27. W. Thomas Boyce et al., "Social Stratification, Classroom Climate, and the Behavioral Adaptation of Kindergarten Children," *Proceedings of the National Academy of Sciences* 109, no. suppl. 2 (October 16, 2012): 17168–17173, doi:10.1073/pnas.1201730109.

28. Boyce, "A Biology of Misfortune"; Megan R. Gunnar et al., "Peer Rejection, Temperament, and Cortisol Activity in Preschoolers," *Developmental Psychobiology* 43, no. 4 (December 1, 2003): 346–368, doi:10.1002/dev.10144.

29. Deborah A. Phillips, Nathan A. Fox, and Megan R. Gunnar, "Same Place, Different Experiences: Bringing Individual Differences to Research in Child Care," *Child Development Perspectives* 5, no. 1 (March 1, 2011): 44–49, doi:10.1111/j.1750-8606.2010.00155.x.

30. Mark Wolery et al., "Mainstreaming in Early Childhood Programs: Current Status and Relevant Issues," *Young Children* 49, no. 1 (1993): 78–84.

31. Virginia Buysse, Barbara Davis Goldman, and Martie L. Skinner, "Setting Effects on Friendship Formation Among Young Children With and Without Disabilities," *Exceptional Children* 68, no. 4 (2002): 503–517.

32. Jason K. Baker et al., "Prediction of Social Skills in 6-Year-Old Children With and Without Developmental Delays: Contributions of Early Regulation and Maternal Scaffolding," *American Journal on Mental Retardation* 112, no. 5 (September 1, 2007): 375–391, doi:10.1352/0895-8017(2007)112[0375:POSSIY]2.0.CO;2; Emily D. Gerstein et al., "Developmental Risk and Young Children's Regulatory Strategies: Predicting Behavior Problems at Age Five," *Journal of Abnormal Child Psychology* 39, no. 3 (April 2011): 351–364, doi:10.1007/s10802-010-9471-5.

33. Michael J. Guralnick, "Family and Child Influences on the Peer-Related Social Competence of Young Children with Developmental Delays," *Mental Retardation and Developmental Disabilities Research Reviews* 5, no. 1 (January 1, 1999): 21–29, doi:10.1002/(SICI)1098-2779(1999)5:1<21::AID-MRDD3>3.0.CO;2-O.

34. Michael J. Guralnick, J. M. Gottman, and M. A. Hammond, "Effects of Social Setting on the Friendship Formation of Young Children Differing in Developmental Status," *Journal of Applied Developmental Psychology* 17, no. 4 (1996): 625–651, doi: 10.1016/S0193-3973(96)90019-2.

35. Walter S. Gilliam, *Prekindergarteners Left Behind: Expulsion Rates in State Prekindergarten Systems* (New York: Foundation for Child Development 2005); W. S. Gilliam and G. Shahar, "Preschool and Child Care Expulsion and Suspension: Rates and Predictors in One State," *Infants & Young Children* 19, no. 3 (2006): 228–245.

36. Linda M. Raffaele Mendez, "Predictors of Suspension and Negative School Outcomes: A Longitudinal Investigation," *New Directions for Youth Development* 2003, no. 99 (September 1, 2003): 17–33, doi:10.1002/yd.52.

37. US Department of Education Office for Civil Rights, "Civil Rights Data Collection, Data Snapshot: School Discipline," Issue Brief No. 1 (March 2014), http://ocrdata.ed.gov/Downloads/CRDC-School-Discipline-Snapshot.pdf.

38. S. Jones, "Classroom-Based Early Childhood Interventions," in *Handbook of Early Childhood Programs, Practices, and Policies*, ed. E. Dearing and E. Votruba-Drzal (New York: Blackwell, in press).

39. Katherine C. Pears and Hyoun K. Kim, "Improving Child Self-Regulation and Parenting in Families of Pre-Kindergarten Children with Developmental Disabilities and Behavioral Difficulties," *Prevention Science: The Official Journal of the Society for Prevention Research* 16, no. 2 (2014), doi:10.1007/s11121-014-0482-2.

40. Melanie Killen, Adam Rutland, and Martin D. Ruck, "Promoting Equity, Tolerance, and Justice in Childhood," *Social Policy Report* 25, no. 4 (2011): 1–33.

41. US Department of Health and Human Services, US Department of Education, "Policy Statement on Expulsion and Suspension Policies in Early Childhood Settings," accessed October 22, 2015, www.acf.hhs.gov/sites/default/files/ecd/expulsion_suspension_final.pdf.

42. National Scientific Council on the Developing Child, "Young Children Develop in an Environment of Relationships," working paper 1 (Cambridge, MA: Harvard University, 2004), http://developingchild.harvard.edu/wp-content/uploads/2015/04/Young-Children-Develop-in-an-Environment-of-Relationships.pdf; National Scientific Council on the Developing Child, "The Science of Neglect: The

Persistent Absence of Responsive Care Disrupts the Developing Brain," working paper (Cambridge, MA: Harvard University, 2012), http://developingchild.harvard.edu/wp-content/uploads/2015/05/The-Science-of-Neglect-The-Persistent-Absence-of-Responsive-Care-Disrupts-the-Developing-Brain.pdf.

43. Jack P. Shonkoff et al., "The Lifelong Effects of Early Childhood Adversity and Toxic Stress," *Pediatrics* 129, no. 1 (January 1, 2012): e232–46, doi:10.1542/peds.2011-2663.

44. C. Howes and S. Spieker, "Attachment Relationships in the Context of Multiple Caregivers," in *Handbook of Attachment: Theory and Research*, ed. Jude Cassidy and Phillip R. Shaver, 3rd ed. (New York: Guilford Press, in press); Lisa S. Badanes, Julia Dmitrieva, and Sarah Enos Watamura, "Understanding Cortisol Reactivity Across the Day at Child Care: The Potential Buffering Role of Secure Attachments to Caregivers," *Early Childhood Research Quarterly* 27, no. 1 (2012): 156–165, doi:10.1016/j.ecresq.2011.05.005.

45. Megan R. Gunnar et al., "The Rise in Cortisol in Family Day Care: Associations with Aspects of Care Quality, Child Behavior, and Child Sex," *Child Development* 81, no. 3 (June 2010): 851–69, doi:10.1111/j.1467-8624.2010.01438.x.

46. Megan R. Gunnar et al., "The Import of the Cortisol Rise in Child Care Differs as a Function of Behavioral Inhibition," *Developmental Psychology* 47, no. 3 (May 2011): 792–803, doi:10.1037/a0021902.

47. Sarah Enos Watamura et al., "Child Care Setting Affects Salivary Cortisol and Antibody Secretion in Young Children," *Psychoneuroendocrinology* 35, no. 8 (September 2010): 1156–1166, doi:10.1016/j.psyneuen.2010.02.001.

48. Boyce et al., "Social Stratification, Classroom Climate."

49. Lieny Jeon, Cynthia K. Buettner, and Anastasia R. Snyder, "Pathways from Teacher Depression and Child-Care Quality to Child Behavioral Problems," *Journal of Consulting and Clinical Psychology* 82, no. 2 (2014): 225–235, doi:10.1037/a0035720; Elles J. de Schipper et al., "Cortisol Levels of Caregivers in Child Care Centers as Related to the Quality of Their Caregiving," *Early Childhood Research Quarterly* 24, no. 1 (2009): 55–63, doi:10.1016/j.ecresq.2008.10.004; Marleen G. Groeneveld et al., "Caregivers' Cortisol Levels and Perceived Stress in Home-Based and Center-Based Childcare," *Early Childhood Research Quarterly* 27, no. 1 (2012): 166–175, doi:10.1016/j.ecresq.2011.05.003; M. G. Groeneveld et al., "Stress, Cortisol and Well-Being of Caregivers and Children in Home-Based Child Care: A Case for Differential Susceptibility," *Child: Care, Health and Development* 38, no. 2 (March 1, 2012): 251–260, doi:10.1111/j.1365-2214.2010.01194.x; C. C. Raver, C. P. Li-Grining, and C. Blair, "Extending Models of Emotional Self-Regulation to Classroom Settings: Implications for Professional Development," in *Effective Early Childhood Professional Development: Improving Teacher Practice and Child Outcomes*, ed. Carollee Howes, Bridget K. Hamre, and Robert C. Pianta (Baltimore: Paul H. Brookes, 2012), 111–130.

50. Institute of Medicine and National Research Council, "The Early Childhood Care and Education Workforce: Challenges and Opportunities: A Workshop Report" (Washington, DC: National Academies Press, 2012).

51. Marcy Whitebook, Deborah A. Phillips, and Carollee Howes, "Worthy Work, Still Unlivable Wages: The Early Childhood Workforce 25 Years After the National Child Care Staffing Study" (Berkeley, CA: Center for the Study of Child Care Employment, 2014), http://ffyf.org/wp-content/uploads/2014/11/Child-Care-Employment-Report-11.18.14.pdf.

52. Dee Baldwin et al., "The Health of Female Child Care Providers: Implications for Quality of Care," *Journal of Community Health Nursing* 24, no. 1 (2007): 1–17, doi:10.1080/07370010709336582; Bridget K. Hamre and Robert C. Pianta, "Self-Reported Depression in Nonfamilial Caregivers: Prevalence and Associations with Caregiver Behavior in Child-Care Settings," *Early Childhood Research Quarterly* 19, no. 2 (2004): 297–318, doi:10.1016/j.ecresq.2004.04.006; A. M. Fish et al., "Epidemiology of Depression in Child Care Workers in a Large Metropolitan Area" (paper presented at Biennial Meeting of the Society for Research in Child Development, Atlanta, 2015); Jeon, Buettner, and Snyder, "Pathways from Teacher Depression"; Christine Li-Grining et al., "Understanding and Improving Classroom Emotional Climate and Behavior Management in the 'Real World': The Role of Head Start Teachers' Psychosocial Stressors," *Early Education and Development* 21, no. 1 (January 28, 2010): 65–94, doi:10.1080/10409280902783509; Robert C. Whitaker et al., "The Physical and Mental Health of Head Start Staff: The Pennsylvania Head Start Staff Wellness Survey, 2012," *Preventing Chronic Disease* 10, no. 181 (October 31, 2013), doi:10.5888/pcd10.130171.

53. Marcy Whitebook, S. Ryan, and L. Sakai, "Economic Insecurity and Early Childhood Teaching: The Relationship Between Teacher Worry and Program Economic Policies, Auspices and Quality Ratings," working paper (Berkeley: Center for the Study of Child Care Employment, University of California, Berkeley, 2014).

54. Bureau of Labor Statistics, "May 2013 National Occupational Employment and Wage Estimates United States" (Washington, DC: Department of Labor, 2013), www.bls.gov/oes/current/oes_nat.htm.

55. Jack P. Shonkoff and Deborah A. Phillips, *From Neurons to Neighborhoods: The Science of Early Child Development* (Washington, DC: National Academy Press, 2000), 390.

56. Whitebook, Phillips, and Howes, "Worthy Work, Still Unlivable Wages."

57. Ibid.

### *Chapter 2*

1. Y. Jiang, M. Ekono, and C. Skinner, *Basic Facts About Low-Income Children* (New York: National Center for Children in Poverty, 2015).

2. UNICEF, "State of the World's Children" (New York: UNICEF, 2014).

3. Jeanne Brooks-Gunn and Greg J. Duncan, "The Effects of Poverty on Children," *Future of Children* 7, no. 2 (July 1, 1997): 55–71, doi:10.2307/1602387; Vonnie C. McLoyd, "Socioeconomic Disadvantage and Child Development," *American Psychologist* 53, no. 2 (1998): 185, doi:10.1037/0003-066X.53.2.185; Susan P. Walker et al., "Child Development: Risk Factors for Adverse Outcomes in Developing

Countries," *Lancet* 369, no. 9556 (January 19, 2007): 145–157, doi:10.1016/S0140-6736(07)60076-2.

4. Brooks-Gunn and Duncan, "Effects of Poverty on Children"; Greg J. Duncan and K. Magnuson, "The Long Reach of Early Childhood Poverty," in *Economic Stress, Human Capital, and Families in Asia: Research and Policy Challenges*, ed. Wei-Jun Jean Yeung and Mui Teng Yap, vol. 4, *Quality of Life in Asia* (Dordrecht: Springer Netherlands, 2013), 57–70; Kathleen M. Ziol-Guest et al., "Early Childhood Poverty, Immune-Mediated Disease Processes, and Adult Productivity," *Proceedings of the National Academy of Sciences* 109, no. suppl. 2 (October 16, 2012): 17289–17293, doi:10.1073/pnas.1203167109.

5. Brooks-Gunn and Duncan, "Effects of Poverty on Children."

6. Clancy Blair, "School Readiness: Integrating Cognition and Emotion in a Neurobiological Conceptualization of Children's Functioning at School Entry," *American Psychologist* 57, no. 2 (2002): 111–127, doi:10.1037/0003-066X.57.2.111.

7. J. P. Bourgeois, "Synaptogenesis, Heterochrony and Epigenesis in the Mammalian Neocortex," *Acta Paediatrica* 86, no. suppl. 422 (July 1, 1997): 27–33, doi:10.1111/j.1651-2227.1997.tb18340.x.

8. Sharon E. Fox, Pat Levitt, and Charles A. Nelson III, "How the Timing and Quality of Early Experiences Influence the Development of Brain Architecture," *Child Development* 81, no. 1 (January 1, 2010): 28–40, doi:10.1111/j.1467-8624.2009.01380.x.

9. E. Knudsen, "Sensitive Periods in the Development of the Brain and Behavior," *Journal of Cognitive Neuroscience* 16, no. 8 (October 2004): 1412–1425, doi:10.1162/0898929042304796.

10. National Scientific Council on the Developing Child, "The Timing and Quality of Early Experiences Combine to Shape Brain Architecture," working paper 4 (Cambridge, MA: Harvard Center on the Developing Child, 2007).

11. Peter J. Gianaros et al., "Prospective Reports of Chronic Life Stress Predict Decreased Grey Matter Volume in the Hippocampus," *NeuroImage* 35, no. 2 (April 1, 2007): 795–803, doi:10.1016/j.neuroimage.2006.10.045; Jamie L. Hanson et al., "Early Stress Is Associated with Alterations in the Orbitofrontal Cortex: A Tensor-Based Morphometry Investigation of Brain Structure and Behavioral Risk," *Journal of Neuroscience* 30, no. 22 (June 2, 2010): 7466–7472, doi:10.1523/JNEUROSCI.0859-10.2010; Rajeev Krishnadas et al., "The Envirome and the Connectome: Exploring the Structural Noise in the Human Brain Associated with Socioeconomic Deprivation," *Frontiers in Human Neuroscience* 7 (2013), doi:10.3389/fnhum.2013.00722; Kimberly G. Noble et al., "Hippocampal Volume Varies with Educational Attainment Across the Life-Span," *Frontiers in Human Neuroscience* 6 (2012): 307, doi:10.3389/fnhum.2012.00307.

12. Kimberly G. Noble et al., "Socioeconomic Disparities in Neurocognitive Development in the First Two Years of Life," *Developmental Psychobiology* 57, no. 5 (July 2015): 535–551, doi:10.1002/dev.21303.

13. Pilyoung Kim et al., "Effects of Childhood Poverty and Chronic Stress on Emotion Regulatory Brain Function in Adulthood," *Proceedings of the National Academy of Sciences* 110, no. 46 (November 12, 2013): 18442–18447, doi:10.1073/pnas.1308240110.

14. McLoyd, "Socioeconomic Disadvantage and Child Development."

15. Bruce S. McEwen, "Stress, Adaptation, and Disease: Allostasis and Allostatic Load," *Annals of the New York Academy of Sciences* 840, no. 1 (May 1, 1998): 33–44, doi:10.1111/j.1749-6632.1998.tb09546.x.

16. National Scientific Council on the Developing Child, "Excessive Stress Disrupts the Architecture of the Developing Brain," working paper 3 (Cambridge, MA: Harvard Center on the Developing Child, 2005).

17. Lisa Eiland and Bruce S. McEwen, "Early Life Stress Followed by Subsequent Adult Chronic Stress Potentiates Anxiety and Blunts Hippocampal Structural Remodeling," *Hippocampus* 22, no. 1 (January 1, 2012): 82–91, doi:10.1002/hipo.20862; Elizabeth Gould et al., "Neurogenesis in the Dentate Gyrus of the Adult Tree Shrew Is Regulated by Psychosocial Stress and NMDA Receptor Activation," *Journal of Neuroscience* 17, no. 7 (April 1, 1997): 2492–2498.

18. A. F. Arnsten, "Stress Impairs Prefrontal Cortical Function in Rats and Monkeys: Role of Dopamine D1 and Norepinephrine Alpha-1 Receptor Mechanisms," *Progress in Brain Research* 126 (2000): 183–192, doi:10.1016/S0079-6123(00)26014-7; Richard J. Davidson, Katherine M. Putnam, and Christine L. Larson, "Dysfunction in the Neural Circuitry of Emotion Regulation: A Possible Prelude to Violence," *Science* 289, no. 5479 (July 28, 2000): 591–594, doi:10.1126/science.289.5479.591.

19. Michela Fagiolini, Catherine L Jensen, and Frances A Champagne, "Epigenetic Influences on Brain Development and Plasticity," *Current Opinion in Neurobiology*, Development, 19, no. 2 (April 2009): 207–212, doi:10.1016/j.conb.2009.05.009; Patrick O. McGowan and Moshe Szyf, "The Epigenetics of Social Adversity in Early Life: Implications for Mental Health Outcomes," *Neurobiology of Disease*, Epigenetics and Neuropsychiatric Disease, 39, no. 1 (July 2010): 66–72, doi:10.1016/j.nbd.2009.12.026.

20. Gary W. Evans and Pilyoung Kim, "Childhood Poverty and Young Adults' Allostatic Load: The Mediating Role of Childhood Cumulative Risk Exposure," *Psychological Science* 23, no. 9 (September 1, 2012): 979–983, doi:10.1177/0956797612441218.

21. National Scientific Council on the Developing Child, "Excessive Stress Disrupts the Architecture of the Developing Brain."

22. Katie A. McLaughlin, Margaret A. Sheridan, and Hilary K. Lambert, "Childhood Adversity and Neural Development: Deprivation and Threat as Distinct Dimensions of Early Experience," *Neuroscience & Biobehavioral Reviews* 47 (November 2014): 578–591, doi:10.1016/j.neubiorev.2014.10.012; Margaret A. Sheridan and Katie A. McLaughlin, "Dimensions of Early Experience and Neural Development: Deprivation and Threat," *Trends in Cognitive Sciences* 18, no. 11 (November 2014): 580–585, doi:10.1016/j.tics.2014.09.001.

23. Stéphane A. De Brito et al., "Reduced Orbitofrontal and Temporal Grey Matter in a Community Sample of Maltreated Children," *Journal of Child Psychology and Psychiatry* 54, no. 1 (January 1, 2013): 105–112, doi:10.1111/j.1469-7610.2012.02597.x; E. E. Edmiston et al., "Corticostriatal-Limbic Gray Matter Morphology in Adolescents with Self-Reported Exposure to Childhood Maltreatment," *Archives of Pediatrics & Adolescent Medicine* 165, no. 12 (December 1, 2011): 1069–1077, doi:10.1001/archpediatrics.2011.565; Hanson et al., "Early Stress Is Associated with Alterations in the Orbitofrontal Cortex"; Philip A. Kelly et al., "Cortical Thickness, Surface Area, and Gyrification Abnormalities in Children Exposed to Maltreatment: Neural Markers of Vulnerability?" *Biological Psychiatry*, Stress: Impact on Brain and Body, 74, no. 11 (December 1, 2013): 845–852, doi:10.1016/j.biopsych.2013.06.020; Eamon J. McCrory et al., "Amygdala Activation in Maltreated Children During Pre-Attentive Emotional Processing," *British Journal of Psychiatry* 202, no. 4 (April 1, 2013): 269–276, doi:10.1192/bjp.bp.112.116624; Eamon J. McCrory et al., "Heightened Neural Reactivity to Threat in Child Victims of Family Violence," *Current Biology* 21, no. 23 (December 6, 2011): R947–R948, doi:10.1016/j.cub.2011.10.015.

24. Mitul A. Mehta et al., "Amygdala, Hippocampal and Corpus Callosum Size Following Severe Early Institutional Deprivation: The English and Romanian Adoptees Study Pilot," *Journal of Child Psychology and Psychiatry* 50, no. 8 (August 1, 2009): 943–951, doi:10.1111/j.1469-7610.2009.02084.x; Margaret A. Sheridan et al., "The Impact of Social Disparity on Prefrontal Function in Childhood," *PLoS ONE* 7, no. 4 (April 26, 2012): e35744, doi:10.1371/journal.pone.0035744.

25. Celia Beckett et al., "VI. Institutional Deprivation, Specific Cognitive Functions, and Scholastic Achievement: English and Romanian Adoptee (ERA) Study Findings," *Monographs of the Society for Research in Child Development* 75, no. 1 (April 1, 2010): 125–142, doi:10.1111/j.1540-5834.2010.00553.x; Karen J. Bos et al., "Effects of Early Psychosocial Deprivation on the Development of Memory and Executive Function," *Frontiers in Behavioral Neuroscience* 3 (2009), doi:10.3389/neuro.08.016.2009; McLaughlin, Sheridan, and Lambert, "Childhood Adversity and Neural Development"; Katie A. McLaughlin et al., "Widespread Reductions in Cortical Thickness Following Severe Early-Life Deprivation: A Neurodevelopmental Pathway to Attention-Deficit/Hyperactivity Disorder," *Biological Psychiatry* 76, no. 8 (October 15, 2014): 629–638, doi:10.1016/j.biopsych.2013.08.016.

26. Charles A. Nelson et al., "Cognitive Recovery in Socially Deprived Young Children: The Bucharest Early Intervention Project," *Science* 318, no. 5858 (December 21, 2007): 1937–1940, doi:10.1126/science.1143921.

27. Center on the Developing Child at Harvard University, "Building the Brain's 'Air Traffic Control' System: How Early Experiences Shape the Development of Executive Function," working paper 11 (Cambridge, MA: Harvard Center on the Developing Child, 2011).

28. Clancy Blair, "Stress and the Development of Self-Regulation in Context," *Child Development Perspectives* 4, no. 3 (December 1, 2010): 181–188, doi:10.1111/j.1750-8606.2010.00145.x.

29. Blair, "School Readiness."

30. Clancy Blair and Rachel Peters Razza, "Relating Effortful Control, Executive Function, and False Belief Understanding to Emerging Math and Literacy Ability in Kindergarten," *Child Development* 78, no. 2 (March 1, 2007): 647–663, doi:10.1111/j.1467-8624.2007.01019.x; Laura L. Brock et al., "The Contributions of 'Hot' and 'Cool' Executive Function to Children's Academic Achievement, Learning-Related Behaviors, and Engagement in Kindergarten," *Early Childhood Research Quarterly* 24, no. 3 (2009): 337–349, doi:10.1016/j.ecresq.2009.06.001; Robin Jacob and Julia Parkinson, "The Potential for School-Based Interventions That Target Executive Function to Improve Academic Achievement: A Review," *Review of Educational Research*, March 4, 2015, 0034654314561338, doi:10.3102/0034654314561338; Terrie E. Moffitt et al., "A Gradient of Childhood Self-Control Predicts Health, Wealth, and Public Safety," *Proceedings of the National Academy of Sciences* 108, no. 7 (February 15, 2011): 2693–2698, doi:10.1073/pnas.1010076108.

31. Jenessa Sprague et al., "Moderators and Mediators of the Stress-Aggression Relationship: Executive Function and State Anger," *Emotion* 11, no. 1 (2011): 61, doi:10.1037/a0021788.

32. Jack P. Shonkoff, "Leveraging the Biology of Adversity to Address the Roots of Disparities in Health and Development," *Proceedings of the National Academy of Sciences* 109, no. suppl. 2 (October 16, 2012): 17302–17307, doi:10.1073/pnas.1121259109.

33. Center on the Developing Child at Harvard University, "Supportive Relationships and Active Skill-Building Strengthen the Foundations of Resilience," working paper 13 (Cambridge, MA: Harvard Center on the Developing Child, 2015).

34. P. Morris et al., "Impact Findings from the Head Start Cares Demonstration: National Evaluation of Three Approaches to Improving Preschoolers' Social and Emotional Competence," OPRE Report (Washington, DC: Office of Planning, Research and Evaluation, Administration for Children and Families, US Department of Health and Human Services, 2014).

35. Stephanie M. Jones and Suzanne M. Bouffard, "Social and Emotional Learning in Schools: From Programs to Strategies," *Social Policy Report* 26, no. 4 (Society for Research in Child Development, 2012), http://eric.ed.gov/?id=ED540203; Susan B. Neuman and Linda Cunningham, "The Impact of Professional Development and Coaching on Early Language and Literacy Instructional Practices," *American Educational Research Journal* 46, no. 2 (June 1, 2009): 532–566, doi:10.3102/0002831208328088.

36. Jack P. Shonkoff and Philip A. Fisher, "Rethinking Evidence-Based Practice and Two-Generation Programs to Create the Future of Early Childhood Policy,"

*Development and Psychopathology* 25 (25th Anniversary Special Issue), no. 4 pt. 2 (November 2013): 1635–1653, doi:10.1017/S0954579413000813.

37. W. S. Barnett, "Effectiveness of Early Educational Intervention," *Science* 333, no. 6045 (August 19, 2011): 975–978, doi:10.1126/science.1204534.

38. Jack P. Shonkoff, "Building a New Biodevelopmental Framework to Guide the Future of Early Childhood Policy," *Child Development* 81, no. 1 (2010): 357–367.

39. Laurie Miller Brotman et al., "Cluster (School) RCT of ParentCorps: Impact on Kindergarten Academic Achievement," *Pediatrics* 131, no. 5 (May 1, 2013): e1521–e1529, doi:10.1542/peds.2012-2632; Carolyn Webster-Stratton and Ted Taylor, "Nipping Early Risk Factors in the Bud: Preventing Substance Abuse, Delinquency, and Violence in Adolescence Through Interventions Targeted at Young Children (0–8 Years)," *Prevention Science* 2, no. 3 (September 2001): 165–192, doi:10.1023/A:1011510923900.

40. Jones and Bouffard, "Social and Emotional Learning in Schools."

### *Chapter 3*

We thank Paula K. S. Yust for her assistance with manuscript preparation.

1. Betty Hart and Todd R. Risley, *Meaningful Differences in the Everyday Experience of Young American Children* (Baltimore: P. H. Brookes, 1995).

2. David K. Dickinson, Roberta M. Golinkoff, and Kathy Hirsh-Pasek, "Speaking Out for Language: Why Language Is Central to Reading Development," *Educational Researcher* 39, no. 4 (May 1, 2010): 308, doi:10.3102/0013189X10370204.

3. A. Wong, "The Case Against Universal Preschool," *Atlantic*, November 18, 2014, www.theatlantic.com/education/archive/2014/11/the-case-against-universal-preschool/382853/.

4. Hirokazu Yoshikawa et al., "Investing in Our Future: The Evidence Base on Preschool Education" (Society for Research in Child Development, and Foundation for Child Development, October 2013), http://home.uchicago.edu/~ludwigj/papers/Investing%20in%20Our%20Future%20Preschool%20Education%202013.pdf.

5. Eunice Kennedy Shriver National Institute of Child Health and Human Development (NICHD), Early Child Care Research Network, "The Relation of Child Care to Cognitive and Language Development," *Child Development* 71, no. 4 (July 1, 2000): 960–980.

6. Dickinson, Golinkoff, and Hirsh-Pasek, "Speaking Out for Language"; Erika Hoff, "Interpreting the Early Language Trajectories of Children from Low-SES and Language Minority Homes: Implications for Closing Achievement Gaps," *Developmental Psychology* 49, no. 1 (2013): 4–14, doi:10.1037/a0027238.

7. Kate Cain, Jane Oakhill, and Peter Bryant, "Children's Reading Comprehension Ability: Concurrent Prediction by Working Memory, Verbal Ability, and Component Skills," *Journal of Educational Psychology* 96, no. 1 (2004): 31–42, doi:10.1037/0022-0663.96.1.31; Kate Nation et al., "Hidden Language Impairments in Children: Parallels Between Poor Reading Comprehension and Specific Language Impairment?"

*Journal of Speech, Language, and Hearing Research* 47, no. 1 (February 1, 2004): 199–211, doi:10.1044/1092-4388(2004/017); W. E. Tunmer and W. A. Hoover, "Cognitive and Linguistic Factors in Learning to Read," in *Reading Acquisition*, ed. Philip B. Gough, Linnea C. Ehri, and Rebecca Treiman (Hillsdale, NJ: L. Erlbaum Associates, 1992).

8. Christopher J. Lonigan and Grover J. Whitehurst, "Relative Efficacy of Parent and Teacher Involvement in a Shared-Reading Intervention for Preschool Children from Low-Income Backgrounds," *Early Childhood Research Quarterly* 13, no. 2 (1998): 263–290, doi:10.1016/S0885-2006(99)80038-6; NICHD Early Child Care Research Network, "Pathways to Reading: The Role of Oral Language in the Transition to Reading," *Developmental Psychology* 41, no. 2 (2005): 428–142, doi:10.1037/0012-1649.41.2.428; H. S. Scarborough, "Connecting Early Language and Literacy to Later Reading (Dis)abilities," in *Handbook of Early Literacy Research*, ed. Susan B. Neuman and David K. Dickinson (New York: Guilford Press, 2001), 97–110; Grover J. Whitehurst and Christopher J. Lonigan, "Emergent Literacy: Development from Prereaders to Readers," in *Handbook of Early Literacy Research*, ed. Susan B. Neuman and David K. Dickinson, (New York: Guilford Press, 2001), 1:11–29.

9. Catherine E. Snow et al., *Unfulfilled Expectations: Home and School Influences on Literacy* (Cambridge, MA: Harvard University Press, 1991); Anne E. Cunningham and Keith E. Stanovich, "Early Reading Acquisition and Its Relation to Reading Experience and Ability 10 Years Later," *Developmental Psychology* 33, no. 6 (1997): 934–945, doi:10.1037/0012-1649.33.6.934; David K. Dickinson and Michelle V. Porche, "Relation Between Language Experiences in Preschool Classrooms and Children's Kindergarten and Fourth-Grade Language and Reading Abilities," *Child Development* 82, no. 3 (May 1, 2011): 870–886, doi:10.1111/j.1467-8624.2011.01576.x; Elana Greenfield Spira, Stacey Storch Bracken, and Janet E. Fischel, "Predicting Improvement After First-Grade Reading Difficulties: The Effects of Oral Language, Emergent Literacy, and Behavior Skills," *Developmental Psychology* 41, no. 1 (2005): 225–234, doi:10.1037/0012-1649.41.1.225; Patton O. Tabors, Catherine E. Snow, and David K. Dickinson, "Homes and Schools Together: Supporting Language and Literacy Development," in *Beginning Literacy with Language: Young Children Learning at Home and School*, ed. David K. Dickinson and Patton Ogden Tabors (Baltimore: P. H. Brookes, 2001), 313–334.

10. Caroline K. P. Roben, Pamela M. Cole, and Laura Marie Armstrong, "Longitudinal Relations Among Language Skills, Anger Expression, and Regulatory Strategies in Early Childhood," *Child Development* 84, no. 3 (May 1, 2013): 891–905, doi:10.1111/cdev.12027.

11. Shannon M. Pruden, Susan C. Levine, and Janellen Huttenlocher, "Children's Spatial Thinking: Does Talk About the Spatial World Matter?" *Developmental Science* 14, no. 6 (November 1, 2011): 1417–1430, doi:10.1111/j.1467-7687.2011.01088.x; Brian Verdine Roberta Michnick Golinkoff, Kathy Hirsh-Pasek, and Nora S. Newcombe, "Spatial Thinking: Fundamental to School Readiness and Early Mathematics," working paper, n.d.

12. Raquel S. Klibanoff et al., "Preschool Children's Mathematical Knowledge: The Effect of Teacher 'Math Talk,'" *Developmental Psychology* 42, no. 1 (2006): 59–69, doi:10.1037/0012-1649.42.1.59.

13. Hart and Risley, *Meaningful Differences*; Erika Hoff, "The Specificity of Environmental Influence: Socioeconomic Status Affects Early Vocabulary Development via Maternal Speech," *Child Development* 74, no. 5 (October 1, 2003): 1368–1378, doi:10.1111/1467-8624.00612; E. Hoff, "Environmental Supports for Language Acquisition," in *Handbook of Early Literacy Research*, ed. Susan B. Neuman and David K. Dickinson, vol. 2 (New York: Guilford Press, 2006a); Erika Hoff, "How Social Contexts Support and Shape Language Development," *Developmental Review* 26, no. 1 (March 2006): 55–88, doi:10.1016/j.dr.2005.11.002; Barbara Alexander Pan et al., "Maternal Correlates of Growth in Toddler Vocabulary Production in Low-Income Families," *Child Development* 76, no. 4 (July 1, 2005): 763–782, doi:10.1111/1467-8624.00498-i1; Meredith L. Rowe, "Child-Directed Speech: Relation to Socioeconomic Status, Knowledge of Child Development and Child Vocabulary Skill," *Journal of Child Language* 35, no. 1 (February 2008): 185–205, doi:10.1017/S0305000907008343; Dale Walker et al., "Prediction of School Outcomes Based on Early Language Production and Socioeconomic Factors," *Child Development* 65, no. 2 (April 1, 1994): 606–621, doi:10.1111/j.1467-8624.1994.tb00771.x.

14. Anne Fernald, Virginia A. Marchman, and Adriana Weisleder, "SES Differences in Language Processing Skill and Vocabulary Are Evident at 18 Months," *Developmental Science* 16, no. 2 (March 1, 2013): 234–248, doi:10.1111/desc.12019; Erika Hoff, "Causes and Consequences of SES-Related Differences in Parent-to-Child Speech," in *Socioeconomic Status, Parenting, and Child Development*, ed. Marc H. Bornstein and Robert H. Bradley, Monographs in Parenting Series (Mahwah, NJ: Lawrence Erlbaum Associates, 2003); Hoff, "Specificity of Environmental Influence."

15. Walker et al., "Prediction of School Outcomes."

16. Fernald, Marchman, and Weisleder, "SES Differences in Language Processing."

17. Martha J. Farah et al., "Childhood Poverty: Specific Associations with Neurocognitive Development," *Brain Research* 1110, no. 1 (September 19, 2006): 166–174, doi:10.1016/j.brainres.2006.06.072; Daniel A. Hackman and Martha J. Farah, "Socioeconomic Status and the Developing Brain," *Trends in Cognitive Sciences* 13, no. 2 (February 2009): 65–73, doi:10.1016/j.tics.2008.11.003; Jamie L. Hanson et al., "Family Poverty Affects the Rate of Human Infant Brain Growth," *PLoS ONE* 8, no. 12 (December 11, 2013): e80954, doi:10.1371/journal.pone.0080954.

18. A. McCabe, C. Tamis-LeMonda, and M. Bornstein, "Multilingual Children: Beyond Myths to Best Practices," SRCD Social Policy Report (Society for Research in Child Development, 2013).

19. M. L. McGillion et al., "The Relation Between Caregiver Contingent Talk, SES, and Language Learning: An Intervention Study," in *Paper Symposium, Understanding the Longitudinal Effects of SES on Language Development in Infancy: Timing,*

*Mechanisms, and Early Intervention* (Berlin: ICIS, 2014); M. L. McGillion et al., "Supporting Early Vocabulary Development: What Sort of Responsiveness Matters?" *IEEE Transactions on Autonomous Mental Development* 5, no. 3 (September 2013): 240–248, doi:10.1109/TAMD.2013.2275949; Dana Suskind et al., "An Exploratory Study of 'Quantitative Linguistic Feedback': Effect of LENA Feedback on Adult Language Production," *Communication Disorders Quarterly* 34 (February 1, 2013): 199–209, doi:10.1177/1525740112473146; Dana Suskind, "Intervention to Close the Word Gap," in Translating Research into Education, Intervention, and Policy Symposium: Shaping the Developing Brain: Prenatal Through Early Childhood, Fifth Annual Aspen Brain Forum, New York, 2014.

20. McGillion et al., "Caregiver Contingent Talk, SES, and Language Learning."

21. Annie E. Casey Foundation, *The 2013 Kids Count Data Book: State Trends in Child Well-Being* (Baltimore: Annie E. Casey Foundation, 2013), www.aecf.org/resources/the-2013-kids-count-data-book/; Margaret R. Burchinal et al., "Relating Quality of Center-Based Child Care to Early Cognitive and Language Development Longitudinally," *Child Development* 71, no. 2 (March 1, 2000): 339–357, doi:10.1111/1467-8624.00149; Eric Dearing, Kathleen McCartney, and Beck A. Taylor, "Does Higher Quality Early Child Care Promote Low-Income Children's Math and Reading Achievement in Middle Childhood?" *Child Development* 80, no. 5 (September 1, 2009): 1329–1349, doi:10.1111/j.1467-8624.2009.01336.x; Greg J. Duncan, "Modeling the Impacts of Child Care Quality on Children's Preschool Cognitive Development," *Child Development* 74, no. 5 (October 1, 2003): 1454–1475, doi:10.1111/1467-8624.00617.

22. Patrice L. Engle et al., "Strategies for Reducing Inequalities and Improving Developmental Outcomes for Young Children in Low-Income and Middle-Income Countries," *Lancet* 378, no. 9799 (October 14, 2011): 1339–1353, doi:10.1016/S0140-6736(11)60889-1.

23. McCabe, Tamis-LeMonda, and Bornstein, "Multilingual Children: Beyond Myths"; Haruka Konishi et al., "Six Principles of Language Development: Implications for Second Language Learners," *Developmental Neuropsychology* 39, no. 5 (July 4, 2014): 404–420, doi:10.1080/87565641.2014.931961.

24. J. Harris, Roberta M. Golinkoff, and Kathy Hirsh-Pasek, "Family Poverty Affects the Rate of Human Infant Brain Growth," in *Handbook of Early Literacy Research*, ed. Susan B. Neuman and David K. Dickinson, vol. 3 (New York: Guilford Press, 2001), 49–65.

25. Dilara Deniz Can, Todd Richards, and Patricia K. Kuhl, "Early Gray-Matter and White-Matter Concentration in Infancy Predict Later Language Skills: A Whole Brain Voxel-Based Morphometry Study," *Brain and Language* 124, no. 1 (January 2013): 34–44, doi:10.1016/j.bandl.2012.10.007; Patricia K. Kuhl, "Early Language Learning and Literacy: Neuroscience Implications for Education," *Mind, Brain, and Education* 5, no. 3 (September 1, 2011): 128–142, doi:10.1111/j.1751-228X.2011.01121.x; Hoff, "How Social Contexts Support"; Erika Hoff and Letitia Naigles,

"How Children Use Input to Acquire a Lexicon," *Child Development* 73, no. 2 (March 1, 2002): 418–433, doi:10.1111/1467-8624.00415; Erika Hoff-Ginsberg, "Mother-Child Conversation in Different Social Classes and Communicative Settings," *Child Development* 62, no. 4 (August 1, 1991): 782–796, doi:10.1111/j.1467-8624.1991.tb01569.x; C. Tamis-LeMonda and Marc H. Bornstein, "Maternal Responsiveness and Early Language Acquisition," *Advances in Child Development and Behavior* 29 (2002): 89–127; Paula J. Clarke et al., "Ameliorating Children's Reading-Comprehension Difficulties: A Randomized Controlled Trial," *Psychological Science* 21, no. 8 (August 1, 2010): 1106–1116, doi:10.1177/0956797610375449; Virginia A. Marchman and Anne Fernald, "Speed of Word Recognition and Vocabulary Knowledge in Infancy Predict Cognitive and Language Outcomes in Later Childhood," *Developmental Science* 11, no. 3 (May 1, 2008): F9–16, doi:10.1111/j.1467-7687.2008.00671.x.

26. Hart and Risley, *Meaningful Differences*; Hoff, "SES-Related Differences"; Meredith L. Rowe, "A Longitudinal Investigation of the Role of Quantity and Quality of Child-Directed Speech in Vocabulary Development," *Child Development* 83, no. 5 (September 1, 2012): 1762–1774, doi:10.1111/j.1467-8624.2012.01805.x; Valerie E. Lee and David T. Burkam, *Inequality at the Starting Gate: Social Background Differences in Achievement as Children Begin School* (Washington, DC: Economic Policy Institute, 2002).

27. Hoff, "How Social Contexts"; Hoff and Naigles, "How Children Use Input"; Hoff-Ginsberg, "Mother-Child Conversation"; Tamis-LeMonda and Bornstein, "Maternal Responsiveness and Early Language Acquisition"; Rose I. Arriaga et al., "Scores on the MacArthur Communicative Development Inventory of Children from Low and Middle-Income Families," *Applied Psycholinguistics* 19, no. 02 (April 1998): 209–223, doi:10.1017/S0142716400010043; Hoff, "Causes and Consequences of SES-Related Differences in Parent-to-Child Speech"; Pan et al., "Maternal Correlates of Growth"; Meredith L. Rowe and Susan Goldin-Meadow, "Early Gesture Selectively Predicts Later Language Learning," *Developmental Science* 12, no. 1 (January 1, 2009): 182–187, doi:10.1111/j.1467-7687.2008.00764.x; Janellen Huttenlocher et al., "Sources of Variability in Children's Language Growth," *Cognitive Psychology* 61, no. 4 (December 2010): 343–365, doi:10.1016/j.cogpsych.2010.08.002; Marina Vasilyeva, Heidi Waterfall, and Janellen Huttenlocher, "Emergence of Syntax: Commonalities and Differences Across Children," *Developmental Science* 11, no. 1 (January 1, 2008): 84–97, doi:10.1111/j.1467-7687.2007.00656.x; Lynne Vernon-Feagans et al., "Early Language and Literacy Skills in Low-Income African American and Hispanic Children," in *Handbook of Early Literacy Research*, ed. Susan B. Neuman and David K. Dickinson (New York: Guilford Press, 2001), 192–210; Walker et al., "Prediction of School Outcomes"; Z. O. Weizman and Catherine E. Snow, "Lexical Input as Related to Children's Vocabulary Acquisition: Effects of Sophisticated Exposure and Support for Meaning," *Developmental Psychology* 37 (2001): 265–279.

28. Fernald, Marchman, and Weisleder, "SES Differences in Language Processing"; Nereyda Hurtado, Virginia A. Marchman, and Anne Fernald, "Does Input Influ-

ence Uptake? Links Between Maternal Talk, Processing Speed and Vocabulary Size in Spanish-Learning Children," *Developmental Science* 11, no. 6 (November 1, 2008): F31–39, doi:10.1111/j.1467-7687.2008.00768.x.

29. Adriana Weisleder and Anne Fernald, "Talking to Children Matters: Early Language Experience Strengthens Processing and Builds Vocabulary," *Psychological Science* 24, no. 11 (November 1, 2013): 2143–2152, doi:10.1177/0956797613488145.

30. Erika Hoff et al., "Dual Language Exposure and Early Bilingual Development," *Journal of Child Language* 39, no. 1 (January 2012): 1–27, doi:10.1017/S0305000910000759.

31. Erika Hoff et al., "Expressive Vocabulary Development in Children from Bilingual and Monolingual Homes: A Longitudinal Study from Two to Four Years," *Early Childhood Research Quarterly* 29, no. 4 (2014): 433–444, doi:10.1016/j.ecresq.2014.04.012.

32. US Census Bureau, "American Community Survey (ACS)," accessed September 20, 2015, www.census.gov/programs-surveys/acs/; Erika Hoff et al., "The Additional Effect of Dual Language Exposure on Disparities in Early Language Experience and Language Development," 2015, https://docs.google.com/viewer?url=http%3A%2F%2Fwww.bwgresnet.res.ku.edu%2Fwp-content%2Fuploads%2F2015%2F04%2FHoff-et-al.pdf.

33. Carol Scheffner Hammer, Frank R. Lawrence, and Adele W. Miccio, "Exposure to English Before and After Entry into Head Start: Bilingual Children's Receptive Language Growth in Spanish and English," *International Journal of Bilingual Education and Bilingualism* 11, no. 1 (January 1, 2008): 30–56, doi:10.2167/beb376.0; Ofelia Garcia, Jo Anne Kleifgen, and Lorraine Falchi, *From English Language Learners to Emergent Bilinguals*, Research Initiative of the Campaign for Educational Equity, Equity Matters: Research Review No. 1 (New York: Teachers College, Columbia University, January 2008), http://deimos3.apple.com/webObjects/Core.woa/DownloadTrackPreview/tc.columbia.edu.1463244836.01463261407.1463634935.pdf.

34. D. August and T. Shanahan, "Developing Literacy in Second-Language Learners: Report of the National Literacy Panel on Language-Minority Children and Youth" (Mahwah, NJ: Erlbaum, 2006).

35. Carol Scheffner Hammer, Gisela Jia, and Yuuko Uchikoshi, "Language and Literacy Development of Dual Language Learners Growing Up in the United States: A Call for Research," *Child Development Perspectives* 5, no. 1 (March 1, 2011): 4–9, doi:10.1111/j.1750-8606.2010.00140.x; Hoff et al., "Dual Language Exposure and Early Bilingual Development."

36. Lois Bloom, *The Transition from Infancy to Language: Acquiring the Power of Expression* (New York: Cambridge University Press, 1993), 19.

37. George J. Hollich et al., "Breaking the Language Barrier: An Emergentist Coalition Model for the Origins of Word Learning," *Monographs of the Society for Research in Child Development* 65, no. 3 (January 1, 2000): i–135; Shannon M. Pruden et al., "The Birth of Words: Ten-Month-Olds Learn Words Through Perceptual Salience,"

*Child Development* 77, no. 2 (March 1, 2006): 266–80, doi:10.1111/j.1467-8624.2006.00869.x.

38. Jessica Markus et al., "Individual Differences in Infant Skills as Predictors of Child-Caregiver Joint Attention and Language," *Social Development* 9, no. 3 (2000): 302–15, doi:10.1111/1467-9507.00127.

39. Philip J. Dunham, Frances Dunham, and Ann Curwin, "Joint-Attentional States and Lexical Acquisition at 18 Months," *Developmental Psychology* 29, no. 5 (1993): 827–31, doi:10.1037/0012-1649.29.5.827; Roberta M. Golinkoff, "The Influence of Piagetian Theory on the Study of the Development of Communication," in *New Directions in Piagetian Theory and Practice*, ed. Irving E. Sigel, David Brodzinsky, and Roberta M. Golinkoff (Hillsdale, NJ: Erlbaum Associates Publishers, 1981), 127–42; Hollich et al., "Breaking the Language Barrier."

40. Katarina Begus, Teodora Gliga, and Victoria Southgate, "Infants Learn What They Want to Learn: Responding to Infant Pointing Leads to Superior Learning," *PLoS ONE* 9, no. 10 (October 7, 2014): e108817, doi:10.1371/journal.pone.0108817.

41. Ibid.

42. Carollee Howes, "Social-Emotional Classroom Climate in Child Care, Child–Teacher Relationships and Children's Second Grade Peer Relations," *Social Development* 9, no. 2 (2000): 191–204, doi:10.1111/1467-9507.00119; Patricia Leigh, M. Angela Nievar, and Laura Nathans, "Maternal Sensitivity and Language in Early Childhood: A Test of the Transactional Model," *Perceptual and Motor Skills* 113, no. 1 (August 1, 2011): 281–99, doi:10.2466/10.17.21.28.PMS.113.4.281-299; Tamis-LeMonda and Bornstein, "Maternal Responsiveness and Early Language Acquisition"; Catherine S. Tamis-LeMonda et al., "Maternal Control and Sensitivity, Child Gender, and Maternal Education in Relation to Children's Behavioral Outcomes in African American Families," *Journal of Applied Developmental Psychology* 30, no. 3 (May 2009): 321–31, doi:10.1016/j.appdev.2008.12.018; Catherine S. Tamis-LeMonda, Yana Kuchirko, and Lulu Song, "Why Is Infant Language Learning Facilitated by Parental Responsiveness?," *Current Directions in Psychological Science* 23, no. 2 (2014): 121–26, doi:10.1177/0963721414522813.

43. Patricia K. Kuhl, Feng-Ming Tsao, and Huei-Mei Liu, "Foreign-Language Experience in Infancy: Effects of Short-Term Exposure and Social Interaction on Phonetic Learning," *Proceedings of the National Academy of Sciences* 100, no. 15 (July 22, 2003): 9096–9101, doi:10.1073/pnas.1532872100; Sarah Roseberry et al., "Live Action: Can Young Children Learn Verbs From Video?," *Child Development* 80, no. 5 (September 1, 2009): 1360–75, doi:10.1111/j.1467-8624.2009.01338.x; Judy S. DeLoache et al., "Do Babies Learn From Baby Media?," Psychological Science 21, no. 11 (November 1, 2010): 1570–74, doi:10.1177/0956797610384145.

44. Tamis-LeMonda, Kuchirko, and Song, "Why Is Infant Language Learning Facilitated by Parental Responsiveness?"

45. Susan H. Landry et al., "Does Early Responsive Parenting Have a Special Importance for Children's Development or Is Consistency Across Early Childhood

Necessary?," *Developmental Psychology* 37, no. 3 (2001): 387–403, doi:10.1037/0012-1649.37.3.387; Tamis-LeMonda and Bornstein, "Maternal Responsiveness and Early Language Acquisition."

46. NICHD Early Child Care Research Network, "Cognitive and Language Development"; Leigh, Nievar, and Nathans, "Maternal Sensitivity and Language in Early Childhood"; Tamis-LeMonda et al., "Maternal Control and Sensitivity"; Kathy Hirsh-Pasek and M. Burchinal, "Putting Language Learning in Context: How Change at Home and in School Affects Language Growth Across Time," *Merrill-Palmer Quarterly* 52 (2006): 449–485; NICHD Early Child Care Research Network, "Nonmaternal Care and Family Factors in Early Development: An Overview of the NICHD Study of Early Child Care," *Journal of Applied Developmental Psychology* 22, no. 5 (September 2001): 457–92, doi:10.1016/S0193-3973(01)00092-2; NICHD Early Child Care Research Network, "Child-Care Effect Sizes for the NICHD Study of Early Child Care and Youth Development," *American Psychologist* 61, no. 2 (2006): 99–116, doi:10.1037/0003-066X.61.2.99; Terri J. Sabol and Robert C. Pianta, "Recent Trends in Research on Teacher-Child Relationships," *Attachment & Human Development* 14, no. 3 (April 27, 2012): 213–231, doi:10.1080/14616734.2012.672262.

47. Sondra H. Birch and Gary W. Ladd, "The Teacher-Child Relationship and Children's Early School Adjustment," *Journal of School Psychology* 35, no. 1 (1997): 61–79, doi:10.1016/S0022-4405(96)00029-5.

48. A. Densmore, D. Dickinson, and M. W. Smith, "The Socioemotional Content of Teacher-Child Interaction in Pre-School Settings Serving Low-Income Children," Annual Meeting of the American Educational Research Association, San Francisco, 1995.

49. Bridget K. Hamre and Robert C. Pianta, "Learning Opportunities in Preschool and Early Elementary Classrooms," in *School Readiness and the Transition to Kindergarten in the Era of Accountability*, ed. Robert C. Pianta, Martha J. Cox, and Kyle LaBrie Snow (Baltimore: Paul H. Brookes, 2007), 49–83; Andrew J. Mashburn et al., "Measures of Classroom Quality in Prekindergarten and Children's Development of Academic, Language, and Social Skills," *Child Development* 79, no. 3 (May 1, 2008): 732–749, doi:10.1111/j.1467-8624.2008.01154.x.

50. Jerome S. Bruner, *Child's Talk: Learning to Use Language* (New York: W. W. Norton, 1983).

51. Dare A. Baldwin and Louis J. Moses, "Links Between Social Understanding and Early Word Learning: Challenges to Current Accounts," *Social Development* 10, no. 3 (August 1, 2001): 309–329, doi:10.1111/1467-9507.00168; Sabol and Pianta, "Teacher-Child Relationships."

52. Alan Fogel, Sueko Toda, and Masatoshi Kawai, "Mother-Infant Face-to-Face Interaction in Japan and the United States: A Laboratory Comparison Using 3-Month-Old Infants," *Developmental Psychology* 24, no. 3 (1988): 398–406, doi:10.1037/0012-1649.24.3.398.

53. Hart and Risley, *Meaningful Differences in the Everyday*; Kathy Hirsh-Pasek et al., "The Contribution of Early Communication Quality to Low-Income Children's

Language Success," *Psychological Science* 26, no. 7 (July 1, 2015): 1071–1083, doi: 10.1177/0956797615581493.

54. Sarah Roseberry, Kathy Hirsh-Pasek, and Roberta M. Golinkoff, "Skype Me! Socially Contingent Interactions Help Toddlers Learn Language," *Child Development* 85, no. 3 (May 1, 2014): 956–970, doi:10.1111/cdev.12166.

55. David K. Dickinson, "Teachers' Language Practices and Academic Outcomes of Preschool Children," *Science* 333, no. 6045 (August 19, 2011): 964–967, doi:10.1126/science.1204526.

56. Catherine A. Haden, Rachel A. Haine, and Robyn Fivush, "Developing Narrative Structure in Parent-Child Reminiscing Across the Preschool Years," *Developmental Psychology* 33, no. 2 (1997): 295–307, doi:10.1037/0012-1649.33.2.295.

57. Frederic C. (Frederic Charles) Bartlett, *Remembering: A Study in Experimental and Social Psychology*, Cambridge Psychological Library (Cambridge: Cambridge University Press, 1932); Endel Tulving, "When Is Recall Higher Than Recognition?" *Psychonomic Science* 10, no. 2 (November 4, 2013): 53–54, doi:10.3758/BF03331403; John D. Bransford and Marcia K. Johnson, "Contextual Prerequisites for Understanding: Some Investigations of Comprehension and Recall," *Journal of Verbal Learning and Verbal Behavior* 11, no. 6 (December 1, 1972): 717–726, doi:10.1016/S0022-5371(72)80006-9.

58. J. Christie and K. Roskos, "Standards, Science, and the Role of Play in Early Literacy Education," in *Play = Learning: How Play Motivates and Enhances Children's Cognitive and Social-Emotional Growth*, ed. Dorothy G. Singer, Roberta M. Golinkoff, and Kathy Hirsh-Pasek (New York: Oxford University Press, 2006).

59. Amy E. Booth and Sandra R. Waxman, "A Horse of a Different Color: Specifying with Precision Infants' Mappings of Novel Nouns and Adjectives," *Child Development* 80, no. 1 (January 1, 2009): 15–22, doi:10.1111/j.1467-8624.2008.01242.x.

60. Jennifer M. Zosh, Meredith Brinster, and Justin Halberda, "Optimal Contrast: Competition Between Two Referents Improves Word Learning," *Applied Developmental Science* 17, no. 1 (January 1, 2013): 20–28, doi:10.1080/10888691.2013.748420.

61. K. Fisher et al., "Playing Around in School: Implications for Learning and Educational Policy," in *The Oxford Handbook of the Development of Play*, ed. Anthony D. Pellegrini, Oxford Library of Psychology (New York: Oxford University Press, 2011), 341–362; Hirsh-Pasek et al., "Contribution of Early Communication Quality"; Deena Skolnick Weisberg, Kathy Hirsh-Pasek, and Roberta Michnick Golinkoff, "Embracing Complexity: Rethinking the Relation Between Play and Learning: Comment on Lillard et Al. (2013)," *Psychological Bulletin* 139, no. 1 (2013): 35–39, doi:10.1037/a0030077.

62. Diane C. Burts et al., "A Comparison of Frequencies of Stress Behaviors Observed in Kindergarten Children in Classrooms with Developmentally Appropriate Versus Developmentally Inappropriate Instructional Practices," *Early Childhood Research Quarterly* 5, no. 3 (September 1990): 407–423, doi:10.1016/0885-2006(90)90030-5; Katrina Ferrara et al., "Block Talk: Spatial Language During Block Play," *Mind, Brain,*

*and Education* 5, no. 3 (September 1, 2011): 143–151, doi:10.1111/j.1751-228X.2011.01122.x; M. Han et al., "Does Play Make a Difference? How Play Intervention Affects the Vocabulary Learning of At-Risk Preschoolers," *American Journal of Play* 3, no. 1 (2011): 82–104; Angeline Lillard and Nicole Else-Quest, "Evaluating Montessori Education," *Science* 313, no. 5795 (2006): 1893–1894, doi:10.1126/science.1132362; Kathleen O. Roskos, Patton O. Tabors, and Lisa A. Lenhart, *Oral Language and Early Literacy in Preschool: Talking, Reading, and Writing* (Newark, DE: International Reading Association, 2004; and 2nd ed., 2009); Lawrence L. Schweinhart, David P. Weikart, and Mary B. Larner, "Consequences of Three Preschool Curriculum Models Through Age 15," *Early Childhood Research Quarterly* 1, no. 1 (March 1, 1986): 15–45, doi:10.1016/0885-2006(86)90005-0.

63. Ferrara et al., "Block Talk."

64. Pruden, Levine, and Huttenlocher, "Children's Spatial Thinking."

65. Elizabeth A. Gunderson and Susan C. Levine, "Some Types of Parent Number Talk Count More Than Others: Relations Between Parents' Input and Children's Cardinal-Number Knowledge," *Developmental Science* 14, no. 5 (September 1, 2011): 1021–1032, doi:10.1111/j.1467-7687.2011.01050.x.

66. Klibanoff et al., "Preschool Children's Mathematical Knowledge."

67. Doris Bergen and Daria Mauer, "Symbolic Play, Phonological Awareness, and Literacy Skills at Three Age Levels," in *Play and Literacy in Early Childhood: Research from Multiple Perspectives*, ed. Kathy Roskos and James F. Christie (Mahwah, NJ: Erlbaum Associates Publishers, 2000), 45–62; Ageliki Nicolopoulou, J. McDowell, and C. Brockmeyer, "Narrative Play and Emergent Literacy: Storytelling and Story-Acting Meet Journal Writing," in *Play = Learning: How Play Motivates and Enhances Children's Cognitive and Social-Emotional Growth*, ed. Dorothy G. Singer, Roberta M. Golinkoff, and Kathy Hirsh-Pasek (New York: Oxford University Press, 2006).

68. See, for example, Roberta Michnick Golinkoff, "'I Beg Your Pardon?': The Preverbal Negotiation of Failed Messages," *Journal of Child Language* 13, no. 03 (October 1986): 455–476, doi:10.1017/S0305000900006826.

69. Susan B. Neuman and Julie Dwyer, "Missing in Action: Vocabulary Instruction in Pre-K," *Reading Teacher* 62, no. 5 (February 1, 2009): 384–392, doi:10.1598/RT.62.5.2; Kathy Hirsh-Pasek et al., *A Mandate for Playful Learning in Preschool: Presenting the Evidence* (New York: Oxford University Press, 2009).

70. E. Newport, H. Gleitman, and L. Gleitman, "Mother, I'd Rather Do It Myself: Some Effects and Non-Effects of Maternal Speech Style," in *Talking to Children: Language Input and Acquisition: Papers from a Conference Sponsored by the Committee on Sociolinguistics of the Social Science Research Council*, ed. Catherine E. Snow, Charles Albert Ferguson, and Charles A. (Charles Albert) Ferguson (New York: Cambridge University Press, 1977), 109–49.

71. Janellen Huttenlocher et al., "Early Vocabulary Growth: Relation to Language Input and Gender," *Developmental Psychology* 27, no. 2 (1991): 236–48, doi:10.1037/0012-1649.27.2.236; C. S. Tamis-LeMonda, M. H. Bornstein, and

L. Baumwell, "Maternal Responsiveness and Children's Achievement of Language Milestones," *Child Development* 72, no. 3 (June 2001): 748–767; Catherine E. Snow, "Conversations with Children," in *Language Acquisition: Studies in First Language Development*, ed. Paul Fletcher and Michael Garman, 2nd ed. (Cambridge: Cambridge University Press, 1986), 69–89.

72. Weizman and Snow, "Lexical Input"; Pan et al., "Maternal Correlates of Growth"; Nadya Pancsofar and Lynne Vernon-Feagans, "Fathers' Early Contributions to Children's Language Development in Families from Low-Income Rural Communities," *Early Childhood Research Quarterly* 25, no. 4 (2010): 450–463, doi:10.1016/j.ecresq.2010.02.001; Rowe, "Child-Directed Speech."

73. Huttenlocher et al., "Sources of Variability in Children's Language Growth."

74. Dickinson and Porche, "Relation Between Language Experiences."

75. Janellen Huttenlocher et al., "Language Input and Child Syntax," *Cognitive Psychology* 45, no. 3 (November 2002): 337–374, doi:10.1016/S0010-0285(02)00500-5.

76. Silvia Place and Erika Hoff, "Properties of Dual Language Exposure That Influence 2-Year-Olds' Bilingual Proficiency," *Child Development* 82, no. 6 (November 1, 2011): 1834–1849, doi:10.1111/j.1467-8624.2011.01660.x.

77. Lynn K. Perry et al., "Learn Locally, Think Globally: Exemplar Variability Supports Higher-Order Generalization and Word Learning," *Psychological Science* 21, no. 12 (December 1, 2010): 1894–1902, doi:10.1177/0956797610389189.

78. Andrew Biemiller and Catherine Boote, "An Effective Method for Building Meaning Vocabulary in Primary Grades," *Journal of Educational Psychology* 98, no. 1 (2006): 44–62, doi:10.1037/0022-0663.98.1.44.

79. Catherine E. Snow, "Input to Interaction to Instruction: Three Key Shifts in the History of Child Language Research," *Journal of Child Language* 41, no. supplement S1 (July 2014): 117–123, doi:10.1017/S0305000914000294.

80. Dedre Gentner, Florencia K. Anggoro, and Raquel S. Klibanoff, "Structure Mapping and Relational Language Support Children's Learning of Relational Categories," *Child Development* 82, no. 4 (July 1, 2011): 1173–1188, doi:10.1111/j.1467-8624.2011.01599.x; Dedre Gentner and Laura L. Namy, "Analogical Processes in Language Learning," *Current Directions in Psychological Science* 15, no. 6 (December 1, 2006): 297–301, doi:10.1111/j.1467-8721.2006.00456.x; Sandra R. Waxman and Raquel S. Klibanoff, "The Role of Comparison in the Extension of Novel Adjectives," *Developmental Psychology* 36, no. 5 (2000): 571–581, doi:10.1037/0012-1649.36.5.571.

81. Susan B. Neuman, "Overcoming the Knowledge Gap: The Case for Content-Rich Instruction," working paper (Ann Arbor: University of Michigan, Education Leadership, n.d.).

82. James A. Dixon and Virginia A. Marchman, "Grammar and the Lexicon: Developmental Ordering in Language Acquisition," *Child Development* 78, no. 1 (January 1, 2007): 209, doi:10.1111/j.1467-8624.2007.00992.x.

83. Barbara T. Conboy and Donna J. Thal, "Ties Between the Lexicon and Grammar: Cross-Sectional and Longitudinal Studies of Bilingual Toddlers," *Child Development* 77, no. 3 (May 1, 2006): 712–735, doi:10.1111/j.1467-8624.2006.00899.x.

84. Mutsumi Imai et al., "Novel Noun and Verb Learning in Chinese-, English-, and Japanese-Speaking Children," *Child Development* 79, no. 4 (July 1, 2008): 979–1000, doi:10.1111/j.1467-8624.2008.01171.x.

85. Ibid.; Letitia Naigles, "Children Use Syntax to Learn Verb Meanings," *Journal of Child Language* 17, no. 2 (June 1990): 357–374, doi:10.1017/S0305000900013817.

86. Kathy Hirsh-Pasek and Roberta M. Golinkoff, *Action Meets Word: How Children Learn Verbs* (New York: Oxford University Press, 2006); Roberta Michnick Golinkoff and Kathy Hirsh-Pasek, "How Toddlers Begin to Learn Verbs," *Trends in Cognitive Sciences* 12, no. 10 (October 2008): 397–403, doi:10.1016/j.tics.2008.07.003.

87. Roberta M. Golinkoff, Kathy Hirsh-Pasek, and Melissa A. Schweisguth, "A Reappraisal of Young Children's Knowledge of Grammatical Morphemes," in *Approaches to Bootstrapping: Phonological, Lexical, Syntactic and Neurophysiological Aspects of Early Language Acquisition*, Language Acquisition & Language Disorders, vols. 23–24, ed. Jürgen Weissenborn and Barbara Höhle (Philadelphia: John Benjamins Pub. Co, 2001), 176–188; Kathy Hirsh-Pasek and Roberta M. Golinkoff, *The Origins of Grammar: Evidence from Early Language Comprehension* (Cambridge, MA: MIT Press, 1996); Yael Gertner and Cynthia Fisher, "Predicted Errors in Children's Early Sentence Comprehension," *Cognition* 124, no. 1 (July 2012): 85–94, doi:10.1016/j.cognition.2012.03.010; J. C. Damonte et al., "Ten- to 12-Month-Old Infants Segment a Common Bound Morpheme from Its Stem," working paper, n.d.

88. Imai et al., "Novel Noun and Verb Learning"; Kyong-sun Jin and Cynthia Fisher, "Early Evidence for Syntactic Bootstrapping: 15-Month-Olds Use Sentence Structure in Verb Learning," in *Boston University Conference on Language Development (BUCLD) Proceedings*, vol. 38, ed. Will Orman and Matthew James Valleau (Boston: Cascadilla Press, 2014), www.bu.edu/bucld/files/2014/04/jin.pdf; Hirsh-Pasek and Golinkoff, *Origins of Grammar*.

89. NICHD Early Child Care Research Network, "Pathways to Reading."

90. R. Stevens and W. R. Penuel, "Studying and Fostering Learning Through Joint Media Engagement" (Principal Investigators Meeting of the National Science Foundation's Science of Learning Centers, Arlington, VA, 2010), 1–75.

91. Ibid.

92. K. Ridge et al., "Supermarket Speak: Increasing Talk Among Low-SES Families," *Mind, Brain, and Education* 9, no. 3 (2015): 127–135.

### *Chapter 4*

1. Erika Hoff, "Interpreting the Early Language Trajectories of Children from Low-SES and Language Minority Homes: Implications for Closing Achievement Gaps," *Developmental Psychology* 49, no. 1 (2013): 4–14, doi:10.1037/a0027238.

2. Camille Ryan, "Language Use in the United States: 2011," *American Community Survey, US Census Bureau*, 2013, https://census.gov/content/dam/Census/library/publications/2013/acs/acs-22.pdf.

3. Patricia K. Kuhl, Feng-Ming Tsao, and Huei-Mei Liu, "Foreign-Language Experience in Infancy: Effects of Short-Term Exposure and Social Interaction on Phonetic Learning," *Proceedings of the National Academy of Sciences* 100, no. 15 (July 22, 2003): 9096–9101, doi:10.1073/pnas.1532872100; Janet F. Werker and Richard C. Tees, "Cross-Language Speech Perception: Evidence for Perceptual Reorganization During the First Year of Life," *Infant Behavior and Development* 7, no. 1 (January 1984): 49–63, doi:10.1016/S0163-6383(84)80022-3.

4. Jeanne Brooks-Gunn and Greg J. Duncan, "The Effects of Poverty on Children," *The Future of Children* 7, no. 2 (July 1, 1997): 55–71, doi:10.2307/1602387; Rand D. Conger and M. Brent Donnellan, "An Interactionist Perspective on the Socioeconomic Context of Human Development," *Annual Review of Psychology* 58, no. 1 (2007): 175–199, doi:10.1146/annurev.psych.58.110405.085551; Martha J. Farah et al., "Childhood Poverty: Specific Associations with Neurocognitive Development," *Brain Research* 1110, no. 1 (September 19, 2006): 166–174, doi:10.1016/j.brainres.2006.06.072; Greg J. Duncan, Kathleen M. Ziol-Guest, and Ariel Kalil, "Early-Childhood Poverty and Adult Attainment, Behavior, and Health," *Child Development* 81, no. 1 (January 1, 2010): 306–325, doi:10.1111/j.1467-8624.2009.01396.x; Donald J. Hernandez, "Demographic Change and the Life Circumstances of Immigrant Families," *The Future of Children* 14, no. 2 (July 1, 2004): 17–47, doi:10.2307/1602792.

5. Hernandez, "Demographic Change and the Life Circumstances of Immigrant Families"; Jeannette Mancilla-Martinez, Joanna A. Christodoulou, and Michelle M. Shabaker, "Preschoolers' English Vocabulary Development: The Influence of Language Proficiency and At-Risk Factors," *Learning and Individual Differences* 35 (October 2014): 79–86, doi:10.1016/j.lindif.2014.06.008.

6. E. Chen and G. E. Miller, "'Shift-and-Persist' Strategies: Why Low Socioeconomic Status Isn't Always Bad for Health," *Perspectives on Psychological Science* 7 (2012): 135–158; N. L. Letourneau et al., "Socioeconomic Status and Child Development: A Meta-Analysis," *Journal of Emotional and Behavioral Disorders* 21 (2011): 211–224, doi:10.1177/1063426611421007; S. R. Sirin, "Socioeconomic Status and Academic Achievement: A Meta-Analytic Review of Research," *Review of Educational Research* 75, no. 3 (2005): 417–453.

7. Betty Hart and Todd R. Risley, Meaningful Differences in the Everyday Experience of Young American Children (Baltimore: P.H. Brookes, 1995).

8. Erika Hoff, "How Social Contexts Support and Shape Language Development," *Developmental Review* 26, no. 1 (March 2006): 55–88, doi:10.1016/j.dr.2005.11.002; Meredith L. Rowe, "A Longitudinal Investigation of the Role of Quantity and Quality of Child-Directed Speech in Vocabulary Development," *Child Development* 83, no. 5 (September 1, 2012): 1762–1774, doi:10.1111/j.1467-8624.2012.01805.x; Keith

Topping, Rayenne Dekhinet, and Suzanne Zeedyk, "Parent–Infant Interaction and Children's Language Development," *Educational Psychology* 33, no. 4 (November 27, 2012): 391–426, doi:10.1080/01443410.2012.744159.

9. Victoria J. Rideout, Elizabeth A. Vandewater, and Ellen A. Wartella "Zero to Six: Electronic Media in the Lives of Infants, Toddlers and Preschoolers" (Menlo Park, CA: Kaiser Family Foundation, 2003), http://eric.ed.gov/?id=ED482302.

10. Helena Duch et al., "Screen Time Use in Children Under 3 Years Old: A Systematic Review of Correlates," *International Journal of Behavioral Nutrition and Physical Activity* 10, no. 1 (2013): 1–10.

11. Suzy Tomopoulos et al., "Infant Media Exposure and Toddler Development," *Archives of Pediatrics & Adolescent Medicine* 164, no. 12 (December 1, 2010): 1105–1011, doi:10.1001/archpediatrics.2010.235.

12. Masako Tanimura, Kanako Okuma, and Kayoko Kyoshima, "Television Viewing, Reduced Parental Utterance, and Delayed Speech Development in Infants and Young Children," *Archives of Pediatrics & Adolescent Medicine* 161, no. 6 (June 1, 2007): 618–619, doi:10.1001/archpedi.161.6.618-b; Marie Evans Schmidt et al., "The Effects of Background Television on the Toy Play Behavior of Very Young Children," *Child Development* 79, no. 4 (July 1, 2008): 1137–1151, doi 10.1111/j.1467-8624.2008.01180.x; Alan L. Mendelsohn et al., "Infant Television and Video Exposure Associated with Limited Parent-Child Verbal Interactions in Low Socioeconomic Status Households," *Archives of Pediatrics & Adolescent Medicine* 162, no. 5 (May 1, 2008): 411–417, doi:10.1001/archpedi.162.5.411; D. A. Christakis et al., "Audible Television and Decreased Adult Words, Infant Vocalizations, and Conversational Turns: A Population-Based Study," *Archives of Pediatrics & Adolescent Medicine* 163, no. 6 (June 1, 2009): 554–558, doi:10.1001/archpediatrics.2009.61.

13. Kuhl, Tsao, and Liu, "Foreign-Language Experience in Infancy."

14. James J. Heckman et al., "The Rate of Return to the Highscope Perry Preschool Program," *Journal of Public Economics* 94, no. 1–2 (February 2010): 114–128, doi:10.1016/j.jpubeco.2009.11.001.

15. Charles A. Nelson et al., "Cognitive Recovery in Socially Deprived Young Children: The Bucharest Early Intervention Project," *Science* 318, no. 5858 (December 21, 2007): 1937–1940, doi:10.1126/science.1143921; Jennifer Windsor et al., "Effect of Foster Care on Language Learning at Eight Years: Findings from the Bucharest Early Intervention Project," *Journal of Child Language* 40, no. 3 (June 2013): 605–627, doi:10.1017/S0305000912000177.

16. Frances Campbell et al., "Early Childhood Investments Substantially Boost Adult Health," *Science* 343, no. 6178 (March 28, 2014): 1478–1485, doi:10.1126/science.1248429; James J. Heckman, "Schools, Skills, and Synapses," *Economic Inquiry* 46, no. 3 (July 1, 2008): 289–324, doi:10.1111/j.1465-7295.2008.00163.x; Pamela Hines et al., "Laying the Foundation for Lifetime Learning," *Science* 333, no. 6045 (August 19, 2011): 951–951, doi:10.1126/science.333.6045.951; Milagros Nores and W. Steven Barnett, "Benefits of Early Childhood Interventions Across the

World: (Under) Investing in the Very Young," *Economics of Education Review*, Special Issue in Honor of Henry M. Levin, 29, no. 2 (April 2010): 271–282, doi:10.1016/j.econedurev.2009.09.001.

17. Adriana Weisleder and Anne Fernald, "Talking to Children Matters Early Language Experience Strengthens Processing and Builds Vocabulary," *Psychological Science* 24, no. 11 (November 1, 2013): 2143–2152, doi:10.1177/0956797613488145; Annie Bernier, Stephanie M. Carlson, and Natasha Whipple, "From External Regulation to Self-Regulation: Early Parenting Precursors of Young Children's Executive Functioning," *Child Development* 81, no. 1 (January 1, 2010): 326–39, doi:10.1111/j.1467-8624.2009.01397.x; Huttenlocher et al., "Sources of Variability in Children's Language Growth"; Eileen T. Rodriguez and Catherine S. Tamis-LeMonda, "Trajectories of the Home Learning Environment Across the First 5 Years: Associations with Children's Vocabulary and Literacy Skills at PreK," *Child Development* 82, no. 4 (July 1, 2011): 1058–1075, doi:10.1111/j.1467-8624.2011.01614.x.

18. Christina Weiland, M. Clara Barata, and Hirokazu Yoshikawa, "The Co-Occurring Development of Executive Function Skills and Receptive Vocabulary in Preschool-Aged Children: A Look at the Direction of the Developmental Pathways," *Infant and Child Development* 23, no. 1 (January 1, 2014): 4–21, doi:10.1002/icd.1829.

19. Janet F. Werker and Krista Byers-Heinlein, "Bilingualism in Infancy: First Steps in Perception and Comprehension," *Trends in Cognitive Sciences* 12, no. 4 (April 2008): 144–151, doi:10.1016/j.tics.2008.01.008; Virginia A. Marchman, Anne Fernald, and Nereyda Hurtado, "How Vocabulary Size in Two Languages Relates to Efficiency in Spoken Word Recognition by Young Spanish–English Bilinguals," *Journal of Child Language* 37, no. 4 (September 2010): 817–840, doi:10.1017/S0305000909990055; Fred Genesee and Elena Nicoladis, "Bilingual First Language Acquisition," in *Handbook of Language Development*, ed. Erika Hoff and Marilyn Shatz (Malden, MA: Blackwell, 2007), 324–342.

20. D. J. Saer, "The Effect of Bilingualism on Intelligence," *British Journal of Psychology. General Section* 14, no. 1 (July 1, 1923): 25–38, doi:10.1111/j.2044-8295.1923.tb00110.x; Madorah E. Smith, "A Study of Five Bilingual Children from the Same Family," *Child Development* 2, no. 3 (September 1, 1931): 184–187, doi:10.2307/1125374.

21. Stefka H. Marinova-Todd, "'Corplum Is a Core from a Plum': The Advantage of Bilingual Children in the Analysis of Word Meaning from Verbal Context," *Bilingualism: Language and Cognition* 15, no. Special Issue 1 (January 2012): 117–127, doi:10.1017/S136672891000043X; Nameera Akhtar et al., "Learning Foreign Labels from a Foreign Speaker: The Role of (Limited) Exposure to a Second Language," *Journal of Child Language* 39, no. 5 (November 2012): 1135–1149, doi:10.1017/S0305000911000481; Li-Jen Kuo and Richard C. Anderson, "Effects of Early Bilingualism on Learning Phonological Regularities in a New Language," *Journal of Experimental Child Psychology* 111, no. 3 (March 2012): 455–467, doi:10.1016/j.jecp

.2011.08.013; Jessica Tsimprea Maluch et al., "The Effect of Speaking a Minority Language at Home on Foreign Language Learning," *Learning and Instruction* 36 (April 2015): 76–85, doi:10.1016/j.learninstruc.2014.12.001; Kathleen Jubenville, Monique Sénéchal, and Melissa Malette, "The Moderating Effect of Orthographic Consistency on Oral Vocabulary Learning in Monolingual and Bilingual Children," *Journal of Experimental Child Psychology* 126 (October 2014): 245–263, doi:10.1016/j.jecp.2014.05.002.

22. Mariëlle J. L. Prevoo et al., "Within- and Cross-Language Relations Between Oral Language Proficiency and School Outcomes in Bilingual Children with an Immigrant Background: A Meta-Analytical Study," *Review of Educational Research*, May 6, 2015, 0034654315584685, doi:10.3102/0034654315584685.

23. Ellen Bialystok et al., "Receptive Vocabulary Differences in Monolingual and Bilingual Children," *Bilingualism: Language and Cognition* 13, no. 4 (October 2010): 525–531, doi:10.1017/S1366728909990423; Erika Hoff et al., "Dual Language Exposure and Early Bilingual Development," *Journal of Child Language* 39, no. 1 (January 2012): 1–27, doi:10.1017/S0305000910000759.

24. Megan Gross, Milijana Buac, and Margarita Kaushanskaya, "Conceptual Scoring of Receptive and Expressive Vocabulary Measures in Simultaneous and Sequential Bilingual Children," *American Journal of Speech-Language Pathology* 23, no. 4 (November 1, 2014): 574–586, doi:10.1044/2014_AJSLP-13-0026; Hoff et al., "Dual Language Exposure and Early Bilingual Development"; Jeannette Mancilla-Martinez and Shaher Banu Vagh, "Growth in Toddlers' Spanish, English, and Conceptual Vocabulary Knowledge," *Early Childhood Research Quarterly* 28, no. 3 (2013): 555–567, doi:10.1016/j.ecresq.2013.03.004.

25. Olusola O. Adesope et al., "A Systematic Review and Meta-Analysis of the Cognitive Correlates of Bilingualism," *Review of Educational Research* 80, no. 2 (June 1, 2010): 207–245, doi:10.3102/0034654310368803; Ellen Bialystok, Fergus I. M. Craik, and Gigi Luk, "Bilingualism: Consequences for Mind and Brain," *Trends in Cognitive Sciences* 16, no. 4 (April 2012): 240–250, doi:10.1016/j.tics.2012.03.001.

26. Leah L. Kapa and John Colombo, "Attentional Control in Early and Later Bilingual Children," *Cognitive Development* 28, no. 3 (July 2013): 233–246, doi: 10.1016/j.cogdev.2013.01.011.

27. J. F. Kroll et al., "Juggling Two Languages in One Mind: What Bilinguals Tell Us About Language Processing and Its Consequences for Cognition," in *The Psychology of Learning and Motivation*, vol. 56, ed. B. Ross (San Diego: Academic Press, 2012), 229–262.

28. Alejandra Calvo and Ellen Bialystok, "Independent Effects of Bilingualism and Socioeconomic Status on Language Ability and Executive Functioning," *Cognition* 130, no. 3 (March 2014): 278–288, doi:10.1016/j.cognition.2013.11.015.

29. "Working-class" here may not be equivalent to low SES in the United States, because there is no systematic measurement of SES status in Canada. The critical point is that there is a distinctive difference in these children's parental education, family income, or both.

30. Pascale M. J. Engel de Abreu et al., "Bilingualism Enriches the Poor Enhanced Cognitive Control in Low-Income Minority Children," *Psychological Science* 23, no. 11 (November 1, 2012): 1364–1371, doi:10.1177/0956797612443836.

31. Aristea I. Ladas, Daniel J. Carroll, and Ana B. Vivas, "Attentional Processes in Low-Socioeconomic Status Bilingual Children: Are They Modulated by the Amount of Bilingual Experience?," *Child Development* 86, no. 2 (March 1, 2015): 557–578, doi:10.1111/cdev.12332.

32. Gigi Luk and Ellen Bialystok, "Bilingualism Is Not a Categorical Variable: Interaction Between Language Proficiency and Usage," *Journal of Cognitive Psychology* 25, no. 5 (May 16, 2013): 605–621, doi:10.1080/20445911.2013.795574.

33. Lisa M. Bedore et al., "The Measure Matters: Language Dominance Profiles Across Measures in Spanish–English Bilingual Children," *Bilingualism: Language and Cognition* 15, no. 3 (July 2012): 616–629, doi:10.1017/S1366728912000090.

34. S. L. Guerrero, S. Smith, and G. Luk, "Home Language Usage and Executive Function in Bilingual Preschoolers," working paper, n.d.

35. National Center for Education Statistics, Common Core of Data (CCD), "State Nonfiscal Survey of Public Elementary/Secondary Education," 2011 and 2012.

36. Shannon B. Wanless et al., "The Influence of Demographic Risk Factors on Children's Behavioral Regulation in Prekindergarten and Kindergarten," *Early Education and Development* 22, no. 3 (May 1, 2011): 461–488, doi:10.1080/10409289.2011.536132.

37. Adam Winsler et al., "Child, Family, and Childcare Predictors of Delayed School Entry and Kindergarten Retention Among Linguistically and Ethnically Diverse Children," *Developmental Psychology* 48, no. 5 (2012): 1299–1314.

38. Ibid.

39. Wanless et al., "Influence of Demographic Risk Factors."

40. US Department of Education, Office of Special Education Programs, "Annual Report to Congress on the Implementation of the Individuals with Disabilities Education Act," Individual with Disabilities Education Act (IDEA) database, selected years 1992 through 2006, http://tadnet.public.tadnet.org/pages/712.

41. Ibid.

### *Chapter 5*

We gratefully acknowledge the input of Jill R. Kavanaugh, MLIS, who constructed and performed the literature search and provided suggestions throughout the development of this chapter.

1. Victoria J. Rideout, "Zero to Eight: Children's Media Use in America 2013," *Common Sense Media*, 2013, www.commonsensemedia.org/research/zero-to-eight-childrens-media-use-in-america-2013.

2. Cleborne Maddux et al., "Fad, Fashion, and the Weak Role of Theory and Research in Information Technology in Education," *Journal of Technology and Teacher Education* 12, no. 4 (2004): 511–533.

3. Heather L. Kirkorian, Ellen A. Wartella, and Daniel R. Anderson, "Media and Young Children's Learning," *Future of Children* 18, no. 1 (2008): 39–61, doi:10.1353/foc.0.0002.

4. Ida Eva Zielinska and Bette Chambers, "Using Group Viewing of Television to Teach Preschool Children Social Skills," *Journal of Educational Television* 21, no. 2 (June 1, 1995): 85–99, doi:10.1080/0260741950210203.

5. Rosemarie T. Truglio et al., "The Varied Role of Formative Research: Case Studies from 30 Years," in *"G" Is for Growing: Thirty Years of Research on Children and Sesame Street*, ed. Shalom M. Fisch and Rosemarie T. Truglio (Mahwah, NJ: Erlbaum, 2001).

6. Marie-Louise Mares and Zhongdang Pan, "Effects of Sesame Street: A Meta-Analysis of Children's Learning in 15 Countries," *Journal of Applied Developmental Psychology* 34, no. 3 (May 2013): 140–151, doi:10.1016/j.appdev.2013.01.001.

7. Shalom M. Fisch, Rosemarie T. Truglio, and Charlotte F. Cole, "The Impact of Sesame Street on Preschool Children: A Review and Synthesis of 30 Years' Research," *Media Psychology* 1, no. 2 (June 1, 1999): 165–190, doi:10.1207/s1532785xmep0102_5.

8. Rupin R. Thakkar, Michelle M. Garrison, and Dimitri A. Christakis, "A Systematic Review for the Effects of Television Viewing by Infants and Preschoolers," *Pediatrics* 118, no. 5 (November 1, 2006): 2025–2031, doi:10.1542/peds.2006-1307.

9. Julianne Lynch and Terri Redpath, "'Smart' Technologies in Early Years Literacy Education: A Meta-Narrative of Paradigmatic Tensions in iPad Use in an Australian Preparatory Classroom," *Journal of Early Childhood Literacy* 14, no. 2 (June 1, 2014): 147–174, doi:10.1177/1468798412453150.

10. Natalia Kucirkova et al., "Children's Engagement with Educational iPad Apps: Insights from a Spanish Classroom," *Computers & Education* 71 (February 2014): 175–184, doi:10.1016/j.compedu.2013.10.003.

11. Eugene A. Geist, "A Qualitative Examination of Two Year-Olds Interaction with Tablet Based Interactive Technology," *Journal of Instructional Psychology* 39, no. 1 (March 2012): 26–35.

12. Kucirkova et al., "Children's Engagement with Educational iPad Apps."

13. Daniel R. Anderson et al., "Researching *Blue's Clues*: Viewing Behavior and Impact," *Media Psychology* 2, no. 2 (May 1, 2000): 179–194, doi:10.1207/S1532785XMEP0202_4.

14. Garry Falloon, "Young Students Using iPads: App Design and Content Influences on Their Learning Pathways," *Computers & Education* 68 (October 2013): 505–521, doi:10.1016/j.compedu.2013.06.006.

15. Anderson et al., "Researching *Blue's Clues*."

16. Geist, "A Qualitative Examination of Two Year-Olds."

17. Falloon, "Young Students Using iPads."

18. Shalom M. Fisch and Rosemarie T. Truglio, eds., *"G" Is for Growing: Thirty Years of Research on Children and Sesame Street* (Mahwah, NJ: Erlbaum 2001).

19. Ibid.

20. Falloon, "Young Students Using iPads."

21. Ibid., 519.

22. Ibid.

23. Cynthia Chiong, Jinny Ree, and Lori Takeuchi, "Print Books Vs. E-Books: Comparing Parent-Child Co-Reading on Print, Basic, and Enhanced E-Book Platforms," report, Joan Ganz Cooney Center, New York, spring 2012, www.joanganz cooneycenter.org/publication/quickreport-print-books-vs-e-books/.

24. Linda D. Labbo and Melanie R. Kuhn, "Weaving Chains of Affect and Cognition: A Young Child's Understanding of CD-ROM Talking Books," *Journal of Literacy Research* 32, no. 2 (June 1, 2000): 187–210, doi:10.1080/10862960009548073.

25. Falloon, "Young Students Using iPads."

26. O. Korat and A. Shamir, "Electronic Books Versus Adult Readers: Effects on Children's Emergent Literacy as a Function of Social Class," *Journal of Computer Assisted Learning* 23, no. 3 (June 1, 2007): 248–259, doi:10.1111/j.1365-2729 .2006.00213.x.

27. National Association for the Education of Young Children, and Fred Rogers Center for Early Learning and Chidren's Media, "Technology and Interactive Media as Tools in Early Childhood Programs Serving Children from Birth Through Age 8," 2012, www.naeyc.org/files/naeyc/PS_technology_WEB.pdf.

28. Anderson et al., "Researching *Blue's Clues.*"

29. Fisch and Truglio, *"G" Is for Growing.*

30. Anderson et al., "Researching *Blue's Clues.*"

31. Cynthia Chiong and Carly Shuler, "Learning: Is There an App for That? Investigations of Young Children's Usage and Learning with Mobile Devices and Apps," report, Joan Ganz Cooney Center, New York, 2010, www.joanganzcooneycenter.org /wp-content/uploads/2010/10/learningapps_final_110410.pdf.

32. Robert Kliegman et al., eds., *Nelson Textbook of Pediatrics*, 19th ed. (Philadelphia: Elsevier/Saunders, 2011).

33. Kucirkova et al., "Children's Engagement with Educational iPad Apps."

34. Anne Edwards and Carmen D'arcy, "Relational Agency and Disposition in Sociocultural Accounts of Learning to Teach," *Educational Review* 56, no. 2 (June 1, 2004): 147–155, doi:10.1080/0031910410001693236.

35. S. Pasnik and C. Llorente, "Study of Preschool Parents and Caregivers Use of Technology and PBS Kids Transmedia Resources: A Report to the CPB-PBS 'Ready to Learn Initiative'" (Education Development Center, 2012).

36. C.-T Hsin, M.-C. Li, and C.-C. Tsai, "The Influence of Young Children's Use of Technology on Their Learning: A Review," *Journal of Educational Technology & Society* 17, no. 4 (2014).

37. Cristián Infante et al., "Co-Located Collaborative Learning Video Game with Single Display Groupware," *Interactive Learning Environments* 18, no. 2 (January 15, 2009): 177–195, doi:10.1080/10494820802489339.

38. Helen Cole and Danaë Stanton, "Designing Mobile Technologies to Support Co-Present Collaboration," *Personal and Ubiquitous Computing* 7, no. 6 (November 5, 2003): 365–371, doi:10.1007/s00779-003-0249-4.

39. Siri Mehus and Reed Stevens, "Ethnographic Field Studies of Joint Media Engagement," in *The New Coviewing: Designing for Learning Through Joint Media Engagement*, ed. Lori Takeuchi and Reed Stevens (New York: Joan Ganz Cooney Center, 2011), www.joanganzcooneycenter.org/wp-content/uploads/2011/12/jgc_coviewing_desktop.pdf.

40. Ibid.

41. Patti M. Valkenburg et al., "Developing a Scale to Assess Three Styles of Television Mediation: 'Instructive Mediation,' 'Restrictive Mediation,' and 'Social Coviewing,'" *Journal of Broadcasting & Electronic Media* 43, no. 1 (January 1, 1999): 52–66, doi:10.1080/08838159909364474.

42. David Wood, Jerome S. Bruner, and Gail Ross, "The Role of Tutoring in Problem Solving," *Journal of Child Psychology and Psychiatry* 17, no. 2 (April 1, 1976): 89–100, doi:10.1111/j.1469-7610.1976.tb00381.x.

43. Shalom M. Fisch, *Children's Learning from Educational Television: Sesame Street and Beyond*, LEA's Communication Series (Mahwah, NJ: L. Erlbaum Associates, 2003).

44. Fisch and Truglio, *"G" Is for Growing*.

45. Robert A. Reiser, Martin A. Tessmer, and Pamela C. Phelps, "Adult-Child Interaction in Children's Learning from 'Sesame Street,'" *Educational Technology Research and Development* 32, no. 4 (December 1984): 217–223, doi:10.1007/BF02768893.

46. The term was cited in Lori Takeuchi and Reed Stevens, eds., *The New Coviewing: Designing for Learning Through Joint Media Engagement* (New York: Joan Ganz Cooney Center, 2011), www.joanganzcooneycenter.org/wp-content/uploads/2011/12/jgc_coviewing_desktop.pdf.

47. Ibid.

48. Chiong, Ree, and Takeuchi, "Print Books Vs. E-Books."

49. Rideout, "Zero to Eight."

50. Council on Communications Media, "Policy Statement: Media Education," *Pediatrics* (September 27, 2010): peds.2010–1636, doi:10.1542/peds.2010-1636.

51. Pooja S. Tandon et al., "Preschoolers' Total Daily Screen Time at Home and by Type of Child Care," *Journal of Pediatrics* 158, no. 2 (February 2011): 297–300, doi:10.1016/j.jpeds.2010.08.005.

52. Ellen Wartella et al., "Technology in the Lives of Teachers and Classrooms: Survey of Classroom Teachers and Family Child Care Providers," 2010, http://cmhd.northwestern.edu/wp-content/uploads/2015/10/TechInTheLivesofTeachers-1.pdf.

53. Tina N. Hohlfeld et al., "Examining the Digital Divide in K–12 Public Schools: Four-Year Trends for Supporting ICT Literacy in Florida," *Computers & Education* 51, no. 4 (December 2008): 1648–1663, doi:10.1016/j.compedu.2008.04.002.

54. Howard P. Parette, Amanda C. Quesenberry, and Craig Blum, "Missing the Boat with Technology Usage in Early Childhood Settings: A 21st Century View of

Developmentally Appropriate Practice," *Early Childhood Education Journal* 37, no. 5 (November 11, 2009): 338, doi:10.1007/s10643-009-0352-x.

55. A. Badia, J. Meneses, and C. Sigales, "Teachers' Perceptions of Factors Affecting the Educational Use of ICT in Technology-Rich Classrooms," *Electronic Journal of Research in Educational Psychology* 11, no. 3 (2013): 787–808; Esther Ntuli and Lydia Kyei-Blankson, "Teacher Assessment of Young Children Learning with Technology in Early Childhood Education," *International Journal of Information and Communication Technology Education* 8, no. 4 (October 2012): 1–10, doi:10.4018/jicte.2012100101.

56. Özlem Yurt and Nılgün Cevher-Kalburan, "Early Childhood Teachers' Thoughts and Practices About the Use of Computers in Early Childhood Education," *Procedia Computer Science*, World Conference on Information Technology, 3 (2011): 1562–1570, doi:10.1016/j.procs.2011.01.050.

57. Leslie J. Couse and Dora W. Chen, "A Tablet Computer for Young Children? Exploring Its Viability for Early Childhood Education," *Journal of Research on Technology in Education* 43, no. 1 (September 1, 2010): 75–96, doi:10.1080/15391523.2010.10782562.

58. Parette, Quesenberry, and Blum, "Missing the Boat with Technology."

59. WordWorld, "Parents & Teachers: Education Philosophy—WordWorld's Research and Curriculum," *PBS Parents*, accessed October 27, 2015, www.pbs.org/parents/wordworld/research.html.

60. Federal Communications Commission, "Children's Educational Television," 2014, www.fcc.gov/guides/childrens-educational-television.

61. Kucirkova et al., "Children's Engagement with Educational iPad Apps."

62. DevTech Research Group, Lifelong Kindergarten Group, and Playful Invention Company, "ScratchJr: About," ScratchJr home page, accessed October 27, 2015, www.scratchjr.org/about.html.

63. Lisa Guernsey, *Screen Time: How Electronic Media—From Baby Videos to Educational Software—Affects Your Young Child* (New York: Basic Books, 2012).

### Chapter 6

1. Division for Early Childhood (DEC) and National Association for the Education of Young Children (NAEYC), "Early Childhood Inclusion," Joint Position Statement, 2009, http://umaine.edu/expandinclusiveopp/files/2014/04/EarlyChildhoodInclusion-04-2009-tag.pdf.

2. Division for Early Childhood, "DEC Recommended Practices in Early Intervention/Early Childhood Special Education 2014," 2014, www.decsped.org/recommendedpractices; National Research Council, *Early Childhood Assessment: Why, What, and How* (Washington, DC: National Academies Press, 2008).

3. Samuel J. Meisels and Sally Atkins-Burnett, *Developmental Screening in Early Childhood: A Guide*, 5th ed. (Washington, DC: NAEYC, 2005).

4. Ibid.

5. M. McLean and K. McCormick, "Assessment and Evaluation in Early Intervention," in *Family-Centered Early Intervention with Infants & Toddlers: Innovative Cross-*

*Disciplinary Approaches*, ed. Wesley Brown, S. Thurman, and L. Pearl (Baltimore: Paul H. Brookes, 1993), 43–79.

6. Stephen J. Bagnato et al., *Linking Authentic Assessment and Early Childhood Intervention: Best Measures for Best Practices*, 2nd ed., ed. Stephen J. Bagnato, John T. Neisworth, and Kristie L. Pretti-Frontczak (Baltimore: Paul H. Brookes, 2010).

7. T. Halle et al., "Understanding and Choosing Assessments and Developmental Screeners for Young Children: Profiles of Selected Measures" (Washington, DC: Office of Planning, Research, and Evaluation, Administration for Children and Families, US Department of Health and Human, 2011).

8. Diane Trister Dodge et al., "Beyond Outcomes: How Ongoing Assessment Supports Children's Learning and Leads to Meaningful Curriculum," *Young Children* 59, no. 1 (January 2004): 22.

9. Division for Early Childhood, "DEC Recommended Practices."

10. National Association for the Education of Young Children (NAEYC) and National Association of Early Childhood Specialists in State Departments of Education (NAECS-SDE), "Early Childhood Curriculum, Assessment, and Program Evaluation: Building an Effective, Accountable System in Programs for Children Birth Through Age 8" (Washington, DC: NAEYC, 2003); Division for Early Childhood, "Promoting Positive Outcomes for Children with Disabilities: Recommendations for Curriculum, Assessment, and Program Evaluation" (Missoula, MT: Division for Early Childhood, 2007).

11. J. Squires et al., *Ages and Stages Questionnaires*, 3rd ed. (Baltimore: Paul H. Brookes, 2009).

12. Division for Early Childhood, "Promoting Positive Outcomes."

13. Michael Conn-Powers et al., "The Universal Design of Early Education," *Beyond the Journal: Young Children on the Web* 1 (September 2006), http://nceln.fpg.unc.edu/sites/nceln.fpg.unc.edu/files/resources/Universal%20Design%20of%20Early%20Education.pdf.

14. Child Trends Data Bank, "Racial and Ethnic Composition of the Child Population," 2014, www.childtrends.org/?indicators=racial-and-ethnic-composition-of-the-child-population; National Clearinghouse for English Language Acquisition and Language Instruction Educational Programs (NCELA), "How Many School-Aged English Language Learners (ELLS) Are There in the U.S.?" November 2007.

15. Debra Giambo, Tunde Szecsi, and Maryann Manning, "Teaching Strategies: Opening Up to the Issues: Preparing Preservice Teachers to Work Effectively with English Language Learners," *Childhood Education* 82, no. 2 (December 2005): 107–110, doi:10.1080/00094056.2006.10521358.

16. Linda Espinosa and Michael L. López, "Assessment Considerations for Young English Language Learners Across Different Levels of Accountability," *National Early Childhood Accountability Task Force and First* 5 (2007), www.researchgate.net/profile/Linda_Espinosa/publication/253312187_Assessment_Considerations_for_Young_English_Language_Learners_Across_Different_Levels_of_Accountability/links/54412f110cf2a76a3cc7ce52.pdf.

17. Paul L. Morgan et al., "Are Minority Children Disproportionately Represented in Early Intervention and Early Childhood Special Education?" *Educational Researcher* 41, no. 9 (December 1, 2012): 339–351, doi:10.3102/0013189X12459678.

18. National Research Council, *Early Childhood Assessment.*

19. NAEYC, "Screening and Assessment of Young English Language Learners," Position Statement (Washington, DC: NAEYC, 2005), www.naeyc.org/files/naeyc/file/positions/ELL_SupplementLong.pdf.

20. NAEYC and NAECS/SDE, "Early Childhood Curriculum, Assessment"; Division for Early Childhood, "Promoting Positive Outcomes."

21. J. Woods and K. McCormick, "Toward an Integration of Child- and Family-Centered Practices in the Assessment of Preschool Children: Welcoming the Family," *Young Exceptional Children* 5, no. 3 (2002): 2–11.

22. Carol Copple and Sue Bredekamp, *Developmentally Appropriate Practice in Early Childhood Programs Serving Children from Birth Through Age 8*, 3rd ed. (Washington, DC: National Association for the Education of Young Children, 2009); Division for Early Childhood, "DEC Recommended Practices."

23. W. Steven Barnett et al., *The State of Preschool 2013: First Look* (NCES 2014-078) (Washington, DC: National Center for Education Statistics, 2014).

24. Rashida Banerjee and John L. Luckner, "Assessment Practices and Training Needs of Early Childhood Professionals," *Journal of Early Childhood Teacher Education* 34, no. 3 (July 1, 2013): 231–248, doi:10.1080/10901027.2013.816808.

25. Carolyn R. Kilday et al., "Accuracy of Teacher Judgments of Preschoolers' Math Skills," *Journal of Psychoeducational Assessment* 30, no. 2 (April 1, 2012): 148–159, doi:10.1177/0734282911412722; Andrew J. Mashburn et al., "Teacher and Classroom Characteristics Associated with Teachers' Ratings of Prekindergartners' Relationships and Behaviors," *Journal of Psychoeducational Assessment* 24, no. 4 (December 1, 2006): 367–380, doi:10.1177/0734282906290594.

26. Jennifer Grisham-Brown, Rena A. Hallam, and Kristie Pretti-Frontczak, "Preparing Head Start Personnel to Use a Curriculum-Based Assessment: An Innovative Practice in the 'Age of Accountability,'" *Journal of Early Intervention* 30, no. 4 (September 1, 2008): 271–281, doi:10.1177/1053815108320689.

27. Stephen J. Bagnato et al., "Authentic Assessment as 'Best Practice' for Early Childhood Intervention National Consumer Social Validity Research," *Topics in Early Childhood Special Education* 34, no. 2 (August 1, 2014): 116–127, doi:10.1177/0271121414523652.

28. Katherine M. Barghaus and John W. Fantuzzo, "Validation of the Preschool Child Observation Record: Does It Pass the Test for Use in Head Start?" *Early Education and Development* 25, no. 8 (May 22, 2014): 1118–1141, doi:10.1080/10409289.2014.904646; National Research Council, *Early Childhood Assessment.*

29. Daniel J. Berry, Lisa J. Bridges, and Martha J. Zaslow, *Early Childhood Measures Profiles* (Washington, DC: Child Trends, 2004), http://ectacenter.org/eco/assets/pdfs/early_childhood_measures_profiles.pdf; Halle et al., "Understanding and Choosing Assessments."

30. Barghaus and Fantuzzo, "Validation of the Preschool Child."

31. Beth Rous et al., "The Transition Process for Young Children with Disabilities: A Conceptual Framework," *Infants and Young Children* 20, no. 2 (2007): 135–148.

32. M. B. Bruder and T. Bologna, "Collaboration and Service Coordination for Effective Early Intervention," in *Family-Centered Early Intervention with Infants & Toddlers: Innovative Cross-Disciplinary Approaches*, ed. Wesley Brown, S. Thurman, and L. Pearl (Baltimore: Paul H. Brookes, 1993), 103–127; Mabel L. Rice and Marion O'Brien, "Transitions: Times of Change and Accommodation," *Topics in Early Childhood Special Education* 9, no. 4 (January 1, 1990): 1–14, doi:10.1177/027112149000900402; Beth Rous, Mary Louise Hemmeter, and John Schuster, "Evaluating the Impact of the STEPS Model on Development of Community-Wide Transition Systems," *Journal of Early Intervention* 22, no. 1 (1999): 38–50, doi:10.1177/105381519902200105; Beth Rous, Christine Teeters Myers, and Sarintha Buras Stricklin, "Strategies for Supporting Transitions of Young Children with Special Needs and Their Families," *Journal of Early Intervention* 30, no. 1 (2007): 1–18, doi:10.1177/105381510703000102; Rous et al., "Transition Process for Young Children with Disabilities."

33. Beth Rous et al., "Practices That Support the Transition to Public Preschool Programs: Results from a National Survey," *Early Childhood Research Quarterly* 25, no. 1 (2010): 17–32, doi:10.1016/j.ecresq.2009.09.001.

34. Barnett et al., *State of Preschool 2013*.

35. S. L. Kagan, "Moving from Here to There: Rethinking Continuity and Transitions in Early Care and Education," in *Yearbook in Early Childhood Education*, ed. B. Spodek and O. Saracho (New York: Teachers College Press, 1991), 132–151.

36. Marci J. Hanson et al., "Entering Preschool: Family and Professional Experiences in This Transition Process," *Journal of Early Intervention* 23, no. 4 (October 1, 2000): 279–293, doi:10.1177/10538151000230040701; Rous, Myers, and Stricklin, "Strategies for Supporting Transitions."

37. Rous et al., "Transition Process for Young Children with Disabilities"; Doris R. Entwisle and Karl L. Alexander, "Facilitating the Transition to First Grade: The Nature of Transition and Research on Factors Affecting It," *Elementary School Journal* 98, no. 4 (March 1, 1998): 351–364; Elizabeth Hair et al., "Childrens School Readiness in the ECLS-K: Predictions to Academic, Health, and Social Outcomes in First Grade," *Early Childhood Research Quarterly* 21, no. 4 (2006): 431–454, doi: 10.1016/j.ecresq.2006.09.005.

38. Beth Rous et al., "Practices That Support."

### Chapter 7

The authors thank agency collaborators Steven Dow, Monica Barczak, the Career-Advance team, and especially the parents and the children of the Community Action Project of Tulsa County, Oklahoma (CAP Tulsa), as well as research collaborators Hirokazu Yoshikawa of New York University, Christopher King of University of Texas at Austin, and Amanda Morris of Oklahoma State University. We also thank these funders: the Administration for Children and Families; the US Department of Health and Human Services (Grant 90YR0073 and Grant 90PH0020); the W.K. Kellogg Foundation; Ascend at the Aspen Institute; and the Bill and Melinda Gates Foundation.

1. James J. Heckman, "Skill Formation and the Economics of Investing in Disadvantaged Children," *Science* 312, no. 5782 (June 30, 2006): 1900–1902, doi:10.1126/science.1128898.

2. W. S. Barnett, "Effectiveness of Early Educational Intervention," *Science* 333, no. 6045 (August 19, 2011): 975–978, doi:10.1126/science.1204534.

3. Christina Weiland and Hirokazu Yoshikawa, "Impacts of a Prekindergarten Program on Children's Mathematics, Language, Literacy, Executive Function, and Emotional Skills," *Child Development* 84, no. 6 (November 1, 2013): 2112–2130, doi:10.1111/cdev.12099; Vivian C. Wong et al., "An Effectiveness-Based Evaluation of Five State Pre-Kindergarten Programs," *Journal of Policy Analysis and Management* 27, no. 1 (December 1, 2008): 122–154, doi:10.1002/pam.20310.

4. Children's Bureau, "Summary of the Title IV-E Child Welfare Waiver Demonstrations" (Washington, DC: US Department of Health and Human Services, Administration for Children and Families, 2010); Children's Bureau, "The AFCARS Report: Preliminary FY 2009 Estimates as of July 2010" (Washington, DC: US Department of Health and Human Services, Administration for Children and Families, 2010).

5. Mark W. Lipsey et al., "Evaluation of the Tennessee Voluntary Prekindergarten Program: End of Pre-K Results from the Randomized Control Design," Research Report (Nashville, TN: Vanderbilt University, Peabody Research Institute, 2013); Mike Puma et al., "Third Grade Follow-Up to the Head Start Impact Study: Final Report," OPRE Report 2012-45 (Washington, DC: Office of Planning, Research and Evaluation, Administration for Children and Families, 2012), http://eric.ed.gov/?id=ED539264; Hirokazu Yoshikawa et al., *Investing in Our Future: The Evidence Base on Preschool Education*, vol. 9 (Society for Research in Child Development and Foundation for Child Development, 2013), http://home.uchicago.edu/~ludwigj/papers/Investing%20in%20Our%20Future%20Preschool%20Education%202013.pdf.

6. Sophia Addy, Will Engelhardt, and Curtis Skinner, "Basic Facts About Low-Income Children: Children Under 18 Years, 2011," Fact Sheet (New York: Columbia University Mailman School of Public Health: National Center for Children in Poverty, January 2013). The poverty threshold in 2014 was $23,850 for a four-person household (US Census, 2015). Poor families are defined as below the federal poverty threshold. Low-income families are defined as those who are at or above 200 percent of the federal poverty threshold (or $47,700 for a four-person household). In the United States, 47 percent of families with children three years old or younger live in low-income families, and 25 percent live in poor families. Sophia Addy and Vanessa R. Wight, "Basic Facts About Low-Income Children, 2010: Children Under Age 18," Fact Sheet (New York: Columbia University School of Public Health: National Center for Children in Poverty, February 2012).

7. Lawrence Bernstein et al., "Impact Evaluation of the U.S. Department of Education's Student Mentoring Program: Final Report," NCEE 2009-4047 (Washington, DC: National Center for Education Evaluation and Regional Assistance, 2009), http://eric.ed.gov/?id=ED504310; Tamara Halle et al., *Disparities in Early Learning and Development: Lessons from the Early Childhood Longitudinal Study—Birth Cohort (ECLS-B)* (Washington, DC: Child Trends, 2009), www.elcmdm.org/Knowledge%20Center/reports/Child_Trends-2009_07_10_FR_DisparitiesEL.pdf; Julia B. Isaacs, "Economic Mobility of Families Across Generations," in *Getting Ahead or Losing Ground: Economic Mobility in America*, ed. Ron Haskins, Julia B. Isaacs, and Isabel V. Sawhill (Washington, DC: Brookings Institution, 2008), http://growthandjustice.typepad.com/my_weblog/files/Economic_Mobility_in_America_Full.pdf.

8. P. Lindsay Chase-Lansdale and Jeanne Brooks-Gunn, "Helping Parents, Helping Children: Two-Generation Mechanisms," *Future of Children* 24, no. 1 (2014): 13–39.

9. Ibid.

10. Pamela E. Davis-Kean, "The Influence of Parent Education and Family Income on Child Achievement: The Indirect Role of Parental Expectations and the Home Environment," *Journal of Family Psychology* 19, no. 2 (2005): 294–304, doi:10.1037/0893-3200.19.2.294; Lisa A. Gennetian, Katherine Magnuson, and Pamela A. Morris, "From Statistical Associations to Causation: What Developmentalists Can Learn from Instrumental Variables Techniques Coupled with Experimental Data," *Developmental Psychology* 44, no. 2 (2008): 381–394, doi:10.1037/0012-1649.44.2.381; Narayan Sastry and Anne R. Pebley, "Family and Neighborhood Sources of Socioeconomic Inequality in Children's Achievement," *Demography* 47, no. 3 (2010): 777–800.

11. Katherine A. Magnuson, Christopher Ruhm, and Jane Waldfogel, "Does Prekindergarten Improve School Preparation and Performance?" *Economics of Education Review*, *The Economics of Early Childhood Education*, 26, no. 1 (February 2007): 33–51, doi:10.1016/j.econedurev.2005.09.008.0/0/00 0:00 AM

12. Robert Crosnoe and Ariel Kalil, "Educational Progress and Parenting Among Mexican Immigrant Mothers of Young Children," *Journal of Marriage and Family* 72, no. 4 (August 1, 2010): 976–990, doi:10.1111/j.1741-3737.2010.00743.x; Jonathan Guryan, Erik Hurst, and Melissa Schettini Kearney, "Parental Education and Parental Time with Children," working paper (Cambridge, MA: National Bureau of Economic Research, May 2008), www.nber.org/papers/w13993; A. Kalil, R. Ryan, and M. Corey, "Diverging Destinies: Maternal Education and Investments in Children," *Demography* 49, no. 4 (2012): 1361–1383; Katherine Magnuson, "Maternal Education and Children's Academic Achievement During Middle Childhood," *Developmental Psychology* 43, no. 6 (2007): 1497–1512, doi:10.1037/0012-1649.43.6.1497.

13. Chase-Lansdale and Brooks-Gunn, "Helping Parents, Helping Children."

14. Robert C. Granger and Rachel Cytron, "Teenage Parent Programs: A Synthesis of the Long-Term Effects of the New Chance Demonstration, Ohio's Learning, Earning, and Parenting Program, and the Teenage Parent Demonstration," *Evaluation Review* 23, no. 2 (April 1, 1999): 107–145, doi:10.1177/0193841X9902300201.

15. Lashawn Richburg-Hayes et al., "Rewarding Persistence: Effects of a Performance-Based Scholarship Program for Low-Income Parents," Social Science Research Network Scholarly Paper (Rochester, NY: Social Science Research Network, 2009), http://papers.ssrn.com.ezp-prod1.hul.harvard.edu/abstract=1353360.

16. Ascend at the Aspen Institute, "Two Generations, One Future: Moving Parents and Children Beyond Poverty Together" (Washington, DC: Aspen Institute, 2012), www.aspeninstitute.org/publications/two-generations-one-future-moving-parents-children-beyond-poverty-together; Chase-Lansdale and Brooks-Gunn, "Helping Parents, Helping Children"; Mario Luis Small, *Unanticipated Gains: Origins of Network Inequality in Everyday Life* (New York: Oxford University Press, 2009).

17. Teresa Eckrich Sommer et al., "Early Childhood Education Centers and Mothers' Postsecondary Attainment: A New Conceptual Framework for a Dual-Generation Education Intervention," *Teachers College Record* 114, no. 10 (2013).

18. Edward Zigler and Sally J. Styfco, "Moving Head Start to the States: One Experiment Too Many," *Applied Developmental Science* 8, no. 1 (January 2004): 51–55, doi:10.1207/S1532480XADS0801_7; Edward Zigler and Jeanette Valentine, eds., *Project Head Start: A Legacy of the War on Poverty* (New York: Free Press, 1979), http://eric.ed.gov/?id=ED183266.

19. Terri J. Sabol and P. Lindsay Chase-Lansdale, "The Influence of Low-Income Children's Participation in Head Start on Their Parents' Education and Employment," *Journal of Policy Analysis and Management* 34, no. 1 (January 1, 2015): 136–161, doi:10.1002/pam.21799.

20. Chase-Lansdale and Brooks-Gunn, "Helping Parents, Helping Children."

21. Emmalie Dropkin and Sylvia Jauregui, "Two Generations Together," National Head Start Association Initiative (Alexandria, VA: National Head Start Association, 2015), www.nhsa.org/two-generations-together.

22. Chris M. Herbst and Erdal Tekin, "Child Care Subsidies and Child Development," *Economics of Education Review* 29, no. 4 (August 2010): 618–638, doi:10.1016/j.econedurev.2010.01.002; Anna D. Johnson, Anne Martin, and Jeanne Brooks-Gunn, "Child-Care Subsidies and School Readiness in Kindergarten," *Child Development* 84, no. 5 (September 1, 2013): 1806–1822, doi:10.1111/cdev.12073; Anna D. Johnson, Rebecca M. Ryan, and Jeanne Brooks-Gunn, "Child-Care Subsidies: Do They Impact the Quality of Care Children Experience?" *Child Development* 83, no. 4 (July 1, 2012): 1444–1461, doi:10.1111/j.1467-8624.2012.1780.x.

23. Chase-Lansdale and Brooks-Gunn, "Helping Parents, Helping Children"; Granger and Cytron, "Teenage Parent Programs"; Ron Haskins, "Welfare Reform, 10 Years Later," *Poverty Research Insights*, (fall 2006): 1–7; Martha Zaslow and Kathryn Tout, "Child-Care Quality Matters," *American Prospect* 13, no. 7 (April 2002): 149.

24. Davis Jenkins, "Redesigning Community Colleges for Student Success: Overview of the Guided Pathways Approach" (New York: Columbia University, Teachers College, Community College Research Center, 2014).

25. Thomas R. Bailey, Shanna Smith Jaggars, and Davis Jenkins, *Redesigning America's Community Colleges: A Clearer Path to Student Success* (Cambridge, MA: Har-

vard University Press, 2015); Jenkins, "Redesigning Community Colleges for Student Success."

26. Bailey, Jaggars, and Jenkins, *Redesigning America's Community Colleges*; Heidi Grant and Carol S. Dweck, "Clarifying Achievement Goals and Their Impact," *Journal of Personality and Social Psychology* 85, no. 3 (2003): 541–553, doi:10.1037/0022-3514.85.3.541; Judith E. Scott-Clayton, "The Shapeless River: Does a Lack of Structure Inhibit Students' Progress at Community Colleges?" working paper 25 (New York: Assessment of Evidence Series, Community College Research Center, Columbia University, 2011), http://academiccommons.columbia.edu/catalog/ac:146662; Richard H. Thaler and Cass R. Sunstein, *Nudge: Improving Decisions About Health, Wealth, and Happiness* (New Haven, CT: Yale University Press, 2008).

27. Carol Clymer et al., *Tuning In to Local Labor Markets: Findings from the Sectoral Employment Impact Study* (Philadelphia: Public/Private Ventures, 2010); Ida Rademacher, Marshall Bear, and Maureen Conway, *Project QUEST: A Case Study of a Sectoral Employment Development Approach* (Washington, DC: Aspen Institute, 2001).

28. Robert W. Glover, Christopher T. King, and Tara Carter Smith, "Expanding the Career*Advance*® Program in Tulsa, Oklahoma" (Austin, TX: Ray Marshall Center, 2012).

29. Bailey, Jaggars, and Jenkins, *Redesigning America's Community Colleges*; Jenkins, "Redesigning Community Colleges for Student Success."

30. Nan Marie Astone et al., "School Reentry in Early Adulthood: The Case of Inner-City African Americans," *Sociology of Education* 73, no. 3 (July 1, 2000): 133–154, doi:10.2307/2673213; James T. Austin et al., "Portable, Stackable Credentials: A New Education Model for Industry-Specific Career Pathways" (New York: McGraw-Hill Research Foundation, 2012); Lauren Eyster, Theresa Anderson, and Christina Durham, "Innovations and Future Directions for Workforce Development in the Post-Recession Era" (Washington, DC: Urban Institute, 2013).

31. Tara Smith, Kristen Christensen, and Christopher T. King, "CareerAdvance® Implementation Study Findings Through July 2013" (Austin, TX: Ray Marshall Center, 2013); Tara Smith, Kristen Christensen, and Christopher T. King, "CareerAdvance® Implementation Study Findings Through July 2014" (Austin, TX: Ray Marshall Center, 2014).

32. Christopher Mazzeo, Sara Y. Rab, and Julian L. Alssid, "Building Bridges to College and Careers: Contextualized Basic Skills Programs at Community College" (New York: Workforce Strategy Center, 2003).

33. Teresa Eckrich Sommer et al., "Strengthening Head Start Impacts for Dual Language Learner Children: A Case Study of a Two-Generation Intervention" (Miami: Association for Public Policy Analysis and Management, 2015).

34. Maureen Conway and Robert P. Giloth, eds., *Connecting People to Work: Workforce Intermediaries and Sector Strategies* (New York: Aspen Institute, 2014); Robert P. Giloth, "Introduction: A Case for Workforce Intermediaries," in *Workforce Intermediaries for the Twenty-First Century*, ed. Robert Giloth (Philadelphia: Temple University Press, 2004), 1–30.

35. Chase-Lansdale and Brooks-Gunn, "Helping Parents, Helping Children."

36. Eric Bettinger and Rachel Baker, "The Effects of Student Coaching in College: An Evaluation of a Randomized Experiment in Student Mentoring," working paper (Cambridge, MA: National Bureau of Economic Research, March 2011), www.nber.org/papers/w16881; Sara Goldrick-Rab and Kia Sorensen, "Unmarried Parents in College," *Future of Children* 20, no. 2 (2010): 179–203; James E. Rosenbaum, Regina Deil-Amen, and Ann E. Person, *After Admission: From College Access to College Success* (New York: Russell Sage Foundation, 2006); Susan Scrivener and Erin Coghlan, "Opening Doors to Student Success: A Synthesis of Findings from an Evaluation at Six Community Colleges—Policy Brief" (New York: MDRC, 2011).

37. Bailey, Jaggars, and Jenkins, *Redesigning American's Community Colleges*; Jenkins, "Redesigning Community Colleges for Student Success."

38. Margo Gardner, Jeanne Brooks-Gunn, and P. Lindsay Chase-Lansdale, "The Two-Generation Approach to Building Human Capital: Past, Present, and Future," in *Handbook of Early Childhood Development Programs, Practices, and Policies: Theory-Based and Empirically-Supported Strategies for Promoting Young Children's Growth in the United States*, Workforce Intermediaries for the Twenty-First Century, ed. Eric Dearing and Elizabeth Votruba-Drzal (New York: John Wiley & Sons, 2015).

39. Richburg-Hayes et al., "Rewarding Persistence."

40. Laura J. Horn and C. Dennis Carroll, Nontraditional Undergraduates: Trends in Enrollment from 1986 to 1992 and Persistence and Attainment Among 1989-90 Beginning Postsecondary Students, Postsecondary Education Descriptive Analysis Reports, Statistical Analysis Report (Washington, DC: US Government Printing Office, 1996), http://eric.ed.gov/?id=ED402857; National Center for Education Statistics, "The Condition of Education 2007" (Washington, DC: National Center for Education Statistics, 2007; Thomas Bailey, Davis Jenkins, and D. Timothy Leinbach, "Is Student Success Labeled Institutional Failure? Student Goals and Graduation Rates in the Accountability Debate at Community Colleges" (New York: Columbia University, Teachers College, Community College Research Center, 2006).

41. Bethany Nelson, Meghan Froehner, and Barbara Gault, "College Students with Children Are Common and Face Many Challenges in Completing Higher Education" (Washington, DC: Institute of Women's Policy Research, 2013).

42. Chase-Lansdale and Brooks-Gunn, "Helping Parents, Helping Children"; P. Lindsay Chase-Lansdale et al., "CAP Family Life Study: Year 3 Report: September, 2012–December, 2013" (Tulsa, OK: Community Action Project of Tulsa County to Expand CareerAdvance, 2014), www.researchconnections.org/childcare/resources/27417; Robert W. Glover and Christopher T. King, "The Promise of Sectoral Approaches to Workforce Development: Towards More Effective, Active Labor Market Policies in the United State," in *Human Resource Economics and Public Policy: Essays in Honor of Vernon M. Briggs Jr.*, ed. Vernon M. Briggs and Charles J. Whalen (Kalamazoo, MI: W. E. Upjohn Institute for Employment Research, 2001), 215–251; King, Smith, and Christensen, "CareerAdvance® Implementation Study"; Terri J. Sabol et al., "Parent's Persistence and Certification in a Two-Generation Education and Training Program," *Children and Youth Services Review* 58 (2015): 1–10.

43. Bailey, Jaggars, and Jenkins, *Redesigning America's Community Colleges*; Jenkins, "Redesigning Community Colleges for Student Success."

44. Sommer et al., "Mothers' Postsecondary Attainment."

45. Sabol et al., "Parent's Persistence and Certification."

46. National Community College Benchmark Process, "Report of 2014 National Aggregate," Overland Park, KS: National Community College Benchmark Process, Johnson County Community College, n.d.

47. US Census, "Who's Minding the Kids? Child Care Arrangements: Spring 2011" (Washington, DC: US Department of Commerce, Bureau of the Census, 2013).

48. Chase-Lansdale and Brooks-Gunn, "Helping Parents, Helping Children."

49. Ascend at the Aspen Institute, "Two Generations, One Future"; Dropkin and Jauregui, "Two Generations Together."

50. Conway and Giloth, "Connecting People to Work"; Giloth, "Introduction: A Case for Workforce Intermediaries."

51. Barnett, "Effectiveness of Early Educational Intervention"; Ron Haskins and Greg Margolis, *Show Me the Evidence: Obama's Fight for Rigor and Results in Social Policy* (Washington, DC: Brookings Institution, 2015); Heckman, "Skill Formation"; Children's Bureau, "Title IV-E Child Welfare Waiver Demonstrations"; Children's Bureau, "AFCARS Report"; Weiland and Yoshikawa, "Impacts of a Prekindergarten Program"; Wong et al., "Effectiveness-Based Evaluation."

52. Dropkin and Jauregui, "Two Generations Together."

53. Ibid.

54. Chase-Lansdale and Brooks-Gunn, "Helping Parents, Helping Children."

55. J. Lombardi et al., "Gateways to Two Generations: The Potential for Early Childhood Programs and Partnerships to Support Children and Parents Together" (Washington, DC: Aspen Institute, 2014).

56. P. Lindsay Chase-Lansdale et al., "Developing a Two-Generation Program in Evanston, Illinois," Final Report (Washington, DC: Ascend at the Aspen Institute, 2014); Jenkins, "Redesigning Community Colleges for Student Success."

57. See, for example, Chase-Lansdale and Brooks-Gunn, "Helping Parents, Helping Children"; Dropkin and Jauregui, "Two Generations Together"; Gardner, Brooks-Gunn, and Chase-Lansdale, "Building Human Capital: Past, Present, and Future."

58. Dropkin and Jauregui, "Two Generations Together."

59. Ibid.

60. Ibid.

61. Chase-Lansdale et al., "Two-Generation Program in Evanston, Illinois"; Bettinger and Baker, "Student Coaching in College"; CFED, "From Aspirations to Achievement: Growing the Children's Savings Movement," Executive Summary (Washington, DC: Corporation for Enterprise Development, 2014); Chase-Lansdale et al., "CAP Family Life Study."

# ACKNOWLEDGMENTS

The inspiration for this book was sparked at a one-day conference at the Harvard Graduate School of Education: The Leading Edge of Early Childhood Education Initiative. The meeting brought together nearly three hundred diverse and influential leaders, scholars, and practitioners involved in early education and hailing from the United States and elsewhere around the globe. This book has benefited immeasurably from the generous support of organizations that made the conference possible, which brought with it participants' wealth of knowledge and their key insights. First, we thank all those who attended—early childhood program teachers and principals, district and state directors of early childhood initiatives and programs, early childhood organization policy analysts, and many others.

We are also indebted to all of those who contributed to the meeting's conversations as plenary speakers, discussants, and supporters. The plenary speakers, many of whom wrote chapters in this book, conveyed the best of what we know about healthy child development and high-quality systems of early learning. We thank Jeanne Brooks-Gunn, Kathy Hirsh-Pasek, Charles Nelson, Deborah Phillips, Michael Rich, Beth Rous, and Teresa Eckrich Sommer. In addition, the discussants and opening speakers at the meeting brought a wealth of knowledge from within the field and from the research and policy sectors: Joseph Blatt, Ola Friday, Thomas Hehir, Jacqueline Jones, Jessica Roth, Jim Ryan, Jason Sachs, Jessica Sager, Catherine Snow, Thomas Weber, Wayne Ysaguirre, and Martha Zaslow.

We are also immensely grateful to the organizations that awarded us the funds enabling us to put our vision into action: Jacqueline Jones and the staff at the Foundation for Child Development; Kim Haskins at the Barr Foundation; and Mary Walachy and Sally Fuller at the Irene E. & George A. Davis Foundation. We also thank Jim Ryan, Dean of Harvard Graduate School of Education, for supporting the effort substantively and financially. The conference's Programs in Professional Education Team, Communications Team, and Keith Collar worked hard behind the scenes to make it all come together, including broadcasting the event to all interested but not in attendance. Finally, we are indebted to our own Leading Edge project team: Frannie Abernethy, Sonia Alves, Julie Harris, Lauren Hay, Robin Kane, Kelly Kulsrud, and Ann Partee.

# ABOUT THE EDITORS

**Nonie K. Lesaux**, Juliana W. and William Foss Thompson Professor of Education and Society, Harvard Graduate School of Education, leads a research program that focuses on promoting the language and literacy skills of today's children and youth from diverse linguistic, cultural, and economic backgrounds. She also leads state-level policy work to improve third-grade reading outcomes in Massachusetts. With Stephanie Jones, Lesaux codirects a project on building capacity in the early education workforce and works across the country with teams of district and state leaders, center directors, administrators, and teachers focused on strengthening their pre-K to grade 3 initiatives. Lesaux authored a state-level literacy report that forms the basis for a reading proficiency bill (An Act Relative to Third Grade Reading Proficiency) passed in the Massachusetts House of Representatives. The legislation established an Early Literacy Expert Panel, which Lesaux cochairs. The panel is charged with developing new policies and policy-based initiatives in a number of domains that influence children's early literacy development. Lesaux is currently Chair of the Massachusetts Board of Early Education and Care.

**Stephanie M. Jones**, Marie and Max Kargman Associate Professor in Human Development and Urban Education Advancement, Harvard Graduate School of Education, is affiliated with the Prevention Science and Practice program. Her research focuses on the long-term effects of poverty and exposure to violence on children's social and emotional development, as well as the impact of school-based interventions aimed at promoting children's social-emotional skills, prosocial behavior, and academic skills. With Nonie Lesaux, Jones codirects a project on building capacity in the early education workforce and works across the country with teams of district and state leaders, center directors, administrators, and teachers focused on strengthening their pre-K to 3 initiatives. Jones was awarded the Grawemeyer Award in Education for her work with Edward Zigler and Walter Gilliam on *A Vision for Universal Preschool Education*; she was also awarded the Joseph E. Zins Early-Career Distinguished Contribution Award for Action Research in Social and Emotional Learning, from the Collaborative for Academic, Social, and Emotional Learning.

# ABOUT THE CONTRIBUTORS

**Jeanne Brooks-Gunn**, Virginia and Leonard Marx Professor of Child Development and Education at Teachers College, Columbia University, and Professor of Pediatrics at the College of Physicians and Surgeons at Columbia University, is a nationally renowned scholar and expert whose research centers on family and community influences on the development of children and youth. She is interested in factors that contribute to both positive and negative outcomes across childhood, adolescence, and adulthood, with a particular focus on key social and biological lifetime transitions. Brooks-Gunn has also designed and evaluated interventions aimed at enhancing the well-being of children living in poverty and associated conditions. She has published over five hundred articles and chapters, written four books, edited thirteen volumes, and received numerous major awards and honors. Brooks-Gunn's research has significantly shaped the understanding of child development and the influence of parents, schools, and other contextual factors; how maternal employment affects child well-being; and the nature of successful pathways through adolescence and various complicating factors, such as early childbearing. She is a member of the National Academy of Medicine and the National Academy of Education and has received lifetime achievement awards from the Association for Psychological Science, the American Psychological Association, the Society for Research in Child Development, the Society for Research on Adolescence, and the Margaret Mead Fellow Award from the American Academy of Political and Social Science.

**P. Lindsay Chase-Lansdale**, Frances Willard Professor of Human Development and Social Policy, Associate Provost for Faculty, Northwestern University, is an expert on the interface between research and social policy for children and families and a former Congressional Science Fellow of the American Association for the Advancement of Science. She is professor of human development and social policy at the School of Education and Social Policy and was founding director for seven years of the Cells to Society (C2S): The Center on Social Disparities and Health, at the Institute for Policy Research, Northwestern University, a center funded by the Eunice Kennedy Shriver National Institute of Child Health and Human Development. She specializes in multidisciplinary research on social issues and how they affect families and the development of children and youth. Specific topics include two-generation educational interventions for young parents and children, early childhood education, postsecondary education and training for low-income young adults, immigration, welfare reform, maternal employment, marriage and cohabitation, parent-child relationships, and social disparities in health.

**Joanna A. Christodoulou**, Assistant Professor in the Department of Communication Sciences and Disorders, MGH Institute of Health Professions, leads the Brain, Education, and Mind (BEAM) Team in the Center for Health and Rehabilitation Research, where she integrates roles as clinician, developmental cognitive neuroscientist, and educator. Her primary research focus has been on the development of reading and cognitive skills and on ways to harness individual variability to improve educational outcomes. To explore these research areas, Christodoulou uses neuroimaging and behavioral tools and works with a developmentally and clinically diverse range of populations. Christodoulou was awarded the Transforming Education Through Neuroscience Award by the Learning & the Brain Foundation and the International Mind, Brain, and Education Society. She joined a select group of researchers at the White House to discuss education neuroscience topics and implications for practice. Her research has been supported by various organizations, including the National Institutes of Health, the Spencer Foundation, and the Fulbright Foundation.

**Roberta Michnick Golinkoff**, Unidel H. Rodney Sharp Chair in Human Services, Education and Public Policy and Professor of Education, University of Delaware, has held the John Simon Guggenheim Fellowship and the James McKeen Cattell prize. More recently, she won the American Psychological Association's Distinguished Service to Psychological Science Award and the Urie Bronfenbrenner Award for Lifetime Contribution to Developmental Psychology in the Service of Science and Society, and was named a Francis Alison Scholar, the highest honor given to faculty at the University of Delaware. Her research on language development, the benefits of play, and preschoolers' early spatial knowledge has resulted in numerous articles and book chapters and twelve books—including books for parents and practitioners. Passionate about the dissemination of psychological science, she cofounded the Ultimate Block Party movement. She was also an associate editor of *Child Development*, and has appeared on numerous radio and television shows and in print media.

**Rena Hallam** is an Associate Professor in the Department of Human Development and Family Studies and serves as Associate Director for the Delaware Institute for Excellence in Early Childhood at the University of Delaware. Her research focuses on strategies for improving the quality of both center-based and family childcare environments with an emphasis on the design and implementation of state systems and policies. She served in a lead investigator role across multiple federally funded research projects on topics of early childhood transition, child assessment, and the intersection of childcare quality and subsidized childcare. Currently, she is Principal Investigator on a federally funded study of professional development approaches to support and enhance the quality of care in family childcare settings and Co-Principal Investigator of the Starting At Home project designed to study the impact of a parent-child intervention implemented by Early Head Start home visitors. Hallam has significant research and practice background in working with low-income, culturally diverse children, families, and staff in both Head Start and childcare settings. She served as Program Coordinator for an Early Head Start program, Director of a university laboratory preschool, and Director of Delaware's Quality Rating and Improvement System.

**Julie Russ Harris**, Manager of the Language Diversity and Literacy Development Research Group, Harvard Graduate School of Education, is a former elementary school teacher and reading specialist in urban public schools. Harris's work continues to be guided by the goal of increasing the quality of culturally diverse children's learning environments. The most recent projects in her portfolio include the development of literacy curricula and interventions and the design and implementation of innovative professional development programs and materials for early educators. With her colleagues, Harris has authored several publications, including book chapters, journal articles, policy briefs, a book on literacy instruction for English language learners, and the widely circulated state literacy report *Turning the Page: Refocusing Massachusetts for Reading Success*, which forms the basis for An Act Relative to Third Grade Reading Proficiency, an education bill passed in Massachusetts.

**Kathy Hirsh-Pasek**, Stanley and Debra Lefkowitz Distinguished Faculty Fellow in the Department of Psychology, Temple University, serves as Director of the Temple University Infant and Child Laboratory. Her research in the areas of early language development, literacy, and infant cognition has been funded by the National Science Foundation, the National Institutes of Health and Human Development, and the

Department of Education and has resulted in eleven books and over 150 other publications. With her longtime collaborator, Roberta Golinkoff, she is a recipient of the APA Bronfenbrenner Award for lifetime contribution to the science of developmental psychology in the service of science and society and the APA Award for Distinguished Service to Psychological Science. She also received Temple University's Great Teacher Award and Paul Eberman Research Award. She is a Fellow of the American Psychological Association and the American Psychological Society, served as the Associate Editor of *Child Development* and Treasurer of the International Association for Infant Studies. Her book *Einstein Never Used Flashcards: How Children Really Learn and Why They Need to Play More and Memorize Less* won the prestigious Books for Better Life Award as the best psychology book in 2003. Hirsch-Pasek also served as a researcher on the NICHD Study of Early Child Care and Youth Development, codeveloped the language and literacy preschool curricula for the State of California, and cofounded the Ultimate Block Party (www.ultimateblockparty.com) and Learn (www.LearnNow.org).

**Jacqueline Jones**, President and CEO of the Foundation for Child Development, served as Senior Advisor on Early Learning to Secretary of Education Arne Duncan and as the country's first Deputy Assistant Secretary for Policy and Early Learning in the US Department of Education. Prior to federal service, Jones was the Assistant Commissioner for the Division of Early Childhood Education in the New Jersey State Department of Education. For over fifteen years, she served as a Senior Research Scientist at the Educational Testing Service in Princeton. Jones has been a visiting faculty member at the Harvard Graduate School of Education and a full-time faculty member at the City University of New York.

**Kristelle Lavallee**, Content Strategist, Center on Media and Child Health (CMCH) at Boston Children's Hospital, was a private school teacher at the Park Street School in Boston, where she founded the Media Literacy Club for fifth and sixth graders. After leaving Park Street, she served as Associate Producer for KickinKitchen.TV (now Kickin Nutrition.TV) at KidsCOOK Productions—a scientifically based multimedia platform dedicated to educating tweens about living healthfully through nutrition and exercise. Currently, Lavallee manages the CMCH's interactive and social media accounts and translates CMCH research into actionable advice, practical health resources, and curricula that promote children's healthy and developmentally appropriate creation and consumption of media. Lavallee's work has been presented at psychological, communications, and education conferences, and she has spoken to clinician, parent, educator, and community groups about the importance and impact of media literacy, social media, and family and child health.

**Gigi Luk** is Associate Professor of Education, Harvard Graduate School of Education. Luk's program of research focuses on the neural and cognitive consequences of bilingualism across the lifespan, from young children to older adults. Her research findings suggest that as a language experience, bilingualism has cognitive benefits and linguistic limitations at all developmental stages. For children in particular, these bilingual consequences entail cognitive and educational implications. Luk was selected as a National Academy of Education/Spencer Foundation postdoctoral fellow during 2013–2014. During this fellowship, she examined how to harness scientific findings on bilingualism to improve educational experience for children from diverse language backgrounds. In particular, she has established a research program investigating: (1) effective ways to measure bilingualism in schools; (2) the relevance of knowledge on bilingualism and executive functions to language and literacy outcomes; and (3) the long-term relationship between academic outcomes and quality and quantity of bilingual experience. Luk has active outreach programs to a number of school districts and Head Start programs in Massachusetts serving children with diverse language backgrounds.

**Dana Charles McCoy** is Assistant Professor, Harvard Graduate School of Education. McCoy's work focuses on how poverty-related risk factors in children's home, school, and neighborhood affect the development of their cognitive and socioemotional skills in early childhood. She is also interested in the development, refinement, and evaluation of early intervention programs designed to promote positive development and resilience in young children, particularly in their self-regulation and executive function. McCoy's work is centered in both domestic and international areas, including Ghana, Tanzania, Zambia, and Jordan. She has a particular interest in interdisciplinary theory, causal methodology, and ecologically valid measurement. McCoy served as an NICHD National Research Service Award postdoctoral fellow at the Harvard Center on the Developing Child, where she studied differential effectiveness of early childhood education programs (e.g., Head Start) across diverse communities in the United States.

**Amy Pace** is Assistant Professor in Speech and Hearing Sciences at the University of Washington. Pace's research focuses on language acquisition, assessment, and intervention in early childhood. She has particular interest in how multiple factors—including brain development, parent-child engagement, and environmental experience—interact to support language learning in typical and at-risk populations. She was a postdoctoral fellow at Temple University with Kathy Hirsh-Pasek and received her PhD in language and communicative disorders from the University of California, San Diego, and San Diego State University in 2013, working with Margaret Friend and Leslie Carver.

**Deborah A. Phillips**, Professor of Psychology and Associated Faculty in the McCourt School of Public Policy, Georgetown University, was the first Executive Director of the Board on Children, Youth, and Families of the National Research Council and the Institute of Medicine and served as Study Director for the Board's report *From Neurons to Neighborhoods*:

*The Science of Early Child Development*. She also served as President of the Foundation for Child Development, Director of Child Care Information Services at the National Association for the Education of Young Children, and Congressional Science Fellow (Society for Research in Child Development) on the staff of Congressman George Miller. Her research focuses on the developmental effects of early childhood programs for both typically developing children and those with special needs, including research on childcare, Head Start, and state pre-K programs.

**Michael Rich**, Founder and Director of the Center on Media and Child Health (CMCH), Boston Children's Hospital, Associate Professor of Pediatrics at Harvard Medical School and of Social and Behavioral Science at Harvard T.H. Chan School of Public Health, is a Fellow of the American Academy of Pediatrics and the Society for Adolescent Health and Medicine. Cognizant of the potency of images and the primacy of mass media as a source of information and influence for young people, Dr. Rich, known as "The Mediatrician," studies media as a powerful influence on child development, behavior, and learning. Founded in 2002, CMCH is an interdisciplinary center that investigates, translates, and innovates with the goal of enhancing the positive and limiting the negative effects of media use on the physical, mental, and social health of children and adolescents.

**Beth Rous**, Professor in the Department of Educational Leadership Studies, University of Kentucky, conducts research on the translation of research to practice to support high-quality programs, specifically investigating the implementation of large-scale systems (policy, practice, professional development) to support quality across sectors (education, health, human services) for children from birth through the early grades. Rous is also the Director for the Kentucky Partnership for Early Childhood Service, which is housed at the Human Development Institute. Through the Kentucky Partnership, Rous oversees over

$7 million annually in grants and contracts to support quality services for young children, families, and the professionals who work with them. She has served as technical advisor/consultant at the national level for both Education and Health and Human Services on initiatives such as congressional mandated studies (National Assessment of IDEA and Study of IDEA Implementation), and national longitudinal studies (Pre-Elementary Education Longitudinal Study; Head Start Family Child Experiences Survey).

**Lauren Rubenzahl**, Communications Specialist, Center on Media and Child Health (CMCH) at Boston Children's Hospital, is a writer, editor, and educator who has served in many capacities at CMCH. In her previous role as Program Administrative Manager, she coordinated center operations at all levels, from strategic planning to content development. To further contribute to the mission and vision of CMCH, she has represented the center on several advisory boards; presented at media literacy and communications conferences; spoken to parent, educator, nurse, and community groups; published articles in the *Journal of Children and Media* and *Scientific American*; and presented testimony on media literacy education at the Massachusetts State House.

**Terri J. Sabol**, Assistant Professor in Human Development and Social Policy, Faculty Associate at the Institute for Policy Research, Northwestern University, is a developmental psychologist by training. Her research explores the individual and environmental factors that lead to healthy child development, with an emphasis on schools and families. In particular, she focuses on ways to assess and improve the quality of early childhood education. She recently received a National Research Service Award from the National Institutes of Health to examine the synergistic relations among increases in parents' education, children's participation in early childhood education, and children's learning. Before entering graduate school, she was a first-grade teacher in Chicago.

**Teresa Eckrich Sommer**, Research Associate Professor at the Institute for Policy Research, Northwestern University, studies the intersection of policy and practice for economically disadvantaged families and their children. She specializes in how social and educational institutions influence the life course of families, especially through investments in human and social capital (including basic life skills, education, and social networks). Her current, federally funded research focuses on two-generation educational investments for parents and children, namely, programs that simultaneously offer training, education, and career support to low-income parents and provide high-quality early education for their young children. Sommer previously worked as a Senior Research Associate at the Chapin Hall Center for Children, University of Chicago, and as a Research Associate at the Wiener Center for Social Policy, Kennedy School of Government, Harvard University.

# INDEX